Beta
Release

W9-CIO-833

Using

Using

MICROSOFT®

Windows® 98

Preview Edition

que®

Beta
Release

Using

Using

MICROSOFT®
Windows® 98
Preview Edition

que®

Michael Miller

Using Windows® 98 Preview Edition

Library of Congress Catalog No.: 97-80710

ISBN: 0-7897-1543-0

99 98   6 5 4 3 2 1

Interpretation of the printing code: the rightmost double-digit number is the year of the book's printing; the rightmost single-digit number, the number of the book's printing. For example, a printing code of 98-1 shows that the first printing of the book occurred in 1998.

Screen reproductions in this book were created using Collage Plus from Inner Media, Inc., Hollis, NH.

Contents at a Glance

Table of Contents

Credits

PUBLISHER
Don Fowley

ASSOCIATE PUBLISHER
Dean Miller

GENERAL MANAGER
Joe Muldoon

MANAGER OF PUBLISHING OPERATIONS
Linda H. Buehler

EDITORIAL SERVICES DIRECTOR
Carla Hall

MANAGING EDITOR
Thomas F. Hayes

ACQUISITIONS EDITORS
Grace M. Buechlein
Jill Byus

PRODUCT DIRECTORS
Melanie Palaisa
Philip Wescott

PRODUCTION EDITOR
Lori A. Lyons

EDITORS
Patricia Kinyon
Tom Stevens
Karen Walsh

PRODUCT MARKETING MANAGER
Kourtnaye Sturgeon

ASSISTANT PRODUCT MARKETING MANAGER
Gretchen Schlesinger

TECHNICAL EDITOR
Ron Ellenbecker

SOFTWARE RELATIONS COORDINATOR
Susan D. Gallagher

EDITORIAL ASSISTANT
Jennifer L. Chisholm

BOOK DESIGNER
Ruth Harvey

COVER DESIGNER
Sandra Schroeder

PRODUCTION TEAM
Jenny Earhart
Laura A. Knox
Heather Stephenson
Donna Wright

INDEXER
Cheryl A. Jackson

Composed in *Century Old Style* and *ITC Franklin Gothic* by Que Corporation.

To my three best friends, who each serve a special role in my life:
To Beth, who makes me think ("And I do appreciate you being round");
To Mike, who makes me laugh ("What would you do if I sang out of tune?");
And to Sherry, who makes me feel ("If you want me to, I will").

About the Author

Michael Miller has been involved with the publishing industry since 1987, as both an executive and an author. He currently serves as Vice President of Business Strategy for Macmillan Publishing, where he helps to develop the company's strategic vision. He is also the author of 22 computer books that, together, have sold more than 500,000 copies and have been reprinted in more than a half-dozen languages. His most recent books are *Using Windows 95* and *Easy Internet, Second Edition,* both for Que.

Acknowledgments

My thanks to the usual suspects at Macmillan Computer Publishing, for helping to get this book to market really, really fast.

We'd Like to Hear from You!

QUE Corporation has a long-standing reputation for high-quality books and products. To ensure your continued satisfaction, we also understand the importance of customer service and support.

Tech Support

If you need assistance with the information in this book or with a CD/disk accompanying the book, please access Macmillan Computer Publishing's online Knowledge Base at **http://www.superlibrary.com/general/support**. If you do not find the answer to your questions on our Web site, you may contact Macmillan Technical Support by phone at **317/581-3833** or via e-mail at **support@mcp.com**.

Also be sure to visit QUE's Web resource center for all the latest information, enhancements, errata, downloads, and more. It's located at **http://www.quecorp.com/**.

Orders, Catalogs, and Customer Service

To order other QUE or Macmillan Computer Publishing books, catalogs, or products, please contact our Customer Service Department at **800/428-5331** or fax us at **800/835-3202** (International Fax: **317/228-4400**). Or visit our online bookstore at **http://www.mcp.com/**.

Comments and Suggestions

We want you to let us know what you like or dislike most about this book or other QUE products. Your comments will help us to continue publishing the best books available on computer topics in today's market.

> **Grace M. Buechlein**
> **Executive Editor**
> **Macmillan Computer Publishing**
> **201 West 103rd Street, 4B**
> **Indianapolis, Indiana 46290 USA**
> **Fax: 317/581-4663**
> **E-mail: gbuechlein@mcp.com**

Please be sure to include the book's title and author as well as your name and phone or fax number. We will carefully review your comments and share them with the author. Please note that due to the high volume of mail we receive, we may not be able to reply to every message.

Thank you for choosing QUE!

Introduction

In this chapter

Windows 98–code-named "Memphis"–is the latest version of Microsoft's popular operating system, due for release mid-year 1998. There have been several major releases of Windows over the years, the last big one being the release of Windows 95 in August of 1995. Windows 95 was quite different from preceding versions of Windows. Microsoft changed the file-handling metaphor and key features of the interface to increase the ease-of-use for new and casual users. In the slightly more than two years since its release, Windows 95 has garnered an installed base of close to 100 million users.

Windows 98 won't be quite the revolutionary change that Windows 95 was; Windows 98 is more an evolution of a good thing. In fact, if you've used Windows 95, you'll know your way around Windows 98 without a lot of prompting–at least on a surface level.

There are many new features in Windows 98, most of which revolve around trying to merge the classic desktop operating metaphor with the content and methodology of the Internet. For example, Windows 98's Help system not only includes the standard Help files located on your hard disk, but can also take you to the Web to search for help on a special Microsoft Technical Support site.

With Windows 98, Microsoft wants you to think of the Web as nothing more than an extension of your desktop computer. To facilitate the merger of desktop and Web, Windows 98 lets you use Web pages as background for your desktop–and lets you single-click desktop icons, just as you do Web links. In fact, with this *True Web Integration*, you navigate through and operate Windows 98 just as you would a Web browser; the lines between desktop and Web computing are truly blurred.

All this talk about Windows 98 might sound interesting, but what use is it to you today? After all, unless you're one of the privileged few who are beta testing the new software, you won't be able to buy or install Windows 98 for several months. You can, however, get a feel for Windows 98 by downloading and installing Internet Explorer 4.0, available free of charge from Microsoft's Web site (**www.microsoft.com/ie/ie40**). Internet Explorer 4.0 includes many of the interface features you'll find in Windows 98, and–with True Web Integration enabled–will transform your Windows 95 desktop into a reasonable looking and operating facsimile of Windows 98.

The intent of this Preview Edition of *Using Windows 98* is, in conjunction with Internet Explorer 4.0, to show you how to use the new features of Windows 98. If you like what you see, you'll probably want to be first in line when Microsoft releases the official Windows 98 software. If you don't like the new features, you can turn off Internet Explorer's interface changes and you're not out anything.

By the way, if you do upgrade to Windows 98, look for the official release version of this book at the retailer of your choice at about the same time. The official release version of *Using Windows 98* will be updated to cover the final version of all Windows 98 features, with additional information garnered between the writing of this edition and the official software release.

Who Should Read This Book

This book was written for anyone interested in Windows 98. You can read this book by itself to get a flavor of Windows 98's new features, or use it in conjunction with Internet Explorer 4.0 to actually try some of the new features on your own computer. There's enough basic information in this book to help you get started, and enough coverage of other tasks to act as a reference for your future use.

What This Book Covers

This book covers the most commonly used end-user features expected to be included in the final release of Microsoft Windows 98. In addition to those features previously found in Windows 95, you'll discover such new Windows 98 features as:

- Active Channels
- Active Desktop
- Desktop Themes
- FAT32
- FrontPage Express
- Internet Explorer 4.0
- Kodak Imaging
- Microsoft Chat
- Microsoft Magnifier

- NetMeeting
- Outlook Express
- Personal Web Server
- True Web Integration
- TV Viewer
- Web Help
- Windows System Update
- Windows Tune-Up Wizard

About This Preview Edition

This is a Preview Edition of Que's upcoming *Using Windows 98* book. As such, it is not meant to be a literal how-to book to operating Windows 98. Instead, it is meant to introduce you to the probable features and operations of the upcoming release of the Windows 98 operating system. The official release version of *Using Windows 98* will differ from this book in offering precise information and instructions on how to use the final release version of Windows 98 when it is available.

As a beta tester for "Memphis"–Microsoft's code name for Windows 98–I get access to pre-release versions of the software not available to the general public. This is how I was able to write this book before Windows 98 was generally available. Because I signed a non-disclosure agreement when I agreed to become a "Memphis" beta tester, there is some confidential testing information that I cannot reveal in these pages. This book contains only that information available to the general public at this point in time.

This book was written in the fall of 1997 on beta version 2.1 (build 1602) of Windows 98. Because this book was written on a pre-release version of the software, it is possible that it will contain information that could be inaccurate when compared to the final release version of Windows 98. The final release version of Windows 98 will likely be somewhat different than the version this book describes. Expect things like dialog boxes and icons to change some-what, and expect some current features to change or be deleted, and some new features to be added.

This Preview Edition reflects the development of the Windows 98 operating system at this point in time, not what it will look like in final release. The official release version of *Using Windows 98* will be updated with coverage of the final release of Windows 98.

The *Using* Philosophy

Que's *Using* books help you, the reader, cover the most ground with the least amount of hassle, and in a minimum of time. We try to pack as much information as possible between the front and back covers, so that whatever your problem, you're likely to find the solution in this single book.

In addition, this book gets to the point *quickly*. Your time is valuable, so each task in this book is written with economy in mind. There's little fluff in these pages; just essential explanations and step-by-step instructions.

Conventions Used in This Book

This book uses certain conventions in order to guide you through the various tasks. For ex-ample, you'll find the following special typefaces used in this book:

Type	Meaning
underline	Shortcut keys for menu commands and dialog box options that appear underlined on-screen.
boldface	Information you are asked to type.
`computer type`	Direct quotations of words that appear on-screen or in a figure.

In addition, you will find special Notes, Tips, and Cautions sprinkled throughout the book; these annotations supply you with additional information not present in the general text.

How to Contact the Author

You can find more information about me at my Web site. The address is **http://www.mcp.com/people/miller/**. In addition, feel free to contact me via e-mail at **mmiller@mcp.com**. I may not be able to answer every question immediately, but I do appreciate your feedback.

Windows 98 Basics

What's New in Windows 98?

Previewing Windows 98 with Internet Explorer 4.0

Although Windows 98 is not yet available to the general public (it's still being put through its paces by a select group of beta testers), you can get a feel for how it will look and act by installing Internet Explorer 4.0 (IE 4). IE 4 is the latest version of Microsoft's popular Web browser, and it incorporates many of the same interface features you'll eventually find in Windows 98. Using IE 4 is the next best thing to using Windows 98, at this point in time.

To install Internet Explorer 4.0, follow these steps:

1. Use any Web browser (Netscape Navigator, a previous version of Internet Explorer, or the built-in browser in America Online) to go to Microsoft's Internet Explorer home page (**www.microsoft.com/ie/ie40**).

2. Follow the instructions on-screen to download and install Internet Explorer 4.0. There are three different versions of IE 4 you can download:

   - *Browser Only.* This is just the basic browser, and does not include any of the new interface features or utilities. The file size is 13Mb.

   - *Standard.* This includes the basic browser, but adds all the new interface changes (including True Web Integration) as well as the Outlook Express e-mail and newsgroup software. This is the basic installation necessary to preview the new interface features in Windows 98. The file size is 16Mb.

   - *Full.* This includes everything in the Standard installation and adds NetMeeting, NetShow, FrontPage Express, the Web Publishing Wizard, and Microsoft Chat. This installation not only gives you a preview of Windows 98's interface features but also lets you check out some of Windows 98's new utilities. The file size is 25Mb.

 If you don't want to take the time to download IE 4 (on a slow modem it can take several hours), you can order a CD-ROM version for just $4.95 direct from Microsoft. See more information on the Internet Explorer home page (**www.microsoft.com/ie/ie40**) or call 1-800-485-2048.

---

3. After IE 4 is installed, you need to turn on the True Web Integration feature. Click the Start menu, select Settings, and then select Folders & Icons. When the Folder Options dialog box appears, select the General tab, choose Web Style, and then click OK.

4. To get the full flavor of Windows 98, you also need to enable IE 4's Active Desktop. Click the Start menu, select Settings, select Active Desktop, and then select View As Web Page.

Windows 98 System Requirements

If you're evaluating whether or not to install Windows 98 on your system, you first need to know whether it will run on your system. As of this writing, here are the *minimum* hardware requirements necessary to run Windows 98:

- 80486DX-66 processor
- 16Mb RAM
- 150Mb free disk space
- Mouse or other pointing device
- VGA or higher resolution display

Based on my experience, here are my *recommended* hardware requirements to satisfactorily run Windows 98:

- Pentium P-75 processor
- 32Mb RAM
- 200Mb disk space
- Mouse or other pointing device
- VGA or higher resolution display
- 28.8 Kbps modem

My increased requirements are based on the fact that you really need as much memory as possible to speed up operation, a lot of hard disk space to "cache" Web documents, and a connection to the Internet to use the Web-based Help system and perform system updates. In fact, the best thing you can do to speed up the performance of Windows 98 is to add more memory—as much as you can afford.

The Biggest Differences Between Windows 98 and Windows 95

Windows 98 is an evolutionary operating system, building on the best that Windows 95 had to offer. If you already know your way around Windows 95, you'll find Windows 98 to be similar in operation—similar enough, anyway, that you can get up and running quickly when you upgrade.

Table 1.1 outlines the most important differences between Windows 98 and Windows 95.

Table 1.1 Major Differences Between Windows 95 and Windows 98		
Task/Item	In Windows 95	In Windows 98
Desktop	Static	Active
Select items	Single-click	Hover
Launch items	Double-click	Single-click
E-mail software	Windows Messaging (Exchange)	Outlook Express

continues

Table 1.1 Continued		
Task/Item	**In Windows 95**	**In Windows 98**
Web browser	Not included	Integrated Internet Explorer
ISDN support	Not included	Integrated
FAT32 support	Not included	Integrated
DVD support	Not included	Integrated
TV tuner support	Not included	Integrated
Help system	Disk-based	Includes online Web Help

Learning New Skills for Windows 98

If you know how to use Windows 95, you also know how to use Windows 98—almost. Some of the skills you learned for Windows 95, however, have changed; you have to learn a few new ways of doing things in Windows 98. Among the more useful new skills to learn are:

- *Hovering*. In Windows 95 you selected an item by single-clicking it. Because single-clicking in Windows 98 actually launches the item, you have to learn a new way to select things. This new technique is called *hovering*, which involves placing the cursor over an item without clicking your mouse. When an object is hovered over, it is automatically highlighted, as shown in Figure 1.1.

FIG. 1.1
Hover your cursor over an object to select it; note that your cursor turns from an arrow into a hand shape.

- *Single-clicking*. When you activate Windows 98's True Web Integration, every object on your desktop—icons, files, folders, and shortcuts—becomes a Web-like object. This means that instead of the old double-clicking operation, you now select desktop objects just like you would links on a Web page—by single-clicking.

■ *Right-clicking.* You learned how to click your right mouse button in Windows 95. But in Windows 98 there are many more context-sensitive pop-up menus available. You can right-click just about any desktop object to display a full-featured, pop-up menu custom-tailored to the task at hand.

■ *Browsing.* With Windows 98 True Web Integration, your desktop takes on Web-like characteristics, so you need to learn some new navigational techniques. In particular, get used to displaying everything in the same window—whether the content is on the Web, on your hard disk, or on a removable disk. You can use My Computer, Windows Explorer, and Internet Explorer to display the same content—content that, when single-clicked, displays its content in the same window. This means that you get to use a Back button in My Computer and Windows Explorer, just like you do when browsing Web pages with Internet Explorer.

The two big things to remember are that anything you used to single-click, you now hover over; anything you used to double-click, you now single-click. Master these few basic new techniques and you're well on your way to learning Windows 98 key operations.

The New Interface Features of Windows 98

There are some significant interface changes in Windows 98; most of them involve the addition of World Wide Web-like navigation to the classic Windows point-and-click desktop. These new features include:

■ *True Web Integration.* The Windows 98 desktop operates much like a Web page. You single-click items to launch them instead of double-clicking; you hover the cursor over items to select them. In addition, all your folders—including My Computer and Windows Explorer—can display their contents in either the classic Windows 95 view or in the new Web Style (see Figure 1.2). With Web Style, each folder is like a Web page; in fact, My Computer can browse your desktop or browse the Web, and you won't know the difference.

FIG. 1.2

Choose to display My Computer in Web Style and see information about any selected item.

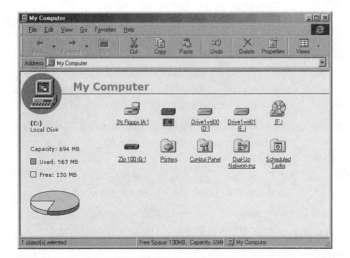

■ *Active Desktop*. This integrated Internet shell turns your desktop into a giant Web page. You can put "live" HTML objects directly on your desktop, and make your desktop background an HTML document.

■ *New Settings menu items*. Windows 98 takes many configuration options that used to be accessed in disparate ways and centralizes them under the Settings menu. Select Settings from the Start menu and you see the new options: Taskbar & Start Menu, Folders & Icons, Active Desktop, and Windows Update.

■ *My Documents folder*. Click this new desktop folder and get instant access to your favorite documents.

■ *New interface animation effects*. Tired of the boring Windows 95 menus? In Windows 98, menus slide out when selected.

■ *New display enhancements*. Windows 98 adds several new ways to personalize your display—including several features from Windows 95's Microsoft Plus! add-on.

■ *Support for multiple displays*. If your software supports it—and if you add a second video card and monitor—Windows 98 lets you run two displays at once. This is great if you're developing Web pages—set up one display to show your HTML code and another to show your output in a Web browser.

The New Internet Features of Windows 98

In addition to the interface changes based on a Web/desktop integration, Windows 98 also includes a wide variety of new Internet programs and utilities, such as:

■ *Internet Explorer 4.0*. The latest version of Microsoft's Web browser is built into Windows 98—complete with new search and history functions.

■ *Active Channels*. Tired of going out to the Web for information? Windows 98 lets you select channels of information to be pushed direct to your desktop (see Figure 1.3).

■ *Outlook Express*. Outlook Express is the new e-mail and newsgroup program; it's versatile and easy to use.

■ *NetMeeting*. This new Internet utility lets you chat with other Internet users—through plain text, audio, or video; it also includes a whiteboard utility that lets you share drawings with other users in real time.

■ *Microsoft Chat*. An Internet chat program with a friendly face; Microsoft Chat takes the messages in a normal Chat channel and uses them to create a continuous comic strip, with different cartoon characters representing the various Chat users.

■ *FrontPage Express*. Also known as FrontPad, this is a "lite" version of the popular FrontPage Web page authoring program that lets you create your own personal Web pages.

■ *Personal Web Server*. After you create your own Web pages with FrontPage Express, publish them to the Web with this step-by-step Wizard.

■ *Global Windows Address Book*. Store all your contact names and addresses in a common Address Book—accessible from all Windows applications.

FIG. 1.3

Choose from any of these active channels in Windows 98's Channel Bar.

- *Online Services folder*. Don't have an Internet connection yet? Windows 98 assembles five major online services—America Online, AT&T WorldNet, CompuServe, the Microsoft Network, and Prodigy Internet—into one convenient desktop folder; subscribing is just a click away!

- *Built-in ISDN support*. Windows 98 now automatically includes support for ISDN modems—one of the fastest ways to connect to the Internet.

One thing is missing from Windows 98 (at least from the beta 2.1 version)—Microsoft Fax. Windows 98 replaces the old Windows Messaging e-mail system with Outlook Express, and whereas Windows Messaging had built-in fax capabilities, Outlook Express doesn't.

The New Utilities in Windows 98

Windows has always included a grab bag of utilities you could use to perform everyday computing tasks; Windows 98 adds some new utilities and updates some existing ones, such as:

- *TV Viewer*. If you install special TV tuner hardware in your system, you can use Windows 98 to receive and display broadcast and cable programs—and the new Program Guide will automatically list upcoming shows.

- *Improved Accessibility options*. Windows 98 includes several new utilities to help the sight and hearing impaired effectively use their computers. Of special note is the Microsoft Magnifier, a utility that turns your display into a large-print readout.

- *Backup*. Windows 98 includes a completely new Backup program—it's easier to use than the old Windows 95 Backup and includes support for more backup devices.

- *Disk Defragmenter*. This essential utility—used to speed up the performance of your hard disks—has been updated to automatically place files for your most frequently used program at the front of your disk, for increased access speed.

■ *DriveSpace 3*. This disk compression utility has been updated to make even better use of your existing disk space.

■ *Registry Scan*. With Registry Scan you can automatically fix errors in the Windows Registry, the critical file that contains all your Windows configuration settings.

■ *Kodak Imaging*. This is a great new fax viewer utility that also doubles as a GIF and JPG graphics viewer.

■ *Windows Tune-Up Wizard*. This Wizard configures the new Task Scheduler to run common maintenance activities—such as Disk Defragmenter and ScanDisk—at preselected times.

■ *Windows System Update*. This new feature makes sure your computer and operating system are always up-to-date, by automatically dialing up the Web and automatically downloading and installing the latest versions of your system files and drivers.

■ *Web Help*. This is an Internet-based component of the standard Windows Help system. If you can't find help from your hard disk, you're sent directly to a special Microsoft Web site to search for technical support.

The New Performance Enhancements in Windows 98

Some of the most useful new features in Windows 98 work behind the scenes to make your system run faster and more efficiently. Among Windows 98's new performance enhancements are:

■ *FAT32*. If you have a large hard disk—more than 2Gb—FAT32 lets you take advantage of every bit of available disk space, without special partitioning. FAT32 also squeezes additional space out of any drive larger than 512Mb.

■ *Enhancements to power management*. Windows now includes preconfigured "schemes" to manage the power consumption of various types of computers, as well as support for new OnNow-compatible computers that power down but never shut off.

■ *Support for DVDs*. DVDs are the latest storage media, the same size CD-ROMs but with much larger capacity. Windows 98 lets your system read DVDs just as it would CDs.

How Windows 98 Differs from Windows 3.x

Although Windows 98 differs only slightly from Windows 95, the differences between Windows 98 and Windows 3.x are much more significant. If you've skipped Windows 95 on your upgrade path, Table 1.2 outlines the major differences between Windows 3.x and Windows 98:

Table 1.2   Major Differences Between Windows 3.x and Windows 98

Task/Item	In Windows 3.x	In Windows 98
Open applications	Program Manager	Start menu
Manage files	File Manager	Windows Explorer or My Computer
Store files in	Directories	Folders
File names	8 characters + 3 character extension	Long file name and extensions (up to 256 characters)
Deleted files	Are deleted	Are sent to the Recycle Bin, from where they can be undeleted
Minimized windows	Become temporary icons at bottom of screen	Become temporary buttons on Taskbar
Close window button	Top-left corner	Top-right corner
Right mouse button	Does nothing	Displays context-sensitive pop-up menu
Installing new hardware	Difficult	Uses Plug and Play technology to automate most hardware installations

Part
I

Ch
1

The big difference between Windows 3.x and Windows 98 is that Program Manager and File Manager no longer exist; you now use the Start button to launch programs and My Computer (or Windows Explorer) to manage your files. In addition, files no longer reside in directories; they're now nestled in folders. Just click a folder to display its contents. Learn these differences, and then turn to Chapter 2, "Navigating the Windows 98 Desktop," for more detail on Windows 98's basic operations. ●

Navigating the Windows 98 Desktop

The New Desktop Features of Windows 98

If you choose not to enable True Web Integration, the Windows 98 desktop is very similar to the Windows 95 desktop. With True Web Integration enabled, however, the desktop changes considerably.

Here are the major new desktop features of Windows 98:

- *Active Desktop with True Web Integration*. This feature makes Windows act like the Web. You single-click objects instead of double-clicking, and you can use My Computer and Windows Explorer to browse the Web. In addition, this feature turns your desktop background into an HTML document—complete with live HTML objects.

- *Multiple toolbars*. You can add toolbars for quick access to various functions, such as the Quick Launch toolbar that provides one-click access to Windows 98's Internet utilities. A toolbar can be docked to the Taskbar, docked to another side of the screen, or left floating in a window on your desktop.

- *Show Desktop*. This button on the Quick Launch toolbar lets you minimize all open windows on your desktop with a single click.

- *New configuration options on the Settings menu*. Centralize many key system settings, including Taskbar & Start Menu, Folders & Icons, and Active Desktop settings.

Starting Windows 98

After Windows 98 is installed on your system, it starts automatically every time you turn on your computer. Although you will see lines of text flashing on-screen during the initial startup, Windows 98 loads automatically and then displays the Windows desktop.

If your installation of Windows has multiple configurations, such as for a laptop or desktop version, a text screen asks you to choose the configuration before Windows starts. If you have configured Windows for multiple users, or you are connected to a network, you see a login dialog box in which you type your password. Windows loads the configuration for the logged in user.

Here is how you start Windows 98:

1. Turn on your computer.
2. Wait for the various text messages to flash by (drivers loading, system memory check, and so on).
3. If multiple configurations are presented, choose one.
4. If the Login dialog box is presented, log in with your password. (Your user name should already be in the dialog box. If this isn't your correct user name, you need to enter that, too.)
5. Windows 98 now displays the desktop with icons, Taskbar, and Start menus.

Logging In on Startup

If your computer is connected to a network, you'll be presented with a dialog box asking you to log in to your network. When you see the Login dialog box, proceed as follows:

1. Enter your password (and user name if needed) in the dialog box.
2. Click OK to proceed.

Eliminating the Need to Login

If you are not on a network but you are still presented with the Login dialog box when Windows starts, you can easily turn this feature off:

 See the sections "Right-Clicking the Mouse for Pop-Up Menus" and "Using Dialog Boxes, Tabs, and Buttons" later in this chapter for more information on how to perform the following steps.

1. Right-click the Network Neighborhood icon on your desktop.
2. When the pop-up menu appears, select Properties.
3. Click the Configuration tab, and then choose Windows Logon from the Primary Network Logon pull-down list. Click OK to proceed.
4. When Windows prompts you to restart your computer, click Yes.
5. If, after Windows restarts, you are still asked for a user name and password, proceed to Step 6.
6. Click the Start button, choose Settings, and then choose Control Panel.
7. When Control Panel opens, click the Passwords icon.
8. When the Password Properties dialog box appears, click the Change Windows Password button.
9. When the Change Windows Password dialog box appears, enter your Old password. Leave New password and Confirm new password blank, and then click OK.
10. Click OK to close the Change Windows Password dialog box. The next time you start Windows, you will not be prompted for a password.

 You may want to retain the Login dialog box even if you're not on a network; requiring a password to start Windows lets multiple users access a single computer with their own unique desktop preferences, as described in Chapter 4, "Personalizing the Windows 98 Desktop."

Part
I

Ch
2

Exiting Windows 98 and Shutting Down Your Computer

When you finish running Windows applications and want to turn off the computer, you first must correctly exit Windows by using the Shut Down command—you can't just turn off your computer with Windows 98 still running.

> **CAUTION**
>
> Don't ever turn your computer off without exiting Windows. You could lose data and settings that are temporarily stored in your system's memory. Wait for the message saying it is safe to turn off your computer. If your system fails to shut down Windows and shut off your computer, see Chapter 33, "Solving Common Problems."

1. Save any documents and other data in applications that are open, and then exit all applications.
2. Click the Start button and select Shut Down.
3. The Shut Down Windows dialog box (see Figure 2.1) appears with the following options (which may vary depending on your configuration):
   - Shut Down
   - Restart
   - Restart in MS-DOS Mode

FIG. 2.1

Exiting Windows; choose Shut Down to exit.

4. Choose Shut Down, and then click OK.
5. When prompted, choose Yes.
6. Turn off your computer when you see the message that says it is safe to do so.

N O T E Some types of computers—including many laptops—automatically shut off your computer without displaying the "safe to shut off" message. ■

 To restart your computer (reboot) without shutting down completely, choose the Restart option in the Shut Down Windows dialog box. To simply restart Windows without restarting your entire computer system, hold down the Shift key when you choose the Restart option, and click OK.

Understanding the Windows 98 Classic Desktop

The desktop is the background on which you work in Windows 98. With Windows 98 you have the choice of two different desktops: The "classic" desktop and the new Active Desktop with True Web Integration. You enable the classic desktop by following these steps:

1. Click the Start button, select Settings, and then select Folders & Icons.

2. When the Folder Options dialog box appears, select the General tab and choose Classic Style. Click OK.

3. Click the Start button, select Settings, select Active Desktop, and then deselect View as Web Page. (If there is no check mark next to View as Web Page, this option is already deselected.)

The classic desktop, shown in Figure 2.2, looks and works just like the desktop in Windows 95. You highlight icons by single-clicking them, and you launch applications by double-clicking icons.

Part

I

Ch

2

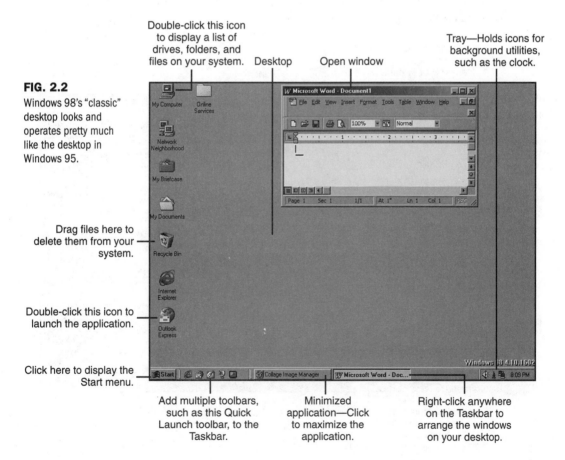

FIG. 2.2
Windows 98's "classic" desktop looks and operates pretty much like the desktop in Windows 95.

Double-click this icon to display a list of drives, folders, and files on your system. Desktop   Open window

Tray—Holds icons for background utilities, such as the clock.

Drag files here to delete them from your system.

Double-click this icon to launch the application.

Click here to display the Start menu.

Add multiple toolbars, such as this Quick Launch toolbar, to the Taskbar.

Minimized application—Click to maximize the application.

Right-click anywhere on the Taskbar to arrange the windows on your desktop.

Understanding the Windows 98 Active Desktop

When you activate True Web Integration, your desktop turns into an Active Desktop, which looks and acts a bit different from the classic desktop. With True Web Integration, all objects behave like Web links—you highlight icons by "hovering" over them (without clicking), and you launch applications by single-clicking icons.

To enable the Active Desktop:

1. Click the Start button, select Settings, and then select Folders & Icons.
2. When the Folder Options dialog box appears, select the General tab and choose Web Style. Click OK.
3. Click the Start button, select Settings, select Active Desktop, and then select View as Web Page.

When the Active Desktop (shown in Figure 2.3) is activated, all objects on your desktop now behave like objects or links on the Web. You highlight icons by hovering over them, and you launch applications by clicking icons.

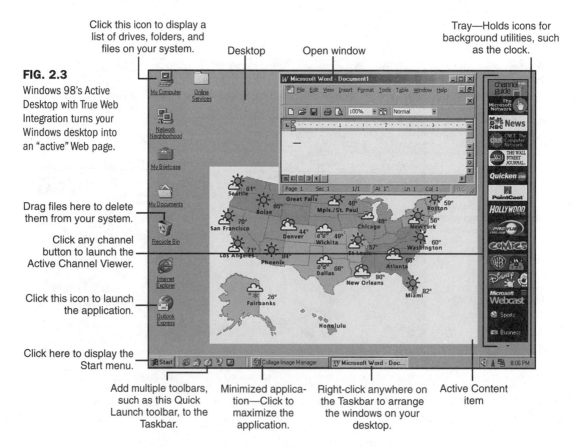

FIG. 2.3

Windows 98's Active Desktop with True Web Integration turns your Windows desktop into an "active" Web page.

Click this icon to display a list of drives, folders, and files on your system.

Desktop

Open window

Tray—Holds icons for background utilities, such as the clock.

Drag files here to delete them from your system.

Click any channel button to launch the Active Channel Viewer.

Click this icon to launch the application.

Click here to display the Start menu.

Add multiple toolbars, such as this Quick Launch toolbar, to the Taskbar.

Minimized application—Click to maximize the application.

Right-click anywhere on the Taskbar to arrange the windows on your desktop.

Active Content item

The major parts of the Active Desktop are:

- *Start button*. Opens the Start menu, which has submenus leading to many other folders and applications.
- *Taskbar*. Displays buttons for your open applications and windows, as well as different toolbars for different tasks.
- *Toolbar*. A separate button bar that can be attached to the main Taskbar. Windows 98 includes toolbars for URL Addresses, Links to favorite Web sites, Desktop icons, and Quick Launch of Web utilities; in addition, you can create your own personalized toolbars.
- *Tray*. The part of the Taskbar that holds the clock, volume control, and icons for other utilities that run in the background of your system.
- *Shortcut icons*. Enable you to launch applications and load documents with a single click of the mouse.
- *Windows*. When open on the desktop, these can be moved around and resized.
- *Active Channels*. These Web-based channels provide access to specific content "pushed" directly to your desktop.

True Web Integration also turns your desktop into a "live" HTML document. This feature lets you add other HTML objects—such as stock or news tickers—directly to your desktop. See Chapter 5, "Configuring the Active Desktop," for more information.

N O T E This book assumes that you're using the Active Desktop with True Web Integration. If you're using the classic desktop, convert all instructions that say "click" to "double-click;" convert all instructions that say "hover" to mean "click." ■

Part I

Ch 2

Using the Start Menu

Whether you're using the classic desktop or the Active Desktop, the Start menu is a straightforward tool for starting applications. Just click the Start button to display the Start menu and associated submenus.

1. Click the Start button. The Start menu pops up (see Figure 2.4).
2. Move the pointer along the menu. Submenus pop up for some of the items: Find, Settings, Documents, Favorites, and Programs.
3. To move to a submenu item, point to the Start menu item, and then move the pointer either left or right to the submenu. Move the pointer up or down in the submenu.
4. When the application, document, or command you want is highlighted, click to select it.

 T I P If you have a newer keyboard, it may have built-in Windows keys. Look between the Ctrl and Alt keys. If you see a key with the Windows logo, press it to open the Start menu. You may also have a key with an icon that looks like a menu. Press it to open a shortcut menu related to the cursor's position onscreen.

FIG. 2.4
The Start menu leads to several submenus, which enable easy organization of your applications.

Using Desktop Shortcuts

Shortcuts are icons on your desktop that represent programs or documents. Single-clicking a desktop shortcut either launches the corresponding program, or launches a program and loads the corresponding document.

 T I P In Windows 95 you had to double-click a shortcut icon to launch its corresponding program. In Windows 98, you only have to single-click the icon.

To launch a program or document from a shortcut:

1. Move your cursor over the icon. As you hover over the icon, the icon will be highlighted.
2. Click the icon once. The program or document now launches automatically.

Opening a Window

Almost every activity in Windows 98 requires opening a window. Although you probably know at least two ways to open a window or application, maybe you haven't tried all the available methods.

Here is the most popular way to open a window or application:

1. Click the Start button.
2. Click a command, menu, folder, or document.

The following are some other ways to open a window or application:

■ Click a shortcut icon on the desktop.
■ From My Computer, click an application or document icon.

- From Windows Explorer, click an application or document icon.
- Click an icon on a separate program's shortcut bar, such as the Microsoft Office Shortcut Bar.

Switching Between Windows

Although you may have multiple applications running, with windows all over your desktop, only one window is active at a time. If you want to work in a window, it must be selected.

You can see which window currently is active because its title bar is a different color—usually brighter or darker—while the other title bars become more faded. (This may not be true if you have customized the window colors.) If windows overlap, the active one is on top. Also, the active window's Taskbar button appears lighter and looks as though it is pressed in.

You can select a window, and therefore switch applications, by using the following steps:

1. Locate the window's button in the Taskbar.
2. Click the window's Taskbar button. This is the best method if some of the open windows are maximized, covering the view of any other windows.

Here are some other ways to select a window:

- Click the window's title bar.
- Click any other part of the window that is visible.
- Hold down the Alt key and then press the Tab key repeatedly until the application window you want is selected. (This cycles through all open windows.) When you're at the window you want, release the Alt key.

Closing a Window

After you've finished using a window or application, you can either leave the window open or you can close it. Your desktop could become very cluttered if you open many windows, however, and a large number of open applications could adversely affect the performance of your system. For these reasons, you should close windows when you are finished using them.

There are a number of ways to close a window:

- Click the x button in the window's upper-right corner (see Figure 2.5).
- Double-click the icon in the window's upper-left corner.
- Click the icon in the window's upper-left corner and select Close.
- Pull down the window's File menu and select Exit, if you're closing an application.
- Right-click the window's Taskbar button and choose Close.
- Press Alt+F4.

FIG. 2.5

Click the X button—also called the "Close" button—to close any window; use the Minimize and Maximize buttons to manipulate the windows on your desktop.

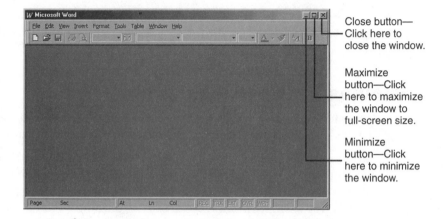

Close button— Click here to close the window.

Maximize button—Click here to maximize the window to full-screen size.

Minimize button—Click here to minimize the window.

CAUTION

If you attempt to close an application window without saving a document, the application will warn you and give you an opportunity to save the document. You must choose to save or not save the document before the application window will close.

Minimizing and Maximizing Windows

You can *minimize* or *maximize* a window. If you minimize a window for an application, a temporary button for the application continues to appear on the Taskbar.

Within an application, minimizing a document window reduces the document within the application window. Maximizing a document window enlarges the document to the full size of the application window, which may or may not be full-screen size.

There are a number of ways to minimize or maximize a window:

- Click the Minimize or Maximize buttons in the window's upper-right corner (refer to Figure 2.5).
- Click the icon in the window's upper-left corner and choose Minimize to minimize the window, or choose Maximize to maximize the window.
- Right-click the Taskbar button that represents the window. Choose Minimize to minimize the window, or choose Maximize to maximize the window.

Restoring a Minimized or Maximized Window

When you minimize a window, it becomes a button on the Taskbar. When you maximize a window, it takes up the full screen or the full size of its application window if it is a document.

To restore a minimized window, just click the Taskbar button that represents the window. To restore a minimized document within an application, click its minimized button in the application window.

Here are some other ways to restore a minimized or maximized window to its former state:

- Click the Restore button in the window's upper-right corner.
- Right-click the Taskbar button that represents the window. Choose Restore.
- Click the icon in the window's upper-left corner to open the Control menu, and then choose Restore to return the window to its previous size.

Clearing All Windows from the Desktop

Windows 98 includes a Quick Launch toolbar on the Taskbar, as shown in Figure 2.6. (To display this toolbar, right-click anywhere on the Taskbar, select Toolbars, and then select Quick Launch.) Follow these steps to minimize all open windows on your desktop:

1. To automatically minimize all open windows, click the Show Desktop button.
2. To return your desktop to its previous state, click the Show Desktop button again.

FIG. 2.6
Click the Show Desktop button on the Quick Launch toolbar to quickly clear your desktop of all open windows.

Show Desktop button

 T I P   You can also minimize all windows by right-clicking a blank area of the Taskbar and then choosing Minimize All Windows from the pop-up menu.

Moving Windows

Often, you will want to move a window out of the way so that you can access a desktop icon or view the contents of another window. The easiest way to move a window on the desktop is to drag it with your mouse.

1. Position the mouse pointer on the title bar of the window.
2. Hold down the left mouse button.
3. Drag the item to the desired position.
4. Release the mouse button.

N O T E   If an application is maximized to full-screen size, you can't move it; the application needs
to be minimized to a smaller window before it can be moved on your desktop. ▪

You can also use the keyboard to move a window. Press Alt+space bar to open the Control
menu icon in the upper-left corner of the window. The window is surrounded by a gray border.
Choose <u>M</u>ove and then use the keyboard arrow keys to position the window. Press Enter to
complete the move.

Resizing Windows

Resizing a window lets you custom-fit the window to a selected space on your desktop. Just
follow these steps:

1. Position the mouse pointer on any corner or side of the window. The pointer changes to
   a double-headed arrow.

2. Hold down the left mouse button.

3. Drag the item to the desired size. Drag toward the window to reduce the size; drag away
   from the window to enlarge it. An outline shows the proposed size.

4. Release the mouse button.

You can use the keyboard to size a window. Press Alt+space bar to open the Control menu icon
in the upper-left corner of the window. Choose <u>S</u>ize and then use the keyboard arrow keys to
size the window. Press Enter to quit sizing the window.

Arranging Windows

Use a special pop-up menu on the Taskbar to automatically rearrange windows on your desktop. (Of course, you can always move and resize any window manually; these commands just
make it easier to deal with multiple windows.)

1. Position your cursor somewhere in a blank area of the Taskbar and then click your right
   mouse button. This displays a pop-up menu (see Figure 2.7).

2. Choose a command from the menu, as described in Table 2.1.

FIG. 2.7

Right-click the Taskbar
to arrange the windows
on your desktop.

Table 2.1   Taskbar Menu Commands

Command	Description
Cascade Windows	Displays windows overlapped from left to right, or top to bottom.
Undo Cascade	Returns cascaded windows to their previous sizes (available only after using Cascade).
Tile Windows Horizontally	Displays windows top to bottom without overlapping.
Tile Windows Vertically	Displays windows left to right without overlapping.
Undo Tile Windows	Returns windows to their previous sizes. (Available only after a Tile command.)
Minimize All Windows	Reduces all open windows to buttons on the Taskbar.
Properties	Displays the Taskbar Properties sheet where you can change options for the Taskbar and the Start menu. (This doesn't have anything to do with arranging windows.)
Toolbars	Enables you to add other toolbars to the main Windows Taskbar.

Part

I

Ch

2

Right-Clicking the Mouse for Pop-Up Menus

One of the more useful features of Windows 98 is the concept of context-sensitive *pop-up menus*. These are menus that pop-up when you click the *right* mouse button, offering you a set of commands appropriate to the current task at hand (such as the Taskbar's pop-up menu discussed in the previous section).

Displaying a pop-up menu is easy. For example, position your cursor over an empty portion of the desktop and click your right (not the normal left) mouse button. (This is also referred to as *right-clicking*.) A pop-up menu appropriate to your task at hand—the desktop—is displayed. If you right-click while your cursor is over a shortcut icon, a different pop-up menu is displayed; and so on.

With Windows 98, one thing is sure—when in doubt, click your right mouse button and see what pops up!

Using Dialog Boxes, Tabs, and Buttons

When Windows or an other application requires a complex set of inputs, you are often presented with a *dialog box*. A dialog box is like a form where you can input various parameters and make various choices—and then register those inputs and choices when you click the OK button.

There are various types of dialog boxes, each one customized to the task at hand. However, most dialog boxes share a set of common features, including:

- *Buttons*. Most buttons either register your inputs or open an auxiliary dialog box. The most common buttons are OK (to register your inputs and close the dialog box), Cancel (to close the dialog box without registering your inputs), and Apply (to register your inputs without closing the dialog box).

- *Tabs*. These enable a single dialog box to display multiple "pages" of information. Think of each tab, arranged across the top of the dialog box, as a "thumbtab" to the individual "page" in the dialog box below it. Click a tab to change to that particular "page" of information.

- *Text boxes*. These are empty boxes where you type in a response. Position your cursor over the empty input box, click your left mouse button, and begin typing.

- *Lists*. These are lists of available choices; lists can either scroll or drop down from what looks like an input box. Select an item from the list with your mouse; select multiple items by holding down the Ctrl key while you click with your mouse.

- *Check boxes*. These are boxes—sometimes called "radio buttons" or "option buttons"— that let you select (or deselect) various stand-alone options.

- *Sliders*. These are sliding bars that let you select increments between two extremes— like a sliding volume control on an audio system.

Figure 2.8 shows a common dialog box—the Display Properties dialog box. (To display this dialog box, right-click an empty part of the desktop, and then select Properties from the pop-up menu.) This dialog box includes buttons, tabs, lists, and check boxes —everything *except* a text box and a slider.

NOTE If an option in a dialog box is dimmed (or "grayed"), that means it isn't available for the current task. ■

Using Wizards

A *wizard* is a kind of interactive dialog box that automates a complex task. Wizards pop up automatically when you choose certain tasks, such as adding a new piece of hardware to your system or creating a new shortcut on your desktop.

When you see a wizard, follow the instructions and click the Next button as appropriate; click the Finish button when you reach the end of the task. As with any dialog box, clicking the Cancel button cancels the current operation and closes the wizard; clicking the Back button lets you back up through any completed steps.

FIG. 2.8

The Display Properties dialog box—where you can set all sorts of parameters for your desktop and display.

List—Click the down arrow and select an item

Check box

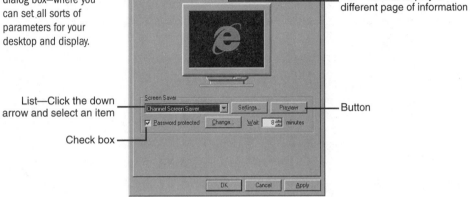

Tab—click to display a different page of information

Button

Part

I

Ch

2

Figure 2.9 shows the Create Shortcut wizard. To access this wizard, right-click anywhere on your desktop; when the pop-up menu appears, select <u>N</u>ew, and then select <u>S</u>hortcut.

FIG. 2.9

The Create Shortcut wizard automates a tedious task.

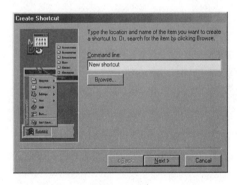

Configuring and Personalizing Windows 98

Configuring Windows 98

In this chapter

The New Configuration Features of Windows 98

Windows 98 includes many more configuration options than you are used to with Windows 95. Among the most notable new options are:

- *Display options*. Windows 98 includes many display options that were part of the optional Windows 95 Plus! pack, including font smoothing and wallpaper stretching. Just click the Display icon in Control Panel.

- *Desktop themes*. You can install unified "themes" for your desktop wallpaper, cursors, system sounds, and screen saver. (This was formerly a feature in the Windows 95 Plus! pack.)

- *Multiple-monitor support*. Windows 98 lets you hook up two monitors to your system, and display different items on each screen.

- *Internet options*. Because Internet Explorer is now an integral part of the operating system, Windows 98 lets you configure various browser settings by clicking the Internet icon in the Control panel.

- *Dialing options*. All of Windows' dialing-related settings can now be accessed by clicking the Telephony icon in the Control Panel.

- *Multiple users*. With Windows 98 it's easier to configure your system for multiple users— just click the Users icon in the Control Panel. (You can also click the Passwords icon in Control Panel to assign passwords to each user.)

- *Power management options*. Windows 98 includes several power management schemes that let you minimize the energy use of your computer system—especially if you use a portable computer.

- *Accessibility options*. Windows 98 includes several new features to make it easier for users with various impairments to use their computers, including the new Microsoft Magnifier utility.

Using Control Panel

Windows 98's Control Panel is a folder that contains a number of individual utilities that let you adjust and configure various system properties. Most items that you can configure with Windows 98 are located in the Control Panel.

By default, Control Panel includes a variety of standard Windows 98 utilities, such as Add New Hardware and Printers. In addition, many applications and utilities install their own Control Panel items. For example, if you install TweakUI (see Chapter 4, "Personalizing the Windows 98 Desktop"), a TweakUI icon is automatically added to Control Panel. When you click an icon in the Control Panel, a dialog box opens specific to the settings of that control. For example, clicking the Date/Time icon opens the Date/Time Properties dialog box, which enables you to set the date and time of the Windows 98 system clock.

To open the Control Panel folder:

1. Click the Start button.
2. From the Start menu select Settings, and then select Control Panel.

Some of the standard items in the Control Panel (see Figure 3.1) are shown in Table 3.1.

FIG. 3.1
Windows 98's Control Panel—click any icon to configure a specific aspect of your system.

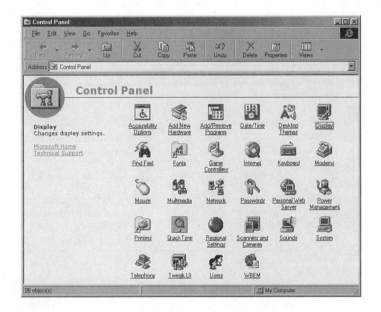

Table 3.1 Standard Control Panel Items

Icon	Name	Description
	Add New Hardware	Adds new hardware devices to your system. See Chapter 14, "Installing and Configuring Peripheral Devices."
	Add/Remove Programs	Adds new software to your system, or removes old software programs. See Chapter 10, "Installing New Software."
	Date/Time	Adjusts Windows 98's time and date settings. See "Setting the Time and Date," later in this chapter.
	Desktop Themes	Lets you install a unified "theme" for your desktop wallpaper, cursors, system sounds, and screen saver. See Chapter 4, "Personalizing the Windows 98 Desktop."

continues

Table 3.1 Continued

Icon	Name	Description
	Display	Configures settings for your desktop display and monitor. See "Configuring Your Desktop Display," later in this chapter.
	Fonts	Manages your system's fonts. See "Installing New Fonts," later in this chapter.
	Game Controllers	Configures any joysticks connected to your system. See Chapter 20, "Configuring and Using Keyboards, Mice, and Joysticks."
	Internet	Manages the settings for the Internet Explorer Web browser. See Chapter 22, "Surfing the Internet with Internet Explorer."
	Keyboard	Configures your PC's keyboard. See Chapter 20.
	Modems	Configures any modems connected to your PC. See Chapter 16, "Configuring and Using Modems."
	Mouse	Configures the operation of your mouse or other pointing devices. See Chapter 20.
	Multimedia	Sets up your system's audio, video, MIDI, and music CD properties. See "Setting Multimedia Options," later in this chapter.
	Network	Configures your PC's connection to a local area network or the Internet. See Chapter 28, "Network Computing with Windows 98."
	Passwords	Secures your system with a password and determines how multiple users can use your computer. See "Securing Your System with Passwords," later in this chapter.
	Power Management	Determines how and when your computer powers down when not in use. See "Conserving Energy with Power Management," later in this chapter.
	Printers	Configures Windows 98 to work with your printer. See Chapter 15, "Configuring and Using Printers."

Icon	Name	Description
	Regional Settings	Adjusts currency and number formats for where you live. See "Setting Up Windows for Your Locality," later in this chapter.
	Sounds	Changes the sounds you hear when you initiate certain operations. See Chapter 18, "Configuring and Using Sound Options."
	System	Lets you view and configure technical aspects of your computer system. See Chapter 9, "Basic System Maintenance."
	Telephony	Configures the universal dialing properties for any programs that use a modem. See "Configuring Your System's Dialing Options," later in this chapter.
	Users	Sets up your computer to be used by multiple users. See "Setting Up Windows for Multiple Users," later in this chapter.

Part

II

Ch

3

Setting the Time and Date

One of the first things you should do after you initially install Windows 98 or purchase a new computer is set the system's time and date. You do this from the Date/Time icon in the Control Panel.

1. Click the Start button, select Settings, and then select Control Panel.

2. Click the Date/Time icon in Control panel.

3. When the Date & Time Properties dialog box appears (see Figure 3.2), select the Date & Time tab. Choose the correct month and year from the pull-down lists, click the correct day of the month on the calendar, and set the correct time on the clock.

FIG. 3.2

Click the Date/Time icon in Control Panel to set your system's date and time.

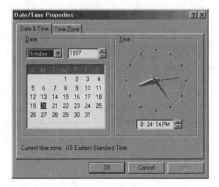

4. Choose the Time Zone tab. Select the correct time zone from the pull-down list; for most states, you should also select Automatically Adjust Clock for Daylight Saving Changes.

5. Click OK to accept the changes and close the dialog box, or click Apply to make the changes while keeping the dialog box open.

 T I P You can also access the Date/Time Properties dialog box by double-clicking the time in the Toolbar tray.

Setting Up Windows for Your Locality

Copies of Windows 98 sold in English-speaking countries, by default, are configured for American-style currency and number formats. By changing Regional Settings properties, you can switch between different international character sets, number formats, currency formats, and date and time displays—essentially setting up Windows 98 for use in other countries.

> **CAUTION**
>
> Changing the language and country formats does not change the language used in Windows menus and dialog boxes (for that you need a local-language version of Windows), but does affect the data in applications that take advantage of these regional features.

To change the regional settings of Windows 98:

1. Click the Start button, select Settings, and then select Control Panel.

2. Click the Regional Settings icon to display the Regional Settings Properties dialog box.

3. Click the tabs described in the Table 3.2 and make the selections you want.

4. Click OK to accept the changes and close the dialog box, or click Apply to make the changes while keeping the dialog box open.

Table 3.2 Regional Settings

Tab	Description
Regional Settings	Select the desired region from the drop-down list. This selection changes settings in the other pages; therefore, you should set this property first.
Number	Notice the Appearance Samples boxes at the top that illustrate the number format selected below. Make changes to the settings by choosing from their drop-down lists or by typing in the boxes. (You can observe the effect your changes will have on the samples by clicking the Apply button.)

Tab	Description
Currency	Change the currency properties by choosing from the drop-down lists or by typing in the boxes.
Time	Change the style of the time by choosing from the drop-down lists or by typing in the boxes. The change is shown in the Time Sample box.
Date	Change long date, short date, and date separator styles by choosing from the drop-down lists or by typing in the boxes. The change is shown in the Long Date Sample box or the Short Date Sample box. These date formats will be the default formats in the programs you use.

N O T E   To type the currency symbols in any given application, you may also have to change the language in the Keyboard Properties dialog box (see Chapter 20, "Configuring and Using Keyboards, Mice, and Joysticks"). Also, many Windows programs let you set currency and number formats that will override these regional settings; if you only need these formats temporarily or infrequently, you can change them in the application when they are needed. ▪

Part

II

Ch

3

Previewing Fonts

Windows 98 comes with numerous fonts preinstalled for use in your favorite software programs. You use these fonts to both display text on-screen and to print out text from your printer. Use the Fonts dialog box to preview the fonts installed on your system.

1. Click the Start button, select Settings, and then select Control Panel.
2. Click the Fonts icon.
3. When the Fonts window is displayed, double-click any font icon to view a sample of that font at various type sizes (see Figure 3.3).
4. Click the Print button to print a sample of the font; click the Done button to close the display window.

Installing New Fonts

Although Windows installs many font files during setup, you may want to add additional fonts from the Windows disks or CD-ROM, from third-party vendors, or even from online services. To install a new font:

1. Click the Start button, select Settings, and then select Control Panel.
2. Click the Fonts icon in Control Panel. The Fonts window displays all fonts currently installed on your system.

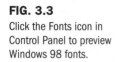

FIG. 3.3
Click the Fonts icon in
Control Panel to preview
Windows 98 fonts.

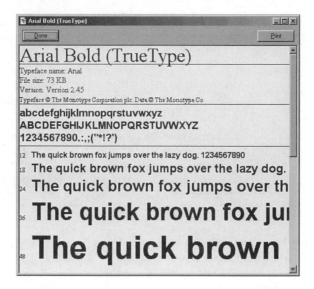

3. Pull down the File menu and select Install New Font to display the Add Fonts dialog box.

4. Select the drive and folder that holds the fonts you want to install.

5. Fonts available at the location you specified will now be listed. Select the font(s) you want to add. (To select multiple fonts, hold down the Ctrl key while clicking additional listings.)

6. Select the Copy Fonts to Fonts Folder check box.

7. Click OK to add the fonts you selected.

 You can also install fonts directly from My Computer or Windows Explorer. Simply drag font files from an installation disk and drop them into the \Windows\Fonts folder.

 Installing too many fonts on your system not only can consume large amounts of hard disk space, but can also eat up system memory and cause your system to run slower. You may want to periodically remove unused fonts to enhance system performance and free up disk space.

Removing Unwanted Fonts

If you find you have too many fonts installed on your system—or find there are fonts you seldom if ever use—you can use Control Panel to delete these font files from your system.

1. Click the Start button, select Settings, and then select Control Panel.

2. Click the Fonts icon in Control Panel. The Fonts window displays all fonts currently registered on the system.

3. Right-click the icon for the font you want to delete and select <u>D</u>elete from the pop-up menu. Windows asks if you're sure you want to delete these fonts. Choose <u>Y</u>es to delete. The font files are uninstalled from your system and sent to the Recycle Bin.

 TIP You can also delete fonts directly from My Computer. Just drag selected font files from the \Windows\Fonts folder and drop them onto the Recycle Bin icon.

Setting Multimedia Options

The Multimedia Properties dialog box lets you adjust various audio and video playback settings for your system. This is also where you configure your system if you've attached a MIDI-compatible device, or you want to play music CDs.

▶ **See** "Setting Up MIDI Output," **p. 196**

To configure your system for multimedia use:

1. Click the Start button, select <u>S</u>ettings, and then select <u>C</u>ontrol Panel.
2. Click the Multimedia icon.
3. When the Multimedia Properties dialog box appears (see Figure 3.4), click the tabs described in Table 3.3 and make the selections you want.

FIG. 3.4
Click the Multimedia icon in Control Panel to adjust your system's audio settings.

4. Click OK to accept the changes and close the dialog box, or click <u>A</u>pply to make the changes while keeping the dialog box open.

Part

II

Ch

3

Table 3.3 Multimedia Settings

Tab	Description
Audio	Adjust playback and recording volume, select the preferred playback and recording devices, and choose to show a volume control icon in the Toolbar's tray.
Video	Select whether full-motion video is shown in a window or full-screen.
MIDI	Select which instruments are used for MIDI playback and recording.
CD Music	Select the volume settings for music CD playback through headphones; if you have more than one CD-ROM drive, you can choose different settings for each drive.
Advanced	Lists the various multimedia devices installed on your system by type of device. Click the "+" sign to show devices for each category type. To reconfigure a device, highlight it and click the Properties button.

TIP Displaying a volume control icon in the Toolbar's tray lets you easily change your system's volume; when you single-click the icon, a sliding volume control appears.

Configuring Your System's Dialing Options

If you have a modem connected to your computer—for connecting to the Internet or a commercial online service—you need to configure your system's telephony, or dialing, properties. These properties include options such as your area code, access numbers, and calling card number.

▶ **See** "Creating a New Connection with the Internet Connection Wizard," **p. 221**

1. Click the Start button, select Settings, and then select Control Panel.

2. Click the Telephony icon.

3. When the Dialing Properties dialog box appears (see Figure 3.5), click the My Locations tab. Select the correct country, enter your area code, and then select the other options appropriate for your location.

4. If you want to use a calling card for your long-distance calls, click the Calling Card button and enter the appropriate information in the Calling Card dialog box.

5. Click OK to register your information.

FIG. 3.5
Click the Telephony icon in Control Panel to adjust your system's dialing settings.

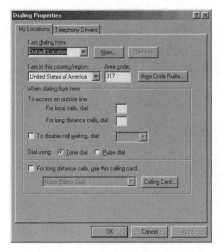

Configuring Your Desktop Display

Assuming you have a powerful enough video card, you can configure your display to run at a variety of screen resolutions. Make sure you've selected the proper display setup for your video card, however—if you set up your display to run at a higher-resolution than your card is capable, you could end up with a lot of gibberish on your screen.

 To best view most Web-based content, configure your system to at least 800×600 resolution with at least 256 colors.

To change the resolution of your desktop display:

1. Click the Start button, select Settings, and then select Control Panel.
2. Click the Display icon.
3. When the Display Properties dialog box appears (see Figure 3.6), click the Settings tab, and then click the Advanced button to display the Advanced Display Properties dialog box.
4. To confirm or change your video card configuration, click the Adapter tab. If your adapter type is correctly displayed, go to step 5. If your adapter type is not correct, click the Change button and follow the instructions in the Upgrade Device Driver Wizard. When you have finished upgrading your video adapter, proceed to step 5.
5. If your monitor is capable of displaying 256 or more colors, return to the main Display Properties dialog box, select the Settings tab, and choose the desired setting from the Colors drop-down list.

FIG. 3.6

Access the Display Properties dialog box from Control Panel or by right-clicking the desktop and choosing Properties.

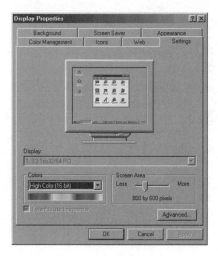

6. To change the resolution of your display, go to the Settings tab and choose the desired setting from the Screen Area slider. (The sample display changes to reflect your new settings.)

7. Click OK to activate your new display settings.

> **CAUTION**
>
> Never try to select a monitor type that is beyond the capability of your monitor. You could cause damage to the monitor or make the display unreadable. If your selection made the screen unreadable, shut off the computer. Turn on the computer; press F8 when you see the phrase `Starting Windows 98`. Choose the Safe Mode selection from the menu. When the Safe Mode Windows desktop is displayed, repeat the preceding steps, but choose a resolution you are certain your monitor can display.

N O T E Some video drivers add new tabs to the Display Properties dialog box. If so, you'll need to click this driver-specific tab to make changes to certain video and display properties. ■

Setting Up Windows for Two Monitors

If you perform any activities that involve both input and output—such as desktop publishing, programming, or Web page design—you should investigate adding a second monitor and configuring Windows 98 to run two separate displays. With such a system setup, you can configure your primary display for the input (entering HTML code, for example) and the secondary display for the final output (the final Web page displayed in a browser, continuing the example).

N O T E To run multiple displays, you must have two compatible video cards installed on your system. ■

To configure Windows 98 to support multiple displays:

1. Make sure that when you install Windows 98, you have only one video card installed in your system. After Windows 98 installation is complete, shut down your computer and add the second display card to your system, following the installation instructions from the card's manufacturer.

2. Click the Start button, select Settings, and then select Control Panel. When Control Panel starts, click the Display icon.

3. After you've installed your second video card, the Display Settings dialog box has a new tab, labeled Monitors, that replaces the standard Settings tab. Select the Monitors tab.

4. Your primary monitor should already be configured properly. Select the secondary display/monitor combination, and choose to Use This Device as Part of the Desktop. Set the other properties as appropriate, dragging the screen images to set relative screen placement for the two monitors.

5. To change the resolution of the second monitor, click the Settings button and make the appropriate changes.

6. Click OK to register changes.

N O T E   If you're running a DOS application in full-screen mode, it will only be visible on your primary display. ■

Part
II

Ch
3

Setting Up Windows for Multiple Users

If you share a computer with someone else, you can set up user profiles to store each person's custom settings. Each user will have a logon name that activates custom settings when Windows is reset for their use.

To configure your system for multiple users:

1. Click the Start button, select Settings, and then select Control Panel.

2. Click the Passwords icon.

3. When the Passwords Properties dialog box is displayed, select the User Profiles tab.

4. If you are the only user on this PC, or if all users use the same preferences, select All Users of This PC Use the Same Preferences and Desktop Settings.

5. If you want to set up separate settings for different users, select Users Can Customize Their Preferences and Desktop Settings. If you select the later option, determine whether users can choose their own desktop icons and/or Start menu groups.

6. Click OK. You will then be asked to restart your computer. Click Yes.

Adding New Users to Your System

After you've configured your system to accept additional users (see the preceding section, "Setting Up Windows for Multiple Users"), you can now add new users to your system.

1. Click the Start button, select Settings, and then select Control Panel.
2. From within Control panel, click the Users icon.
3. The first time you add a second user to your system, you will be prompted by the Enable Multi-User Settings Wizard. Click the Next button to proceed.
4. On the second screen of the Wizard, enter the new User Name and click Next.
5. On the next screen, enter and confirm the new user's password and click Next.
6. When the Personalized Item Settings dialog box appears (see Figure 3.7), select the items you want to personalize, and then click Next.

FIG. 3.7
When you add new users to your system, you can determine how much of the system you want them to personalize.

7. When you see the final screen of the Wizard, click Finish.
8. After you've added your first additional user, you are no longer presented with the Enable Multi-User Settings Wizard when you click the Users icon in Control Panel. Instead, you're taken directly to the User Settings dialog box. To add a new user from the User Settings dialog box, click the New User button and you're launched into the Add User Wizard. Follow steps 4 to 7 to add a new user from this Wizard.

After you add new users following these steps, they can customize their own desktop settings the next time they log onto Windows.

 TIP To change users without shutting off your PC, click the Start button and select Log Off. Windows will log off the current user and then ask for a new user name and password for the next user.

Securing Your Computer with Passwords

If you work in an environment where you need to limit access to data on your computer, you can configure Windows to require a password before it will start. To add a password to your system's startup routine, follow these steps:

1. Click the Start button, select <u>S</u>ettings, and then select <u>C</u>ontrol Panel.

2. Click the Users icon.

3. You will be asked to type the supervisor password; this should be your general Windows password.

▶ **See** "Logging In at Startup," **p. 19**

4. When the User Settings dialog box appears, select the User List tab and highlight the user whose password you want to add or change. Click the <u>S</u>et Password button to display the Change Windows Password dialog box.

5. If you had previously selected a password, it will appear in the <u>O</u>ld password box, and you'll need to enter it again to make changes. If you did not previously select a password, the <u>O</u>ld password box will be empty—and you should leave it empty.

6. Type the new password in the <u>N</u>ew Password and Con<u>f</u>irm Password text boxes. Click OK when done.

To remove a password, type your old password in the <u>O</u>ld password box and leave the other two boxes blank.

N O T E If you have network passwords, they are listed when you open the Change Windows Password dialog box. You can change them to match your Windows password. ■

Enhancing Performance with Virtual Memory

Windows 98 lets you augment your system's random access memory (RAM) with *virtual memory*. Virtual memory is hard disk space that is viewed by Windows as random access memory, so when Windows runs low on RAM it simply begins to store transient data on your hard drive.

Windows 98 automatically configures itself to use your hard disk for virtual memory. If you are running low on hard drive space, however, you can decrease the amount of hard drive used for virtual memory and give yourself more storage room for your permanent data.

> **CAUTION**
>
> In general, you should let Windows determine how to best manage virtual memory, because Windows 98 is built to use it as efficiently as possible. Because specifying the wrong settings can impair your system's performance, inexperienced users should not change Windows' default virtual memory settings.

To configure your system's virtual memory:

1. Click the Start button, select <u>S</u>ettings, and then select <u>C</u>ontrol Panel.

2. Click the System icon to display the System Properties dialog box, and then select the Performance tab.

Part

II

Ch

3

3. Click the Virtual Memory button. By default, Let Windows Manage my Virtual Memory Settings is selected. If you want to override the automatic settings, select Let Me Specify My Own Virtual Memory Settings.

4. Choose the hard disk you want to use for virtual memory, and then specify the Minimum and Maximum number of megabytes you want Windows to use for virtual memory. Click the OK button when done.

CAUTION

You can also choose to disable virtual memory, but this could prevent your computer from running certain applications or opening large files—or, in some instances, running Windows itself.

The hard disk you specify for virtual memory must have at least as much free space as the maximum amount of virtual memory you set. If you are low on hard disk space, a large virtual memory space can cause problems, such as not having enough space to save or copy a file.

Conserving Energy with Power Management

Windows 98 can be configured to work with so-called "green" computer systems. Green systems are built to conserve energy and automatically turn off different devices—such as the monitor or hard drive—when your system is turned on but not in use.

The power management settings vary between different computer manufacturers. The following settings are representative of one of the most common systems used by many manufacturers, where the PC uses a local bus motherboard with an Award BIOS chip set.

To configure your system's power management features:

1. Click the Start button, select Settings, and then select Control Panel.

2. Click the Power Management icon to open the Power Management Properties dialog box.

3. Select the Power Schemes tab, choose the proper Power Scheme from the drop-down list, and then determine how many minutes of inactivity you want to allow before your monitor automatically shuts off.

4. While still in the Power Schemes tab, determine how many minutes of inactivity you want to allow before your hard disk(s) power down, and then click OK.

5. Click OK to close the Power Management Properties dialog box.

Making Windows Accessible for the Impaired

Accessibility options are included in Windows 98 to make computers more available to the millions of people with hearing, sight, and movement disabilities. You can adjust the sound, display, keyboard, and mouse interface from the Accessibility Properties dialog box.

1. Click the Start button, select Programs, select Accessories, select Accessibility, and then select Accessibility Settings Wizard.

2. When the Accessibility Wizard appears, you're asked to select the smallest text that you can read. Do so and then click Next.

3. When the second screen of the Wizard appears, select the desired options to change the size of the on-screen text, and then click Next.

4. When the third screen of the Wizard appears (see Figure 3.8), select those items that you need help with: Items are Too Small, Seeing Colors, Hearing Sounds, Using the Keyboard, and Using or Seeing the Mouse. Click Next and the Wizard will guide you through a custom setup for your individual needs.

 TIP You can also adjust Windows' accessibility options—in a slightly less user-friendly manner—by clicking the Accessibility Options icon in the Control Panel.

Part

II

Ch

3

FIG. 3.8

Use the Accessibility Wizard to optimize Windows for your individual vision, hearing, and mobility needs.

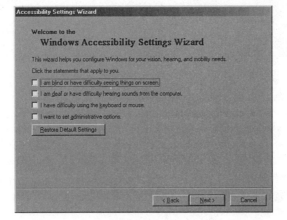

Using Microsoft Magnifier to Enlarge Small Type

If you have trouble seeing small type, Windows 98 includes a special utility called the Microsoft Magnifier. This utility works somewhat like a magnifying glass, enlarging selected portions of the screen so you can see them better.

1. Click the Start button, select Programs, select Accessories, select Accessibility, and then select Microsoft Magnifier.

2. As you can see in Figure 3.9, Magnifier now launches, taking up the top half of your screen. The Magnifier window displays the area around your cursor at a level of magnification. You can resize the Magnifier window just as you would any window on your desktop.

FIG. 3.9

Use Microsoft Magnifier to enlarge selected areas of your desktop display; the Microsoft Magnifier dialog box lets you change key Magnifier options, including magnification level.

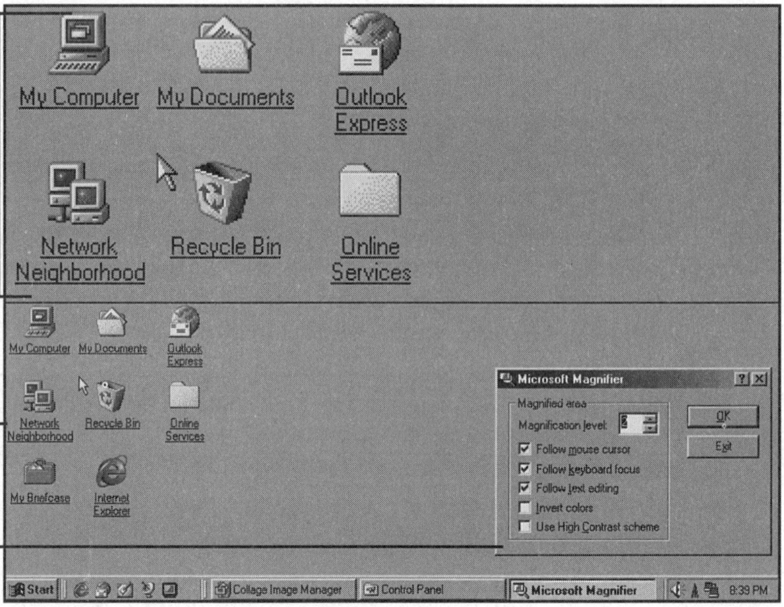

A Magnifier window— Enlarging the area around your cursor

Your normal desktop— The area around your cursor is enlarged in the Magnifier window

Microsoft Magnifier dialog box—Use this to change key configuration options

3. A special dialog box is always displayed when Magnifier is operational, so you can change important configuration options. Go to the Microsoft Magnifier dialog box to change Magnification Level (automatically set at 2X normal) and what screen elements Magnifier should track (mouse cursor, keyboard focus, and text editing). In addition, you can elect to have the text colors inverted in the Magnifier window for better viewing. Click OK when done.

4. To close Magnifier, click the Exit button in the Microsoft Magnifier dialog box.

Personalizing the Windows 98 Desktop

The New Personalization Features of Windows 98

There are numerous new ways to personalize your system with Windows 98. In fact, one of the great things about Windows 98 is how easily you can make the desktop look like *your* desktop, different from anybody else's. Here are some of the best new personalization features of Windows 98:

- *Drag and drop organization of the Programs menu.* With Windows 98, you can move items from place to place in the Programs menu by selecting and dragging them to a new location.

- *HTML documents as desktop background.* Windows 98's Active Desktop mode lets you use a Web page—complete with links to other Web pages—as your desktop background.

- *Gradated title bars.* The title bars in a Windows 98 window can now fade between two selected colors.

- *Desktop Themes.* Windows 98 includes Desktop Themes, formerly found in the Windows 95 Plus! pack. Desktop Themes let you coordinate the look of your desktop's colors, cursors, background, system sounds, and screen savers.

- *New screen savers.* With True Web Integration enabled, you can choose to display your Active Desktop or Active Channels as a screen saver.

- *Toolbars.* Windows 98 lets you add multiple toolbars to your desktop—either docked to the standard Taskbar, docked to another side of your screen, or free-floating in a window on your desktop. Toolbars are comprised of buttons that let you access common functions with a single click. The most popular toolbar is the Quick Launch toolbar, which includes buttons that let you launch Internet Explorer and Outlook Express, as well as a Show Desktop button that automatically minimizes all open windows on your desktop.

Creating New Shortcuts on the Desktop

Desktop icons, called *shortcuts*, are just that—shortcuts for starting applications and opening documents. Placing a shortcut on your desktop is an alternative to locating items on the Start menu and its associated submenus. Clicking a shortcut icon starts the associated application and automatically loads the selected document.

To create a new shortcut on your desktop:

1. Launch My Computer by clicking the My Computer icon on your desktop.
2. Navigate to the application or document for which you want to create a shortcut.
3. Right-drag the file onto the desktop, and then release the right mouse button. (Right-dragging is dragging while holding down the right mouse button.) A pop-up menu appears.
4. From the pop-up menu, select Create Shortcut(s) Here. The shortcut icon is placed on your desktop.

TIP You can also create a shortcut by right-clicking a file or folder, selecting Se_n_d To from the pop-up menu, and then selecting Desktop as Shortcut.

To remove a shortcut icon from the desktop, just drag it into the Recycle Bin.

Changing a Shortcut Icon's Name

When you create a new shortcut icon, its name is automatically prefixed with the words "Short-cut to." To change the name of a shortcut:

1. Right-click the shortcut on your desktop.
2. When the pop-up menu appears, select Re_n_ame.
3. The shortcut's name is now highlighted on your desktop. Use your keyboard's Delete key to erase parts of the existing name, and then type a new name. Press Enter when you've finished entering the new name.

Changing Shortcut Properties

You can change certain things about the way a shortcut behaves. To change the properties of a shortcut:

1. Right-click the shortcut icon and select P_r_operties from the pop-up menu.
2. When the Shortcut Properties dialog box appears, click the Shortcut tab (see Figure 4.1).

FIG. 4.1
Right-click a shortcut icon to change its properties.

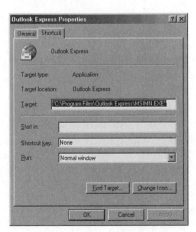

3. Choose the property you want to change, as detailed in Table 4.1.
4. Click OK to accept the changes and close the dialog box, or click _A_pply to make the changes while keeping the dialog box open.

Table 4.1 Shortcut Properties

Tab	Description
Target	Identifies the file that the shortcut opens.
Start In	Identifies the specific folder from which the program starts.
Shortcut Key	Identifies the shortcut keys that activate the shortcut.
Run	Determines whether the program is launched in a normal, maximized, or minimized window.
Change Icon	Click this button to change the icon used for the shortcut.
Find Target	Click this button to find the specific program file for this shortcut, if not correctly listed in the Target box.

Arranging Icons on the Desktop

Desktop shortcut icons give you easy access to your programs, especially when you arrange them in a way that works best for you. To arrange your icons:

1. Right-click a blank area of the desktop to display a pop-up menu.

2. From the pop-up menu, select Arrange Icons and then choose from the cascading menu items shown in Table 4.2.

Table 4.2 Options for Arranging Icons on Your Desktop

Command	Action
By Name	Sort items alphabetically by file name.
By Type	Sort items by file type. Files with the same extension are grouped together.
By Size	Sort items by file size, from smallest to largest.
By Date	Sort items by date, from oldest to the most recent.
Auto Arrange	When checked, this choice automatically arranges icons at the left side of the desktop—and when you move an icon, it will snap into a new position, moving the other icons to make room.

If you want to simply straighten up the icons on your desktop, not change their order, right-click the desktop and select the Line Up Icons command from the pop-up menu.

N O T E   The Line Up Icons command does nothing if the Auto Arrange option is toggled because auto arranging keeps the icons aligned automatically. Turn off Auto Arrange if you want to arrange your icons spread across the desktop, not crowded to the left side. Then use the Line Up Icons command to line them up on the invisible grid in their same general vicinity. ■

Changing the Size of Start Menu Icons

Windows 98 lets you choose from two sizes of icons in the Start menu.

1. Right-click a part of the Taskbar where no buttons appear.
2. When the pop-up menu appears, select Properties.
3. When the Taskbar Properties dialog box appears, select the Taskbar Options tab. Check Show Small Icons in Start Menu to display smaller icons in the Start menu; uncheck this option to display the standard larger icons.
4. Click OK.

 Choosing to display smaller icons also eliminates the display of the Windows banner in the Start menu, therefore making the menu smaller.

Part
II

Ch
4

Adding Items to the Start Menu

When you install most new Windows applications, either a folder or an icon for the application is automatically added to either the Start or the Programs menus. You can also manually add items to the Start menu—either to the first level of the Start menu or to the Programs submenu. Just follow these steps:

 Add a program to the top of the Start Menu quickly by dragging it from My Computer and dropping it on the Start button. You can also drag and drop a desktop icon to the Start button to put the shortcut on the Start menu.

1. Click the Start button, select Settings, and then select Taskbar & Start Menu.
2. When the Taskbar Properties dialog box appears, click the Start Menu Programs tab (see Figure 4.2).
3. Click Add to display the Create Shortcut dialog box.
4. Click Browse to open the Browse dialog box. Select the file you want to add to the Start menu and then choose Open. The selected path and file should now appear in the Command Line text box.
5. Click Next to display the Select Program Folder dialog box, shown in Figure 4.3.

FIG. 4.2
Use the Start Menu
Programs tab to
customize the Start
menu.

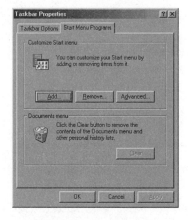

FIG. 4.3
Determine where on the
Start menu you want to
add the item.

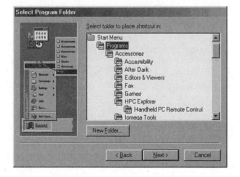

6. Select the folder location where you want the program to appear. If you want the program to appear at the top of the Start menu, select the Start Menu folder. If you want the program to appear on the Programs menu, select the Programs folder. You also can select any subfolders you may have created under the Programs folder.

7. If you want to create a new folder in the Programs menu for this shortcut, click the New Folder button. A new folder now appears in the folder window. Enter a name for this folder, and then click Next.

8. In the Select a Name For The Shortcut text box, type the label for the item that you want to appear on the Start (or Programs) menu.

9. Click Finish, and then click OK to close the Taskbar Properties dialog box.

Creating New Folders on the Programs Menu

After you've been using Windows 98 for a while, you may want to create some new folders on the Programs menu.

1. Right-click the Start button and select Open.

2. When the Start Menu window opens, click the Programs icon.

3. When the Programs window opens (see Figure 4.4), pull down the File menu, select New, and then select Folder.

FIG. 4.4
All the folders on the Programs menu are shown in this window; from here you can add new folders, as well as drag and drop existing items and folders into other folders.

4. When the new folder is added to the Programs menu, type a name for the folder and then press Enter.

Part
II
Ch
4

Reorganizing the Programs Menu

From time to time you might find it helpful to move items from one Program menu folder to another, or to change the order of items on the menu; this is a good way to keep your Programs menu organized. Fortunately, Windows 98 lets you easily drag and drop items into new order and into new folders.

1. Click the Start button and select Programs to display the contents of the Programs menu.
2. Select the item you want to move, and then click the left mouse button and hold it down.
3. Drag the selected item to a new location on tm]s menu or in another folder.
4. Drop the item in its new location and release the mouse button.

When you're done, click the Start button and select the Programs submenu to check the appearance of your changes as they appear on the actual menu.

Removing Items from the Start Menu

When you uninstall a program, its shortcut on the Start or Programs menu is removed automatically—most of the time. If a shortcut is not removed automatically, or if you just want to downsize the number of items on your Start menu, you can remove items manually. Just follow these steps:

1. Click the Start button and select Programs to display the contents of the Programs menu.
2. Select the item you want to delete, and then click the right mouse button to display the pop-up menu.
3. Select Delete from the pop-up menu.

Clearing All Documents from the Documents Menu

A menu of shortcuts to the 15 most recently opened documents is displayed on the Start menu under the Documents submenu. If you want to clear the list—maybe you no longer access some of the documents or have moved or deleted them—here's what to do:

1. Click the Start button, select Settings, and then select Taskbar & Start Menu.
2. When the Taskbar Properties dialog box appears, click the Start Menu Programs tab.
3. In the Documents Menu section of the dialog box, click the Clear button, and then click OK.

 TIP To remove only selected document shortcuts from the Documents menu, open the \Windows\Recent folder from My Computer and drag the document shortcuts to the Recycle Bin.

Launching Programs When Windows 98 Starts

If there are certain applications you want to run every time you turn on your computer, you can add them to the StartUp folder. Programs in the StartUp folder appear in the StartUp menu, a submenu of the Programs menu. To add a program to the StartUp menu:

1. Click the Start button, select Settings, and then select Taskbar & Start Menu.
2. Select the Start Menu Programs tab and click Add to display the Create Shortcut dialog box.
3. Click Browse to open the Browse dialog box. Select the file you want to add to the Start menu and then choose Open. The selected path and file should now appear in the Command Line text box.
4. Click Next to display the Select Program Folder dialog box.
5. Click the StartUp folder (you will probably need to scroll down to see it) and click Next.
6. In the Select a Name For The Shortcut text box, type the label for the item.
7. Click Finish, and then click OK to close the Taskbar Properties dialog box.

The next time you start Windows, the program you added to the StartUp folder will be launched automatically.

Personalizing the Send To Menu

When you right-click a file or folder in My Computer, one of the items on the pop-up menu is the Send To menu. The Send To menu can be used to move, fax, e-mail, print, and accomplish other actions with the selected item.

You can create new options for the Send To menu. For example, you might want to create a Send To item for a Zip drive or commonly used folder—this way you can highlight a file in My Computer, click the right mouse button to display the pop-up menu, and then use the Send To command to copy the file automatically.

To add options to the Send To menu:

1. Click the My Computer icon on your desktop to launch My Computer.
2. In My Computer, navigate to the \Windows\SendTo folder.
3. Pull down the File menu, select New, and then select Shortcut.
4. When the Create New Shortcut wizard appears, enter the name of the file, folder, or drive you want to add to the Send To menu. (Click the Browse button to search your system for the item.) Click Next to proceed.
5. Enter the name you want to appear on the Send To menu, and then click Finish.

Personalizing Your Desktop's Background Pattern and Wallpaper

To keep your desktop interesting, you can select a background pattern or wallpaper to display, and change the design whenever you like. You can also use your own bitmap file, such as a logo, for wallpaper instead of the collection in Windows 98.

In addition, if you've activated Windows 98's Active Desktop, you can use any HTML document or Web page as your desktop wallpaper. If you do this, you can click a hyperlink directly on your desktop to launch Internet Explorer and go to the linked Web page.

▶ **See** "Understanding the Windows 98 Active Desktop," **p. 22**

> **CAUTION**
> You can choose a pattern or a wallpaper, but not both. If you have tiled the wallpaper over the entire screen, it covers the pattern selection.

To select a new pattern or wallpaper:

1. Right-click the desktop and choose Properties from the pop-up menu.
2. When the Display Properties dialog box appears, click the Background tab; the current Background (see Figure 4.5) is displayed.

Part

II

Ch

4

FIG. 4.5
Change the look of your desktop from the Display Properties dialog box.

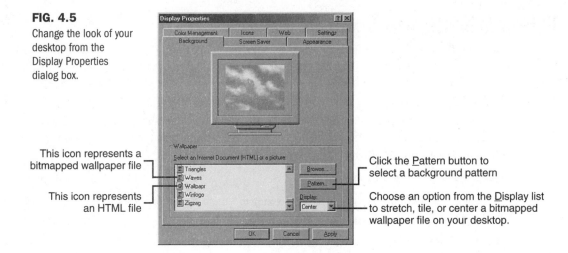

This icon represents a bitmapped wallpaper file

This icon represents an HTML file

Click the Pattern button to select a background pattern

Choose an option from the Display list to stretch, tile, or center a bitmapped wallpaper file on your desktop.

3. To use an HTML file as your desktop background, select a file from the Wallpaper list, or click Browse to find a file elsewhere on your hard disk. Make sure the Disable All Web-Related content option is left unselected, and then click OK.

4. To use a bitmapped wallpaper file as your desktop background, select a file from the Wallpaper list or click the Browse button to find a file elsewhere on your hard disk. To determine how the file is displayed on your desktop, choose one of the options from the Display pull-down list: Center, Tile, or Stretch. Click the Apply button if you want to see the wallpaper on the desktop, and then click OK.

5. To use a pattern as your desktop background, select [None] from the Wallpaper list and then click the Pattern button. When the Pattern dialog box appears, choose a pattern and click OK.

Changing Your Desktop's Color Scheme

The default Windows desktop uses a predefined combination of colors and fonts. If you don't like this combination, you can choose from several other predefined schemes, as described in the following steps:

1. Right-click the desktop and then choose Properties from the pop-up menu.

2. When the Display Properties dialog box appears, click the Appearance tab (see Figure 4.6).

3. In the Scheme drop-down list, select a color and text scheme. The sample box changes to show how items in Windows will appear in the new scheme.

4. Choose OK to use the displayed color scheme.

FIG. 4.6

Use the Display Properties dialog box to change your desktop's color scheme.

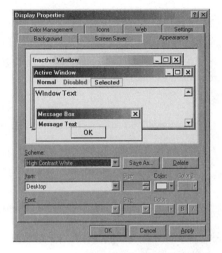

Creating a New Desktop Color Scheme

Although Windows provides a number of predefined color schemes, you can also create and save your own custom color schemes by following these steps:

1. Right-click the desktop and choose Properties from the pop-up menu.

2. When the Display Properties dialog box appears, click the Appearance tab.

3. In the Item list, choose the screen element that you want to change—or click the part of the screen in the sample box, which automatically selects the item's name in the Item list.

4. In the Size, Color, Font, Size, Color 1, and Color 2 (when available) lists, select new settings for the selected element. Notice also that you can click the Bold and Italic buttons for text items. Each time you make a change, the sample box displays it. Choose Apply if you want to see the color scheme applied to your current desktop.

N O T E Color 1 is the left-hand color in a window's title bar; Color 2 is the right-hand color. The color of the title bar gradates from Color 1 to Color 2, left to right. ■

5. To save the scheme so that it will appear on the Scheme list, click Save As. Type a name, and then choose OK.

6. Click OK to change your desktop to the new scheme.

 T I P To find additional colors, choose Other in the drop-down Color palette. Select a color from the expanded palette or create your own custom color.

Part

II

Ch

4

Changing the Look of Your Cursors

Another item you can personalize with Windows 98 is the *cursor scheme* that appears on-screen. Different schemes use different kinds of cursors; you can choose from normal cursors, 3-D cursors, extra-large cursors, and animated cursors.

To change your cursor scheme:

1. Click the Start button, select Settings, and then select Control Panel to open Control Panel.

2. Click the Mouse icon to open the Mouse Properties dialog box.

3. Click the Pointers tab, shown in Figure 4.7.

FIG. 4.7

Choose a new cursor scheme from the Mouse Properties dialog box.

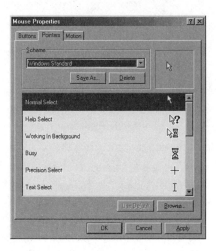

4. Select a new cursor scheme from the Scheme pull-down list. Alternatively, you can change a specific cursor by highlighting the cursor in the cursor list and clicking the Browse button to select a new cursor from the Cursor folder.

5. Click OK when you've finished.

Installing Desktop Themes

Desktop themes are specific combinations of background wallpaper, colors, fonts, cursors, sounds, and screen savers—all arranged around a specific theme, such as Mystery, Science, or Sports. To change desktop themes:

1. Click the Start button, select Settings, and then select Control Panel to open the Control Panel.

2. Click the Desktop Themes icon.

3. When the Desktop Themes dialog box opens (see Figure 4.8), select a theme from the Theme list.

FIG. 4.8
Choose from one of the many Desktop Themes available with Windows 98.

4. If you choose *not* to include all aspects of a chosen theme, deselect the appropriate item(s) from the Settings section.

5. To preview a theme's screen saver, click the Screen saver button; to preview other scheme features (Pointers, Sounds, and more), click the appropriate button.

6. Click Apply to apply the theme to your desktop while keeping the dialog box open for additional changes; click OK to accept the new theme and close the dialog box.

N O T E Choose a Theme that matches the resolution of your video display. For example, if your system displays only 256 colors, choose a 256-color Theme, not a HiColor Theme. ■

Using Screen Savers

Screen savers display moving designs on-screen when you haven't typed or moved the mouse for a preset time. Screen savers were originally created to prevent the screen image from burning onto the screen if the display did not change frequently enough. While this is rarely a problem with newer monitors, screen savers can still be entertaining and will hide the work on your screen when you leave your desk. You can even assign a password to the screen saver so that only you can reactivate the screen.

To configure your system for screen saver operation:

1. Right-click the desktop and choose Properties from the pop-up menu.

2. When the Display Properties dialog box appears, click the Screen Saver tab.

3. Select a screen saver from the Screen Saver drop-down list. A sample of the screen saver appears on the sample display. (For a full-screen view, click the Preview button; click the screen to return from the preview.)

4. Change the properties of the selected screen saver by choosing Settings. The options available differ for each screen saver you choose, but usually include things like speed and colors. Make your selections and then choose OK.

Part
II

Ch
4

5. In the <u>W</u>ait section, select the number of minutes you want the screen to be idle before the screen saver activates. Choose <u>A</u>pply to accept the settings but keep the Display Properties sheet open.

6. If you want to set a password for reactivating the screen, check <u>P</u>assword Protected and then click the Change button. In the Change Password dialog box, enter your password and then choose OK. Choose OK again for confirmation, and then choose OK to apply the changes and close the Display Properties dialog box.

Using a Third-Party Screen Saver

In addition to the screen savers included with Windows 98, there are two types of third-party screen savers that you can add to your system:

■ Screen saver *modules* that work with the standard Windows 98 screen saver engine. These modules are either sold as add-ons at retail or distributed over the Internet as shareware. If a module comes without a standard installation program, simply copy its files to the \Windows\System folder and it will appear automatically as a choice in the <u>S</u>creen Saver drop-down list.

■ Screen saver *programs* that include their own engines that replace the standard Windows 98 screen saver engine. An example of this type of software is the popular After Dark® program. Programs like After Dark come with their own installation routines and install just like any other type of Windows software. Some add-on screen saver programs even install their own tab in the Display Properties dialog box; click this tab to configure the screen saver.

 TIP If you've activated Windows 98's Active Desktop, you can use the Active Desktop itself (or your Active Channel content) as a screen saver. Just select Active Desktop Screen Saver or Channel Screen Saver from the <u>S</u>creen Saver list.

▶ **See** "Using the Active Desktop as a Screen Saver," **p. 79**

Moving the Taskbar

The default position for the Taskbar is horizontally across the bottom of the screen (see Figure 4.9). If you don't like it there, you can move it to the top or to either side of the screen (vertically, as shown in Figure 4.10). Just follow these steps:

FIG. 4.9
The standard Taskbar resides at the bottom of the screen.

FIG. 4.10

A little dragging moves the Taskbar to the left side of the screen.

1. Point to a part of the Taskbar where no buttons appear.

2. Click with the left mouse button and drag the Taskbar to another edge of the screen. You will see a shaded line that indicates the new position of the Taskbar.

3. Release the mouse button.

Hiding the Taskbar

If you're running a small display (640×480 resolution, for example), you might not want the Taskbar taking up screen space all the time. For these situations, Windows 98 lets you hide the Taskbar and recall it only when you need it.

1. Click the Start button, select Settings, and then select Taskbar & Start Menu.

2. When the Taskbar Properties dialog box appears, uncheck Always on Top and check Auto Hide.

3. Click OK when finished.

This configuration automatically hides the Taskbar so that your applications can use the entire screen. To display the Taskbar again, all you have to do is minimize any applications currently running, and then move your cursor to the very bottom of the screen. The Taskbar will then pop up for your use.

Resizing the Taskbar

When the Taskbar is positioned horizontally, you may have noticed that the Taskbar buttons become smaller when you open multiple applications. If you open too many applications, the Taskbar buttons become so small that you cannot read much of the application names. By adjusting the size of the Taskbar, you can create a taller Taskbar that enables multiple buttons to stack on top of each other.

In addition, if you choose to position the Taskbar along one of the sides of the desktop, you may want to adjust the Taskbar width to display wider or narrower buttons. Wherever your Taskbar is positioned, you can resize it by following the same steps:

1. Position your cursor at the edge of the Taskbar, where the pointer becomes a double arrow. (If the Taskbar is at the bottom of the screen, you will point to the upper edge of the Taskbar.)

2. Click the left mouse button and drag the edge to the size you want.

3. Release the mouse button.

 You can make the vertical Taskbar so narrow that only the application icons show, without words. (If you point to the icons, a ToolTip pops up to show you its name.)

Adding Toolbars to the Taskbar

Windows 98 adds something new to the Taskbar—the ability to dock additional *toolbars* to the Taskbar itself. Each toolbar lets you perform selected tasks—such as launching programs or connecting to Web sites—directly from the Windows Taskbar.

Windows 98 comes with several predefined toolbars:

- *Address.* This toolbar is an URL box. Type the address for any Web page into this box, press Enter, and Windows will connect to the Internet, launch Internet Explorer, and display the Web page you entered.

- *Links.* This toolbar displays five selected links (by default, five links on Microsoft's Web site).

- *Desktop.* This toolbar displays all the shortcut icons currently on your desktop; it's a good way to have ready access to your shortcuts if your desktop is perpetually cluttered.

- *Quick Launch.* This toolbar (toggled on by default, and shown in Figure 4.11) displays four icons for basic Internet use: Internet Explorer, Outlook Express, Show Desktop (which minimizes all windows on your desktop), and View Channels (which launches the Active Channel Viewer).

FIG. 4.11

Use the Quick Launch toolbar to launch Internet Explorer or Outlook Express, as well as minimize all windows on your desktop or display the Active Channel Viewer.

To dock a toolbar to the Taskbar:

1. Right-click anywhere on the Taskbar.
2. When the pop-up menu appears, select Toolbars, and then select the toolbar you want to display.

To remove a toolbar from the Taskbar, right-click anywhere on the toolbar to display the pop-up menu. Select Toolbars, and then deselect that particular toolbar.

 You can resize any toolbar you've added to the Taskbar. Just move your cursor to the far left of the toolbar until the cursor changes to a double-arrow, click the left mouse button, and drag the toolbar to the desired size.

Creating a New Toolbar

In addition to the four preselected toolbars discussed in the previous section, you can also create your own toolbars to dock with the Taskbar.

1. Right-click anywhere on the Taskbar.
2. When the pop-up menu appears, select Toolbars, and then select New Toolbar.
3. When the New Toolbar dialog box appears, choose a disk or folder—or enter a Web address—and click OK.
4. The new toolbar now appears, docked to the Taskbar. If you selected a disk or folder, the contents of that disk/folder appear in the toolbar. If you entered a Web address, that address appears in the toolbar.

 You can also create a toolbar by dragging a disk or folder from My Computer onto the Taskbar. If you drag a disk or folder from My Computer to another side of the screen, a new toolbar will be created there instead of on the Taskbar.

Part
II

Ch
4

Configuring Toolbars

Windows 98 provides several ways for you to view your toolbars. You can adjust the size of the icons and how the icons appear.

1. Right-click in an open area of the toolbar you want to configure to display the pop-up menu.
2. To display the title of the toolbar, check Show Title. Uncheck this option to hide the name of the toolbar.
3. To display large icons on the toolbar, select View and check Large. To display small icons, select View and check Small.
4. To display a label for each icon, check Show Text. Uncheck this option to hide labels.

 TIP To move a toolbar to another side of the screen, simply drag the toolbar to the desired spot and then release the mouse button. If you drop the toolbar into the middle of your screen, it becomes an open window on your desktop.

Advanced Customization with Tweak UI

Tweak UI is a Power Toy from Microsoft—a special utility, designed for power users, that lets you further customize your desktop beyond what Windows 98 normally lets you do. Although Tweak UI is available from Microsoft's Web site, but is not officially supported by Microsoft.

CAUTION
Because Tweak UI is not an officially supported program, the installation and use of Tweak UI is recommended only for more experienced users.

When Tweak UI is installed, a Tweak UI icon is automatically created in Control Panel. This makes it easy to start the utility when you want to reconfigure some parameter of your system.

To install and run Tweak UI:

1. Click the Internet icon on your desktop to launch Internet Explorer. After IE connects to the Internet, go to Microsoft's Web site at **http://www.microsoft.com.**
2. Click the Search link at the top of the main page, then enter **tweak ui** in the Search Wizard dialog box and click the Search Now! Button. From the search results page, go to the Tweak UI page and download the program. Follow the on-screen instructions to install Tweak UI on your system.
3. After Tweak UI is installed, click the Start menu, select Settings, and then select Control Panel. Click the Tweak UI icon to display the Tweak UI dialog box, shown in Figure 4.12.
4. Click the tabs described in Table 4.3 and make the selections you want.
5. Click OK to accept the changes and close the dialog box, or click Apply to make the changes while keeping the dialog box open.

FIG. 4.12

The Tweak UI dialog box with the Desktop tab selected; this is how you get rid of unwanted system icons from your desktop

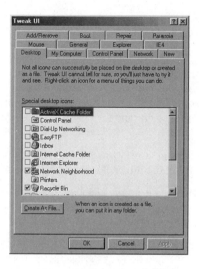

Table 4.3   Tweak UI Settings

Tab	Description
Desktop	Lets you determine which standard system icons are displayed on your desktop. This is the way to get rid of pre-installed icons—such as the icon for the Microsoft Network—that you can't delete normally.
My Computer	Lets you determine which drives are displayed in the My Computer window.
Control Panel	Lets you determine which icons are displayed in the Windows Control Panel.
Network	Lets you choose to Log on to your network automatically at system startup and eliminates the need to type your user name and password every time you start your computer.
New	Adds or removes items from the New submenu displayed when you right-click the desktop. (The New submenu lets you create new documents of the selected types.)
Mouse	Lets you adjust the speed at which submenus extend from main menus, as well as calibrate your mouse's double-clicking and dragging sensitivity. You can also choose to have whichever window the mouse is over be your active window (the Activation Follows Mouse option).
General	Lets you turn on or off various Windows effects (such as window animation and smooth scrolling). Also lets you change the location of various system folders and choose which search engine Internet Explorer uses when you enter **? keyword** in the Address bar.

Part

II

Ch

4

continues

Table 4.3 Continued

Tab	Description
Explorer	Lets you change the way shortcuts are displayed on the desktop (from small arrows to large arrows to no arrows); turn on or off the "Click here to begin" animation and tip of the day displayed when Windows first starts; and turn on or off the "Shortcut to" prefix on new shortcuts.
IE 4	Lets you turn on or off various Internet Explorer settings, including whether or not the Internet icon is displayed on your desktop.
Add/Remove	Removes listings from the installed programs listing in the Add/Remove Programs dialog box, which is quite useful if you are left with listings of programs that you deleted manually.
Boot	Lets you turn on or off various options for Windows behavior at start-up: make function keys available for a preset number of seconds, start the Windows GUI automatically, display the Windows splash screen while loading, allow the F4 key to boot another operating system, and to always show the boot menu. You can also select how to run ScanDisk on startup if you have a system failure: never, with prompting, or without prompting.
Repair	Lets you rebuild any damaged icons on your desktop, repair a damaged font folder, repair any corrupted or overwritten system files, reset Registry Editor to its default parameters, and restore the default file type icons and associations—a great tool in case things go wrong with your system that you can't fix otherwise.
Paranoia	Lets you clear various system tracking mechanisms (Run history, Document history, Find Files history, Find Computer history, Internet Explorer history, and Last User settings). Also lets you turn on or off the ability to play audio or data CDs automatically, and the ability to log errors to the FAULTLOG.TXT files.

N O T E Because Tweak UI is in beta testing as this book is written, it's likely that some features could change or be deleted when it is released in its final version. ■

An entire chapter could have been devoted to Tweak UI. If you're an experienced and interested computer user, I recommend you install it and play with it awhile to discover all the power it adds to your system. ●

Configuring the Active Desktop

The New Active Desktop Features of Windows 98

One of the key new features of Windows 98 is the Active Desktop. This is a new feature that, quite simply, makes the entire Windows interface active, just like a page on the World Wide Web. This means that instead of the background of your desktop being static and decorative, it can now be active and functional. You can choose to use a Web page as your desktop background, complete with links to other Web pages. You can also put live HTML-based objects on your desktop, like stock or news tickers. Best of all, these live objects can contain up-to-date information pushed to your computer over the Internet.

This move to what Microsoft calls True Web Integration has one other effect. Where classic Windows involved double-clicking to launch items, on the Web you only have to single-click items. True Web Integration embraces the Web operating method, so when you choose to enable True Web Integration in Windows 98, items are now launched by single-clicking—and items are selected by simply hovering your cursor over them.

Should you enable True Web Integration in Windows 98? I recommend it; it's an easier way to use Windows, and offers many more options, should you choose to take advantage of them. The only downside is that you have to train yourself to hover and single-click, instead of single-clicking and double-clicking. But once you get past that, it's nice to have a desktop background that can actually be functional rather than decorative.

Activating True Web Integration and the Active Desktop

If you're currently using the classic Windows desktop, follow these steps to switch to the Active Desktop with True Web Integration:

1. Click the Start button, select Settings, and then select Folders & Icons.
2. When the Folder Options dialog box appears, select the General tab and choose Web Style. Click OK.
3. Click the Start button, select Settings, select Active Desktop, and then select View as Web Page.

Deactivating the Active Desktop and Returning to Classic Windows Operation

If you're currently using the Active Desktop, follow these steps to switch back to the classic Windows interface:

1. Click the Start button, select Settings, and then select Folders & Icons.
2. When the Folder Options dialog box appears, select the General tab and choose Classic Style. Click OK.

3. Click the Start button, select Settings, select Active Desktop, and then deselect View as Web Page. (If there is no check mark next to View as Web Page, this option is already deselected.)

Choosing an HTML Page as Your Desktop Background

The first step to activating your desktop is to replace the static wallpaper or patterned desktop background with an HTML-based background. To select a Web page as your desktop background:

1. Right-click the desktop and then choose Properties from the pop-up menu.

2. When the Display Properties dialog box appears, click the Background tab.

3. Select an HTML file from the Wallpaper list, as shown in Figure 5.1, or click Browse to find a file elsewhere on your hard disk. Make sure the Disable All Web-Related content option is left unselected, and then click OK.

FIG. 5.1

Use the Background tab of the Display Properties dialog box to select an HTML file as your background wallpaper; the file named Wallpapr is the default Active Desktop page.

Part

II

Ch

5

If your new Active Desktop background page contains Web links, clicking one of these links will automatically connect you to the Internet, launch Internet Explorer, and display the linked page.

Downloading a Web Page to Use with Active Desktop

You can choose one of your own HTML pages as an Active Desktop background. You can also download pages from other Web sites, as shown in Figure 5.2. To download a Web page to your hard disk:

FIG. 5.2

The Yahoo! Web page used as desktop background; click one of the underlined links to launch Internet Explorer and go to the linked page.

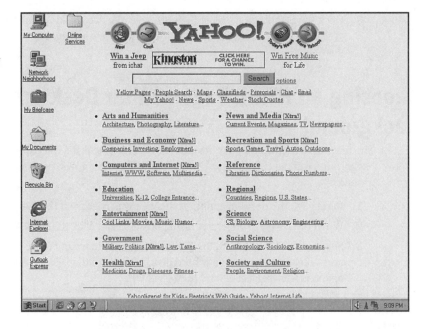

1. Click the Internet icon on your desktop to launch Internet Explorer.

2. After Internet Explorer connects to the Internet, enter the address of the page you want to save in the Address box and press Enter.

3. When the page you want to save is loaded, pull down Internet Explorer's File menu and select Save As.

4. When the Save HTML Document dialog box appears, enter a File Name for the page, select the folder where you want to save the page, and then click Save.

5. If the page includes any graphics, you'll also need to save them to your hard disk. Right-click each graphic and select Save Picture As from the pop-up menu. When the Save Picture dialog box appears, choose to save the picture in the same directory where you saved the main page. Click Save when finished.

After the Web page and its graphics are saved to your hard disk, you can then follow the steps in the previous section to select this page as your Active Desktop background.

Adding the Channel Bar to Your Desktop

You can also place HTML-based objects on your Active Desktop. One example of this type of content is the Internet Explorer Channel Bar, which ships with Windows 98. From the Channel Bar you can choose to subscribe to and view Active Content Channels directly from the Internet.

▶ **See** "Viewing Content Channels with the Active Content Viewer," **p. 248**

To add the Internet Explorer Channel Bar to your desktop:

1. Right-click the desktop and then choose Properties from the pop-up menu.

2. When the Display Properties dialog box appears, click the Web tab.

3. Select Internet Explorer Channel Bar from the Items on the Active Desktop list, and then click OK. The Channel Bar is now installed on your desktop; just click a channel button to connect to the Internet and view that channel's contents.

Adding Active Content to the Desktop

You can also add other types of active content to your desktop. There are many examples of active content on a special Microsoft Web site called the Active Desktop Gallery. To connect to the Active Desktop Gallery and add new items to your desktop:

1. Right-click the desktop and choose Properties from the pop-up menu.

2. When the Display Properties dialog box appears, click the Web tab.

3. Click the New button. The New Active Desktop Item dialog box appears, asking if you want to connect to the Active Desktop Gallery Web site. Click Yes.

4. The Display Properties dialog box closes, and you are connected to the Active Desktop Gallery Web site, shown in Figure 5.3.

FIG. 5.3
Connect to the Active Desktop Gallery Web site to download new active content items.

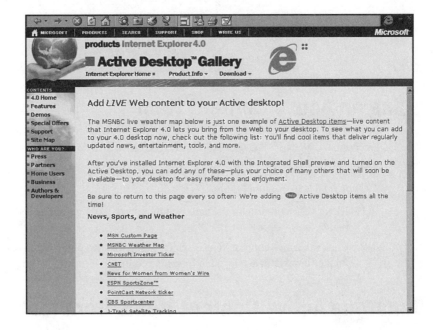

Part

II

Ch

5

5. Click a specific link to go to a specific page for the selected active content item. For example, you can select from an Investor Ticker, a Weather Map, and various news-oriented items.

6. When the page for the selected active content item is displayed, click the Add to My Desktop button.

7. The Add Item to Active Desktop dialog box now appears. To customize your subscription to this item, click the Customize Subscription button.

8. You now see the first screen of the Subscription Wizard, shown in Figure 5.4. If you are connecting to the Internet over your company's network, select Scheduled and accept the Publisher's Recommended Schedule; if you're connecting through a normal dial-up connection, select Manually. Click Finish to return to the Add Item to Active Desktop dialog box, and then click OK.

9. The new active content item is now added to your desktop.

FIG. 5.4
Schedule when to update your active content with the Active Desktop Item dialog box.

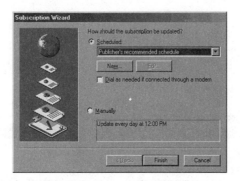

Using an Active Content Item

Most active content items are truly active and can lead you to further content on the Web. For example, the MSNBC Weather Map, when clicked, leads you to a Web site with more detailed weather forecasts.

To launch an active content item:

1. Hover your cursor over the active content item. Your cursor turns into the shape of a hand.

2. Click the active content item. You are automatically connected to the Internet, and further content is displayed in Internet Explorer.

Removing Active Content Items from Your Desktop

To remove an active content item from your desktop, follow these steps:

1. Right-click the desktop and choose Properties from the pop-up menu.

2. When the Display Properties dialog box appears, click the Web tab.

3. In the Items on the Active Desktop list, deselect the item you want to remove from your desktop. You can later add the item back to your desktop by reselecting it.

4. If you want to permanently delete an active content item from your system, highlight it and click the Delete button.

5. Click OK when finished.

Using the Active Desktop as a Screen Saver

Windows 98 also lets you turn your Active Desktop into a screen saver. In this operation, your active content items are displayed when your computer isn't being used.

▶ **See** "Using Screen Savers," **p. 65**

To enable the Active Desktop Screen Saver:

1. Right-click the desktop and choose Properties from the pop-up menu.

2. When the Display Properties dialog box appears, click the Screen Saver tab.

3. From the Screen Saver list, select Active Desktop Screen Saver.

4. Click the Settings button to configure the display options for this screen saver.

5. Click OK when finished.

Part

II

Ch

5

Managing Files, Folders, and Disks

CHAPTER 6

Using My Computer and Windows Explorer: Classic and Web Views

The New File Navigation Features of Windows 98

When you activate True Web Integration in Windows 98, you change the way you navigate through folders and files. Although you still use My Computer and Windows Explorer, the way they look and operate change dramatically; both tools now work similar to the way a Web browser works.

Here are the major navigational changes resulting from the switch to True Web Integration:

- *Single-clicking*. To open a folder or file, you now single-click instead of double-clicking it.
- *Hovering*. To select a folder or file, you now hover over it with your cursor instead of single-clicking it.
- *Web Style file information*. With the Web Style option activated, the backgrounds of the My Computer and Windows Explorer windows become interactive. When you select a disk, folder, or file, information about the selected item appears to the left of the item in the My Computer or Windows Explorer windows. Certain file types, when selected, display as a thumbnail graphic in this informational section.
- *Toolbars*. Both My Computer and Windows Explorer include new toolbars that make it easier to perform common operations.
- *Web browsing*. Both My Computer and Windows Explorer can be used to browse not only your desktop, but also the World Wide Web. Just type a Web URL in the Address Bar and Windows connects you to the Internet and displays the selected Web page in the main window.
- *Back and Forward buttons*. Because My Computer and Windows Explorer now use a single window to display the contents of selected items (instead of the multiple windows used in Windows 95), you use Back and Forward buttons to move back and forth between the contents of previously selected disks and folders.

Understanding My Computer

My Computer is a file-management tool that lets you manage your hard drive(s), mapped network drives, peripheral drives, folders, and files. My Computer is extremely versatile; you can use My Computer to view the contents of the Control Panel and Printers folders, as well as to browse pages on the World Wide Web.

You can easily access almost all of your computer's resources from My Computer by following these steps:

1. Start My Computer by clicking its icon on the desktop.
2. You can open any drive or folder by clicking its icon (see Figure 6.1.) When you hover your cursor over an icon, My Computer displays the contents of the item you opened.

FIG. 6.1

Click any icon in My Computer to show the contents of the selected device.

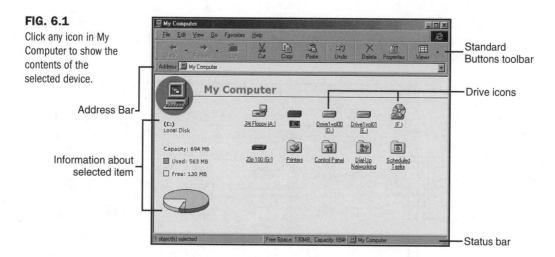

Address Bar

Information about selected item

Standard Buttons toolbar

Drive icons

Status bar

3. To open a file, just click its icon. In addition, you can move, copy, rename, or delete any file or folder in My Computer by right-clicking the corresponding icon and using the steps described in Chapter 7, "Organizing Files and Folders."

4. If you hover your cursor over a folder or file, details about that item will be displayed. If you hover over a popular file type (such as a Word or Excel document), a thumbnail view of the first page of the file will also be displayed.

5. To view other parts of your system from the My Computer window, pull down the Address Bar and select an item. For example, if you select Control Panel, the My Computer window turns into the Control Panel window.

6. To view Web pages with My Computer, enter the address (URL) for a specific page in the Address Bar, and then press Enter. If you are not currently connected to the Internet, you will be automatically connected and the selected Web page then displays within the My Computer window.

7. To close My Computer, pull down the File menu and choose Close.

Understanding Windows Explorer

Windows Explorer is another Windows 98 file-management tool, similar to My Computer. It differs from My Computer in that it displays two different *panes* of information; the contents for any item selected in the left pane are displayed in the right pane.

> **N O T E** Don't confuse Windows Explorer—which you use to view and manipulate folders and files—with Internet Explorer, Microsoft's Web browser. ■

Many users prefer the two-pane approach to managing folders and files used by Windows Explorer. As you can see in Figure 6.2, the left pane contains all the devices on your system, in a tree-like structure. The right pane (called the Contents pane) displays the contents of any

Part

III

Ch

6

item selected in the left pane. Drives or folders that contain folders have a + beside them; click the + to show the contained folders in hierarchical fashion. When the drive or folder is fully expanded, the + changes to a –; click the – to collapse the contents again.

FIG. 6.2

The contents of any item highlighted in the left pane of Windows Explorer are displayed in the right pane, Contents.

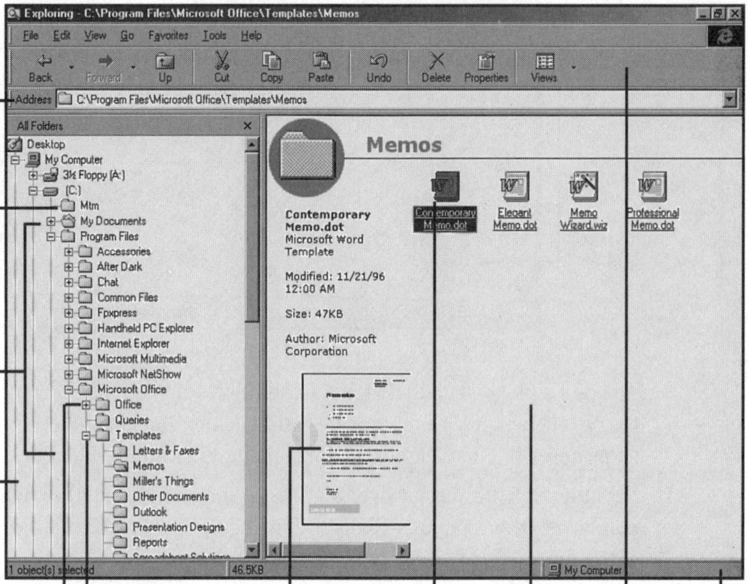

Address Bar —
Folder icon —

Hierarchy of folders —

Left pane —

Expand | Collapse | Information about | File icon | Contents | Standard | Status bar
folder | folder | selected item | | pane | Buttons
button | button | | | | Toolbar

To use Windows Explorer:

1. Start Windows Explorer by clicking the Start button, selecting Programs, and then selecting Windows Explorer.

2. If the folder you want to view contains other folders, click the + button to expand the hierarchy list.

3. Click the folder you want to view and its contents will be displayed in the Contents (right) pane.

4. If you hover your cursor over a folder or file, details about that item will be displayed. If you hover over a popular file type (such as a Word or Excel document), a thumbnail view of the first page of the file will also be displayed.

 TIP If Windows Explorer or My Computer does not display file details, pull down the View menu and select As Web Page.

5. To open a file, just click its icon. In addition, you can move, copy, rename, or delete any file or folder in Explorer by right-clicking the corresponding icon and using the steps described in Chapter 7, "Organizing Files and Folders."

6. To view other parts of your system from the Windows Explorer window, pull down the Address Bar and select an item. For example, if you select Control Panel, the contents of Control Panel appear in the Contents pane.

7. To view Web pages with Windows Explorer, enter the address (URL) for a specific page in the Address Bar, and then press Enter. If you are not currently connected to the Internet, you will be automatically connected and the selected Web page will display within the Contents pane.

8. To close Windows Explorer, pull down the File menu and choose Close.

Navigating with My Computer and Windows Explorer

You navigate through disks and folders in similar fashion with both My Computer and Windows Explorer:

- To view the contents of a disk or folder, click the selected item.
- To move *up* the hierarchy of folders to the next highest folder or disk, click the Up button on the toolbar (see Figure 6.3).

FIG. 6.3

Use the Back, Forward, and Up buttons on the toolbar to navigate through disks and folders.

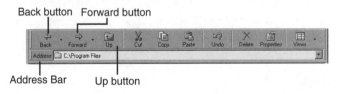

Back button   Forward button

Address Bar   Up button

- To move back to the disk or folder previously selected, click the Back button on the toolbar.
- To choose from the history of disks and folders previously viewed, click the down arrow on the Back button and select a disk or folder.
- If you've moved back through multiple disks or folders, you can move forward to the next folder by clicking the Forward button.
- Go directly to any disk or folder by entering the path in the Address Bar (in the format *x:\folder\subfolder*) and pressing Enter.

Part
III

Ch
6

Activating the Web Style View

Web Style is a way to look at folders and files within My Computer and Windows Explorer as if they were Web pages. If you activate Web Style, you display special Web pages as backgrounds with the My Computer window or Windows Explorer panes—and these special Web page backgrounds provide detailed information about the files and folders you select.

In addition, activating Web Style allows you to treat all icons within My Computer and Windows Explorer as you would objects on a Web page. Instead of double-clicking to launch an object, you now single-click. To select an object, all you have to do is hover your cursor over the object.

To activate Web Style:

1. Click the Start button, select Settings, and then select Folders & Icons.
2. When the Folder Options dialog box appears, select the General tab, select Web Style, and then click OK.

Activating the Classic View

If you prefer to use My Computer and Windows Explorer in the classic Windows mode, follow these steps to turn off Web Style:

1. Click the Start button, select Settings, and then select Folders & Icons.
2. When the Folder Options dialog box appears, select the General tab, select Classic Style, and then click OK.

Adding Toolbars

There are several options you can change that affect how My Computer and Windows Explorer look, the most useful one being the ability to display a variety of toolbars, a status bar, and a series of Internet Explorer bars:

- **Toolbars**. Windows 98 includes three different toolbars:
  - *Standard Buttons toolbar*. Includes buttons for common tasks, like going back and forward, moving up a level in the folder hierarchy, and more.
  - *Address bar*. Used to navigate both your hard disk and the Web.
  - *Links bar*. Includes links to some of Microsoft's most popular Web pages.
- **Status bar**. A horizontal bar at the very bottom of the window that displays information about current selections or actions.
- **Explorer bars**. Actually four different panes of Web-related information that can be displayed within My Computer or Windows Explorer. (Within Windows Explorer, these panes replace the standard left pane.) These panes include:

- *Search*. Includes tools for searching the Web
- *History*. Displays recently visited Web pages
- *Favorites*. Displays a list of your favorite Web pages and documents (see Figure 6.4)
- *Channels*. Lets you access active content channels on the Internet.

FIG. 6.4

Use the Favorites pane to go directly to a favorite document or Web page—like this Web page displayed in My Computer.

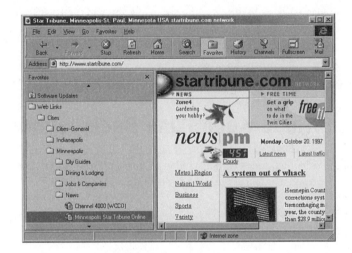

To display these different bars in either My Computer or Windows Explorer, follow these steps:

1. To display a toolbar, pull down the <u>V</u>iew menu and select <u>T</u>oolbar. Select <u>S</u>tandard Buttons to display the Standard Buttons toolbar; select <u>A</u>ddress to display the Address Bar; select <u>L</u>inks to display the Links bar. Deselect any of these options to hide a particular toolbar.

2. If you want to display descriptive labels for the Standard Buttons toolbar, pull down the <u>V</u>iew menu, select <u>T</u>oolbar, and then select <u>T</u>ext Labels. Deselect this option to hide the labels.

3. To display the status bar, pull down the <u>V</u>iew menu and select Status <u>B</u>ar.

4. To display an Internet Explorer bar, pull down the <u>V</u>iew menu and select <u>E</u>xplorer Bar. Select <u>S</u>earch to display the Search pane; select <u>F</u>avorites to display the Favorites pane; select <u>H</u>istory to display the History pane; select <u>C</u>hannels to display the Channels pane; or select <u>N</u>one to hide all Explorer panes.

Part

III

Ch

6

Resizing and Rearranging Toolbars

Any of the three top-of-window toolbars (Standard Button, Address Bar, and Links) can be resized and rearranged:

1. To resize a toolbar, move your cursor to the far left of the toolbar until it changes shape (to a double-headed arrow). Click and hold the left mouse button and drag the end of the toolbar left or right until it is the size you want, and then release the mouse button.

2. To move a toolbar, move your cursor to the far left of the toolbar until it changes shape (to a double-headed arrow). Click and hold the left mouse button while you drag the entire toolbar up or down a level; this way, you can stack toolbars on top of each other. Release the mouse button when the toolbar is located where you want.

Changing Window and Pane Backgrounds

With Web Style enabled, you can now change the backgrounds of the My Computer window and of the individual panes within Windows Explorer. For example, you can add a simple bitmapped graphic or an HTML page as decorative background.

NOTE In Windows Explorer, every folder's Contents pane can have its own individual background. That means you can't universally add backgrounds within Windows Explorer; you have to do it for each folder individually. ▪

To change backgrounds in My Computer and Windows Explorer, follow these steps:

1. Click a drive or folder icon to display its contents, either in the My Computer window or the Windows Explorer contents pane.

2. Right-click the window/pane that displays the drive/folder contents.

3. Select <u>C</u>ustomize This Folder from the pop-up menu. This displays the Customize This Folder wizard (shown in Figure 6.5).

FIG. 6.5
Use the Customize This Folder wizard to add an HTML document or bitmapped graphic as a background to My Computer or Windows Explorer.

4. To add a special HTML document as background, select Create or Edit an HTML Document, and then click Next. When prompted to start your HTML editor, click Next. Your HTML editor (normally Notepad or FrontPage Express) opens, displaying the HTML code for the standard Web Style background. You can edit this code or delete it and insert new HTML code. When you've finished editing the HTML code, pull down the File menu and select Save, and then pull down the File menu and select Exit. When the Wizard displays its final page, click Finish.

5. To add a bitmapped graphic as background, select Choose a Background Picture, and then click Next. When the next screen appears, choose a background picture from the list, or click the Browse button to choose a picture from elsewhere on your system. Click the Text and Background buttons to change text and text background colors accordingly, and then click Next. When the final screen appears, click Finish.

6. To remove all backgrounds, select Remove Customization, and then click Next. Continue clicking Next through the following screens until you reach the final screen. Click Finish to proceed.

Changing the Way Files Are Displayed

You can choose to view items in the My Computer window or the Windows Explorer Content pane in a variety of ways—as icons or as simple file listings. Just pull down the View menu and choose from the following options:

- To view items as large icons, select Large icons.
- To view items as smaller icons, select Small icons.

 T I P For both large and small icon views, the files/folders are arranged in order from left to right in horizontal rows.

- To view items as small icons ordered from top to bottom in vertical columns, select List.
- To view items as small icons in a single, vertical column, complete with information such as size, file type, file date, and modification date (as shown in Figure 6.6), select Details.

 T I P If you have moved, copied, or deleted some files and folders but don't see the changes, update your display by pulling down the View menu and selecting Refresh, or press the F5 key.

Part
III

Ch
6

FIG. 6.6
Files are displayed here
with the Details option.

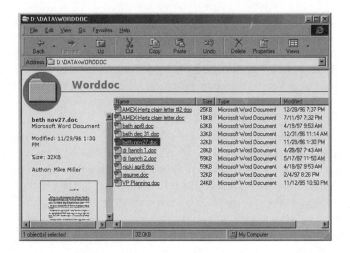

Sorting Files and Folders

When viewing files in My Computer or Windows Explorer, there are a number of ways you can sort your files and folders. Just pull down the <u>V</u>iew menu and choose from the following options:

- To sort files and folders alphabetically by *file name*, select Arrange <u>I</u>cons, and select <u>N</u>ame.

- To sort files and folders by *file type* (applications, configuration files, and so on) and then arranged alphabetically within each file type, select Arrange <u>I</u>cons, and then select <u>T</u>ype.

- To sort files by *file size* (smallest to largest), select Arrange <u>I</u>cons, and then select Si<u>z</u>e.

- To sort files by *date last edited* (most recent to oldest), select Arrange <u>I</u>cons, and then select <u>D</u>ate.

N O T E   If you're displaying files as icons, the Arrange Icons menu will also let you select the <u>A</u>uto Arrange icon, which will force all icons into strict rows and columns so that you cannot have an icon out of line. If you choose not to select this option and your icons become messy, you can realign them by pulling down the <u>V</u>iew menu and selecting Lin<u>e</u> Up Icons. ■

Organizing Files and Folders

In this chapter

The New File Features of Windows 98

Although basic file operations (copying, moving, deleting, renaming, and so on) are unchanged in Windows 98, the way you select files is different when you activate True Web Integration. Basically, you now select folders and files the same way you select Web pages in a Web browser—by hovering and single-clicking.

- *Hovering.* To select a folder or file, you now hover over it with your cursor instead of single-clicking it.
- *Single-clicking.* To open a folder or file, you now single-click it instead of double-clicking it.

Understanding Files and Folders

Every file on your computer has a name and occupies a distinct location. Prior to Windows 95, file names were limited to eight characters plus a three-character "extension," separated by a period. A typical file name looked like this: FILENAME.EXT.

N O T E   Extensions are often assigned automatically to certain types of files. For example, Microsoft Word documents have a .DOC extension. ▪

In Windows 98, however, you're not limited to the old "8+3" convention. Windows 98 file names can include up to 256 characters, and can use spaces and special characters. For example, a file containing information about your 1998 salary might be named 1998 SALARY.DOC.

Files are stored on your disk in *folders*. A folder is like a master file; each folder can contain both files and additional folders. The exact location of a file is called its *path* and contains all the folders leading to the file. For example, a file named FILENAME.DOC that exists in the SYSTEM folder that is contained in the WINDOWS folder on your C:\ drive has a path that looks like this: C:\WINDOWS\SYSTEM\FILENAME.DOC.

N O T E   What Windows 98 calls "folders," Windows 3.x and MS-DOS called "directories." A folder and a directory are the same thing. ▪

Mastering files and folders is a key aspect of using your computer. You may need to copy files from one folder to another, or from your hard disk to a floppy disk. To do this, you use one of the two file-management tools in Windows 98—My Computer or Windows Explorer.

▶ **See** "Understanding My Computer," **p. 84**

▶ **See** "Understanding Windows Explorer," **p. 85**

Selecting Files

Sometimes you'll want to perform an action on a single file. To select a single file, just hover your cursor over the file until it is highlighted; the file name and icon will change color, and information about the selected file will appear in the left part of the window.

Other times, however, you'll want to perform a single action on multiple files. To select multiple files, follow these steps:

1. Start My Computer by clicking the My Computer icon on your desktop.
2. Hover your cursor over the first file you want to select, and then hold down the Ctrl key on your keyboard.
3. Select additional files by hovering your cursor over them until they are highlighted. Keep holding down the Ctrl key until you've selected all desired files.
4. After you've finished selecting files, release the Ctrl key and perform the desired action.

Previewing Files with Quick View

If you would like to view the contents of a file—but you don't want to wait for the associated application to launch—you can take advantage of Quick View. Quick View is a special viewing utility that enables you to see the contents of a file from within My Computer or Windows Explorer.

1. Start My Computer by clicking the My Computer icon on your desktop.
2. Locate the file you want to preview. Right-click the file's icon and choose Quick View from the pop-up menu.
3. This will start the viewer, in which you can look at the contents of the file. If it is a file you want to edit, click the associated application icon on the left side of the toolbar.
4. After you finish viewing the file, click the Close button on the right side of the title bar.

N O T E Windows 98 does not include viewers for all file types. If the Quick View option does not appear on the pop-up menu, no viewer is available for that particular file type. ■

Finding Files

Locating a file can be difficult, especially if you have a large drive or several drives. Windows 98 includes a Find utility to search a drive for you.

To search for a particular file from within My Computer, follow these steps:

1. Start My Computer by clicking the My Computer icon on your desktop. Select the drive you want to search or the drive and folder you want to search.
2. Right-click the drive icon and select Find from the pop-up menu.
3. When the Find: All Files dialog box appears, enter the name of the file or folder you want and click the Find Now button.

4. When the search is complete, a dialog box will appear with any matching files or folders displayed (see Figure 7.1). You can open, move, copy, or delete a file from this display box.

FIG. 7.1
You can search for files by name, by date modified, or by other advanced parameters.

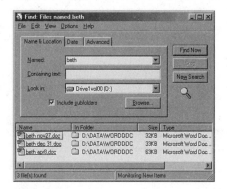

 You can use "wildcard" characters when performing searches with the Find utility. For example, if you use * in place of multiple characters, searching for **FILE*** will find **FILENAME, FILETYPE**, and **FILES**. If you use **?** in place of a single character, searching for **FILE?** will find only **FILES**.

In addition to searching for files by file name, there are other file parameters you can search for:

- *Containing text*. Click the Name & Location tab and enter the specific text within a file you want to search for.
- *Date Modified*. Click the Date tab to search for files created or modified within a specific date range, or during the previous few days or months.
- *File type*. Click the Advanced tab and pull down the Of Type list to specify specific file types to search for.
- *Size*. Click the Advanced tab and select minimum or maximum file sizes from the Size Is lists.

 You can also access the Find utility by selecting Find on the Start menu.

Creating Folders

Folders act as drawers on a hard drive to hold other folders or files. They enable you to organize your hard drive by putting common files or folders together. You can use My Computer to create new folders:

1. Start My Computer by clicking the My Computer icon on your desktop.

2. Click the icon of the drive or folder under which you want your new folder to appear.

3. When the drive or folder's contents appear, right-click in a blank area of the window to display the pop-up menu. Select <u>N</u>ew, and then select <u>F</u>older.

4. A new, empty folder appears, with the file name New Folder highlighted. Type a name for your folder (which overwrites the New Folder name) and press Enter.

▶ **See** "Sorting Files and Folders," **p. 92**

Renaming Files and Folders

File and folder names should always describe the contents of the file or folder. Sometimes, however, the contents may change or the file or folder may contain a revision number that needs to be updated. If you have a file or folder with a name that just isn't right, you can rename it.

1. Start My Computer by clicking the My Computer icon on your desktop.

2. Locate the file or folder you want to rename. Right-click the file or folder icon, and choose Rena<u>m</u>e from the pop-up menu.

3. The file name is now highlighted. Type a new name for your folder (which overwrites the current name) and press Enter.

> **CAUTION**
>
> Folder and file names can include up to 256 characters—including many special characters. Some special characters, however, are "illegal," meaning that you *can't* use them in folder or file names. Illegal characters include the following: \ / : * ? " < > |

Deleting Files and Folders

Because disk space is a resource you don't want to waste, you should delete files and folders you no longer need.

1. Start My Computer by clicking the My Computer icon on your desktop.

2. Select the file or folder you want to delete and press the Delete key, or right-click to display the pull-down menu and select <u>D</u>elete.

 You can also delete a file by dragging it from the My Computer window onto the Recycle Bin icon on the desktop.

Part

III

Ch

7

Restoring Deleted Files

If you delete a file and later decide you made a mistake, you're in luck. Windows 98 stores deleted files in the Recycle Bin for a period of time—if you have deleted the file recently, it should still be in the Recycle Bin.

1. Open the Recycle Bin by clicking its icon on the desktop.

2. When the Recycle Bin opens (see Figure 7.2), locate the file or folder you want to restore. Right-click the item's icon and choose R̲estore from the pop-up menu.

FIG. 7.2

You can restore a deleted file from the Recycle Bin.

Managing the Recycle Bin

The Recycle Bin is where deleted files are stored after you delete them. Files do not stay in the Recycle Bin indefinitely, however. By default, the deleted files in the Recycle Bin can occupy 10 percent of your hard disk space. When you have enough deleted files to exceed 10 percent of your disk space, the oldest files in the Recycle Bin are completely deleted from your hard disk.

If you want to permanently erase files from the Recycle Bin manually, follow these steps:

1. Right-click the Recycle Bin icon.

2. When the pop-up menu appears, select Empty Recycle B̲in.

3. When the Confirm File Delete dialog box appears, click Y̲es to completely erase the files, or click N̲o to continue storing the files in the Recycle Bin.

Copying Files and Folders

Copying a file or folder is the way that you place a copy of it at another location (either in another folder or on another disk) while still retaining the original where it was. Copying is different from moving in that when you copy an item, the original remains; when you move an item, the original is no longer present in the original location.

1. Start My Computer by clicking the My Computer icon on your desktop.

2. Select the file or folder you want to copy. Right-click the icon for this item and choose C̲opy.

3. Select the new location for the item. Right-click in an open space in the new location's window, and then choose <u>P</u>aste from the pop-up menu.

Moving Files and Folders

Moving a file or folder is different from copying a file or folder. Moving deletes the item from its previous location and places it in a new location; copying leaves the original item where it was *and* creates a copy of the item elsewhere. To move a file or folder with My Computer

1. Start My Computer by clicking the My Computer icon on your desktop.

2. Select the file or folder you want to move. Right-click the icon of the folder or file and choose Cu<u>t</u>.

3. Select and open the drive or folder where you want to move the cut item. Right-click in an open space in the new location's Contents pane. Choose <u>P</u>aste from the menu.

Putting Files on the Desktop with Shortcuts

If you have a favorite application or document that you open frequently, you can place a short-cut icon for that item on your desktop. Clicking the shortcut icon launches the application or document.

1. Start My Computer by clicking the My Computer icon on your desktop.

2. Locate the file for which you want to create a shortcut.

3. Right-drag the file onto the desktop, and then release the right mouse button. (Right-dragging is dragging while holding down the right mouse button.) A shortcut menu appears.

4. Choose Create <u>S</u>hortcut(s) Here from the shortcut menu. The shortcut icon is placed on the desktop.

 You can also create a desktop shortcut by highlighting the file in My Computer, right-clicking the mouse, selecting Se<u>n</u>d To from the pop-up menu, and then selecting Desktop As Shortcut.

If you want to delete a desktop shortcut, simply drag it into the Recycle Bin.

Unprotecting Read-Only Files

If you have a file that you want to edit or delete but you can't, chances are the file is designated as *read-only*. Read-only files can't be changed or deleted; you can read them, but you can't touch them. If you need to edit or delete a read-only file, you need to change that file's *attributes*.

1. Start My Computer by clicking the My Computer icon on your desktop.

2. Select the file or folder you want to change and right-click its icon. Choose P<u>r</u>operties from the pop-up menu.

Part

III

Ch

7

3. When the Properties dialog box appears (see Figure 7.3), select the General tab and then select or deselect the desired attributes. For example, to make a read-only file editable, deselect the Read-only check box.

4. After you've made the desired changes, click the OK button.

FIG. 7.3
You can change the attributes of a file from the Properties dialog box.

You can change the following file attributes in the Properties dialog box:

- *Read-only* files are files you can read but not edit or delete.

- *Hidden* files are files—typically sensitive system files—that you normally can't view from My Computer or Windows Explorer.

- *Archive* files are files that have changed since they were last backed up.

- *System* files are sensitive files Windows needs to operate.

Understanding File Types

As you use My Computer to browse files and folders, you'll notice that some files have specific icons. These icons let you know what type the file is.

The file type determines more than just the icon, however; it also determines the description you see if you look at the file's details and the application that will be used to open the file. Windows 98 also uses the characters in the extension of a file name to determine a file's file type.

Table 7.1 shows you some of the icons you'll encounter when you open My Computer or Windows Explorer and their corresponding file types and typical extensions.

Table 7.1 Icons and File Types

Icon	File Type and Typical Extension
	System file (.SYS)
	Configuration settings file (.INI)
	Text file (.TXT)
	Microsoft Word document file (.DOC)
	Microsoft Excel worksheet file (.XLS)
	Microsoft PowerPoint presentation file (.PPT)
	Web page file (.HTM or .HTML)
	Sound file (.WAV)
	MIDI music file (.MID)
	Bitmap image file (.BMP)
	TrueType font file (.TTF)
	System font file (.FON)
	Help file (.HLP)
	MS-DOS application (.EXE)
	Unknown file type

Part
III

Ch
7

Displaying or Hiding File Types

Windows 98 has the capability to hide files that are of a certain type. The types that Windows automatically hides are typically sensitive system files. Because you don't want to accidentally delete or change a system file, hiding them can be a good idea. You may, however, need to edit a system file, so you should know how to unhide the files.

1. Click the Start menu, select Settings, and then select Folders and Icons.
2. When the Folders dialog box appears, click the View tab and double-click the Hidden Files icon to open this section.
3. If you want to see hidden files, select Show All Files. If you don't want system files displayed, select Do Not Show Hidden or System Files.
4. Click Okay to register your changes.

Changing Icons for File Types

Each specific file type is associated with an icon that will be shown whenever files of that type are listed in My Computer. If you don't like a particular file type icon, you can easily choose another icon.

1. Click the Start menu, select Settings, and then select Folders and Icons.
2. When the Folders dialog box appears, select the File Types tab.
3. Choose the file type you want to change from the Registered File Types list and click the Edit button.
4. When the Edit File Type dialog box appears, click the Change Icon button.
5. When the Change Icon dialog box appears (see Figure 7.4), the name of the file that contains the icon is already entered in the File Name box. If you want to use an icon from another file, enter the name of that file into the File Name box; or click the Browse button, select the file, and click Open.
6. Select the appropriate icon in the Current Icon box, and then click OK.

FIG. 7.4
You can change icons for a specific file type in the Change Icon dialog box.

Selecting Which Program Opens a Specific File Type

When you install a new application, it usually registers its file types automatically—that is, Windows associates that file type with a specific application. If you create files with custom or special extensions, however, you need to register these special extensions as a file type.

When you associate a file type with a particular program, you also designate the *actions* that are performed on the file—whether the file can be opened, edited, and so forth. You can have more than one action for any particular file type. These actions will all be displayed when you right-click a file of the registered type; the action that will be performed when you click the file is the *default* action.

To associate a new file type with a particular application, follow these steps:

1. Click the Start menu, select Settings, and then select Folders and Icons.
2. When the Folders dialog box appears, select the File Types tab, and click the New Type button.
3. Enter any comments about the file type in the Description of Type text box, the file type's extension in the Associated Extension text box, and the content type, if applicable, in the Content Type box. (It's okay to leave all but the Associated Extension box blank.)
4. Click New Button under the Actions list. Enter an action (open, edit, close, and so on) into the Action box, and then enter the path and program file used to perform this action into the Application Used to Perform Action box. (You can also click the Browse button to select the application.)
5. Click the OK button when you've finished.

N O T E   The default action for a file type appears as bold in the Actions list when you edit the file type. You can change the default action by selecting the new default action in the Action list and clicking the Set Default button. ■

Removing File Types

If you have file types registered that don't even exist on your system (due to uninstalling a particular program), or if you want to delete the current registration and start again, you can remove the file type from Windows 98.

N O T E   Deleting a file type does not delete any files with that extension from your system. When you delete a file type, all you do is remove the association between that file extension and the corresponding application. ■

To remove a file type association

1. Click the Start menu, select Settings, and then select Folders and Icons.
2. When the Folders dialog box appears, select the File Types tab.
3. Choose the file type you want to remove from the Registered File Types list and click the Remove button.

Part

III

Ch

7

Managing Disks and Disk Drives

The New Disk-Related Features of Windows 98

Formatting, naming, and copying disks in Windows 98 are done the same way they were in Windows 95. The only difference between Windows 95 and Windows 98 is in the contents of the Startup Disk. In Windows 95, the Startup Disk did not include any CD-ROM drivers, making it difficult to use the Startup Disk to reinstall Windows from a CD-ROM. Windows 98 adds CD-ROM drivers to the Startup Disk, so if you need to reinstall the entire operating system from scratch, you can use the CD-ROM version of Windows 98 to do so.

Formatting Floppy Disks

If you have a new disk that is not preformatted, you must format it before you can store any information on it. You also can erase all files from a disk by formatting it; the formatting cleans the disk of all files and prepares it for new information.

> **CAUTION**
>
> Formatting a previously formatted disk will destroy any files previously stored on the disk. Be sure the floppy doesn't contain anything you need before you format it.

1. Insert the disk into the appropriate drive.

2. Click the My Computer icon to start My Computer.

3. Right-click the applicable drive and choose For_mat. When the Format dialog box appears (see Figure 8.1), set the desired options. The first time you format a disk, choose the _F_ull option; when you're reformatting a previously formatted disk, choose the Quick Erase option.

FIG. 8.1

Use My Computer to format floppy disks.

4. Click the _S_tart button. Windows 98 formats your floppy disk and displays the results in a dialog box when complete.

Naming Disks

A volume label is simply a name for a disk. You can change an existing label or name a new disk by following these steps:

1. Click the My Computer icon to start My Computer. If you are changing the volume label for a removable disk, be sure to insert the disk into the appropriate drive.
2. Right-click the drive and choose Properties from the pop-up menu.
3. When the Properties dialog box appears (see Figure 8.2), select the General tab and type the desired volume name into the Label box. Click the OK button.

FIG. 8.2
Change the label of a disk with the Properties dialog box.

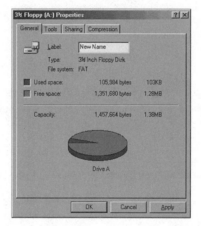

Copying Floppy Disks

You can copy the complete contents of a floppy disk onto another disk with a few simple mouse clicks:

1. Insert the disk you want to copy into the floppy disk drive.
2. Click the My Computer icon to start My Computer.
3. Right-click the floppy drive icon and choose Copy Disk from the menu. Click the Start button in the Copy Disk dialog box.
4. When prompted, remove the source disk and insert the destination disk. Click the OK button.

Creating a Startup Disk

A Startup disk is vital in case you have to restart your computer in an emergency, such as when corrupted system files are detected at normal Windows 98 startup or if your hard disk crashes. With a Startup disk, you essentially start your system from a floppy disk instead of your hard disk.

The Windows 98 Installation Wizard prompts you to make a Startup disk during installation. You can also create a Startup disk at any other time by following these instructions:

1. Click the Start button, select Settings, and then select Control Panel to open the Control Panel.

2. Click the Add/Remove Programs icon to open the Add/Remove Programs Properties dialog box, and then click the Startup Disk tab.

3. Click the Create Disk button to start the process. As Windows prepares to create the Startup disk, it prompts you to label and insert a floppy disk in drive A; do so, and then click the OK button.

4. You are returned to the Add/Remove Programs Properties dialog box (with no additional messages) when the Startup Disk has been successfully created. Click OK to close the dialog box and return to the desktop.

CAUTION

If an error occurs while creating your Startup disk, a Disk Initialization Error information box will be displayed with a message describing the problem, such as `Error: Disk sector was not found`. Insert another disk and click OK.

Open the write-protect notch of your Startup disk to minimize the possibility of erasing or overwriting the disk.

CHAPTER 9

Basic System Maintenance

In this chapter

The New System Maintenance Features of Windows 98

Microsoft completely overhauled almost all of Windows' system maintenance features with Windows 98. Among the new or changed features are:

- *Microsoft Backup.* Windows 98 includes a completely new Backup program—it's easier to use than the old Windows 95 Backup and includes support for more backup devices.

- *Disk Defragmenter.* This essential utility—used to speed up the performance of your hard disks—has been updated to automatically place files for your most frequently used program at the front of your disk, for increased access speed.

- *DriveSpace 3.* This disk compression utility has been updated to make even better use of your existing disk space.

- *Windows Tune-Up Wizard.* This Wizard configures the new Task Scheduler to run common maintenance activities—such as Disk Defragmenter and ScanDisk—at preselected times.

- *Disk Cleanup Manager.* This is a "hidden" utility that identifies unused files on your hard disk that can be deleted to free up more disk space.

- *Windows Update.* This new feature makes sure your computer and operating system are always up-to-date, by automatically dialing up the Web and downloading and installing the latest versions of your system files and drivers.

Backing Up Data

Microsoft Backup is a utility that helps you store important files on floppy disks or backup tapes in the event of a hard drive crash. Even if you've never had a hard drive fail or become corrupted, you should always make regular backup copies of your critical files.

How often you need to back up your files depends on how often the files change and how critical the changes are. For many users, once a month is often enough. If your system crashes, you'll lose some information, but nothing you can't reproduce with a little time. If you store critical information that changes rapidly, however, you should consider backing up more regularly.

You can choose to back up the entire contents of your hard disk, or just selected files. Many users opt to back up just their data files (documents created by Word, Excel, and other applications) on a fairly frequent basis, and do a full hard disk backup at less frequent intervals.

To back up files from your hard disk:

1. To start Microsoft Backup, click the Start button, select Programs, select Accessories, select System Tools, and then select Backup.

2. When Backup launches, you are presented with a dialog box asking you what you'd like to do. Check Create a New Backup Job, and click OK.

3. Windows launches the Backup Wizard. If you want to back up your entire hard disk, select Back Up My Computer and proceed to step 5. If you want to back up only selected files on your computer, select Back Up Selected Files, Folders, and Drives, click Next, and then proceed to step 4.

4. In the left pane of the screen shown in Figure 9.1, select the drives and folders that contain the files you want backed up. In the right pane, select the individual files you want to back up. To back up an entire drive, click the check box next to the drive in the left pane. Click Next to proceed.

FIG. 9.1

To back up files with Microsoft Backup, click the "+" next to each drive and folder to display its contents, and then check the box next to those items you want to back up.

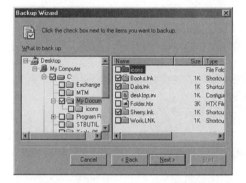

5. When asked *what* you want to back up, specify to back up All Selected Files, or only those New and Changed Files. Click Next to proceed.

 TIP Many users choose to back up only those files that are new or have changed since the last backup. This minimizes the size of your backup file by not backing up files that haven't changed.

6. When asked *where* to back up, select a destination for the backup files. You can back up files to a floppy disk, to a tape drive, to a removable disk, or to a second hard disk. Click Next to proceed.

7. When asked *how* to back up, make sure both options (Compare and Compress) are selected; then click Next to proceed.

8. You are now prompted for a name for this backup job. Enter a name and click Start to begin the backup.

 TIP When labeling the backup set, you should try to include the date so that you know when the files were last backed up.

Restoring Files from a Backup

If you do experience a hard disk problem, you may need to restore to your hard disk the files you previously backed up. While it can be traumatic to lose files in a hard disk failure, restoring files from your backup disks will help to get you up and running in no time.

Part
III

Ch
9

To restore backed-up files to your hard disk, follow these steps:

1. Click the Start button, select <u>P</u>rograms, select Accessories, select System Tools, and then select Backup.

2. When Backup launches, you are presented with a dialog box asking you what you'd like to do. Check <u>R</u>estore Backed Up Files and click OK.

3. When the Restore Wizard appears, select where the backup files are stored, and then click <u>N</u>ext.

4. When the Select Backup Sets dialog box appears, select which backup set you want to restore, and then click OK.

5. When the next dialog box (shown in Figure 9.2) appears, select the files (or folders) you want to restore. Click <u>N</u>ext to proceed.

FIG. 9.2

Check the boxes next to those files or folders you want to restore.

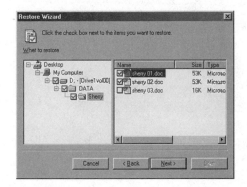

6. When asked *where* you want to restore these files, select either Original Location or Alternate Location. If you select Alternate Location, a new text box appears in this dialog box; enter the location you want for the restored files in this box. Click <u>N</u>ext to proceed.

7. When asked *how* to restore, select one of the following options and then click <u>S</u>tart:

   • *<u>D</u>o Not Replace the File on My Computer.* This prevents you from overwriting existing files.

   • *<u>R</u>eplace the File on My Computer Only if the File Is Older.* This allows you to restore only those files that are newer than those on your computer—that is, those files that have changed recently.

   • *<u>A</u>lways Replace the File on My Computer.* This allows you to replace all files on your computer with the versions contained in your backup set.

8. When the Media Required dialog box appears, make sure you have the right disks/tapes ready for restoration, and then click OK.

9. A Restore Progress dialog box appears during the restore process. When the restoration is complete, a dialog box appears with the message `Operation completed`. Click OK.

Scanning for Viruses

Viruses are programs that harm your computer in some fashion. Some are more annoying than harmful, but others can destroy the contents of your computer system and render it useless. You can protect yourself from viruses by being careful about what you put on your machine and running anti-virus software regularly.

If you have a completely closed system—you never install new software, you never copy files from a floppy, you never communicate with other devices, you're not hooked up to a network, and you never go online—then you don't need a virus checker. Because this is rarely the situation, you should add a virus checker to your start-up folder. This will check your system for viruses each time your system is booted. In addition, if you download files from the Internet or other online services, make sure you download them to a separate directory and scan all files before using them on your system.

You can protect your machine from viruses by performing the following tasks:

- Install an anti-virus software (such as Norton Anti-Virus) according to the directions included with the software. Run the program regularly—and update the software periodically according to instructions included with the software.

- Only accept or purchase software from known vendors.

- If you download files from the Internet, create a special download folder and have the anti-virus software scan the folder each time you download any new files.

Make Your Hard Disk Run Better by Defragmenting

If you notice that opening files seems to take longer than usual or your hard drive light stays on longer then usual, you may need to defragment your hard drive.

You create fragments on your hard drive anytime you run an application or when you edit, move, copy, or delete a file. Fragmentation is like taking the pieces of a puzzle and storing them in different boxes along with pieces from other puzzles; the more dispersed the pieces are, the longer it takes to put the puzzle together. So if you notice your system takes longer and longer to open and close files or run applications, you probably need to defragment your system—in effect, putting all the pieces of the puzzle in one box.

New to Windows 98 is the capability of Disk Defragmenter to rearrange files on your hard drive according to how often you use them. In essence, Disk Defragmenter places those files you use most frequently together near the front of your hard drive, so that they can be accessed more quickly.

To defragment your hard drive:

1. Click the Start button, select Programs, select Accessories, select System Tools, and then select Disk Defragmenter.

2. When the Select Drive dialog box appears, choose the drive you want to defragment and then click OK.

Part
III

Ch
9

T I P You should close all applications and stop working on the system while Disk Defragmenter is running. Defragmenting your drive can take a while, especially if you have a large hard drive or your hard drive is especially fragmented. So you might want to start the utility and let it run while you are at lunch.

Perform a Hard Disk Checkup with ScanDisk

As you run applications, move files, delete files, or accidentally turn the power off while the system is running, you can introduce disk errors. ScanDisk can locate these problems and correct many of them automatically.

Anytime you are having difficulty with your drive, you should run ScanDisk to look for errors. These difficulties include slow access, failure to open a file, or if the system hangs when saving or opening a file. Normally, a standard scan will take care of your difficulties. If you suspect serious errors with the physical mechanics of the drive, you can choose a thorough scan. Thorough scans take much longer, however, so allow extra time when performing one.

N O T E If your system shuts down unexpectedly or if you have to reboot your system manually, Windows runs ScanDisk automatically the next time you start up your system. ■

To run ScanDisk:

1. Click the Start button, select Programs, select Accessories, select System Tools, and then select ScanDisk.

2. When ScanDisk launches (see Figure 9.3), choose the drive you want to scan. Select the Standard option and check Automatically Fix Errors. Click the Start button.

FIG. 9.3
Click Automatically Fix Errors to have ScanDisk fix errors on your hard disk.

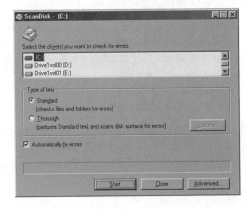

Make More Space on Your Hard Disk with DriveSpace 3

As you add more applications and data to your computer, you may start to run low on free hard drive space. DriveSpace 3 is a *disk compression* utility that comes with Windows 98. It allows you to compress the information that you store on your hard drive, thus giving you more space on the hard drive.

If you're using the FAT32 file system, you won't be able to use DriveSpace 3. FAT32 does a more efficient job of using disk space than the old FAT16 file system, and thus doesn't need disk compression.

Part III

Ch 9

> **CAUTION**
>
> Compressed drives run slower than normal disk drives. If you have an older, slower system, you may find that compressing your hard disk results in unacceptable performance.

If you have a small hard disk—or are simply running out of disk space—you should consider using DriveSpace 3 to compress your existing data and free up space for new programs.

1. Start DriveSpace 3 by clicking the Start button, selecting Programs, selecting Accessories, selecting System Tools, and then selecting DriveSpace.

2. When DriveSpace 3 launches, select the drive you want to compress from the drives listed. (Any drive already compressed will have Compressed drive shown next to it.) Pull down the Drive menu and select Compress.

3. When the Compress a Drive dialog box appears (see Figure 9.4), you can graphically see how much extra disk space you get by compressing the selected drive. Click the Start button to begin compressing the selected disk. (If you haven't already backed up the files on this disk, be sure to click the Back Up Files button when prompted; after backing up, click the Compress Now button.)

 TIP Before you compress your drive with DriveSpace 3, you may want to back up the files on the disk in case any errors occur during the compression activity.

4. After the disk is compressed, you'll be prompted to restart your computer. Click OK; your disk will reflect its compressed status when your computer restarts.

> **CAUTION**
>
> Compressing a drive can take several hours, during which time you cannot use your computer.

FIG. 9.4

The pie charts in the Compress a Drive dialog box indicate how much extra storage space you will create.

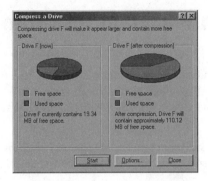

Disabling DriveSpace and Returning Your Hard Drive to Normal

If you are changing machines or operating systems and you need to format your drive, you must decompress the drive before you can format it. In addition, if you decide you really don't need the extra space given with disk compression, you should consider decompressing the drive to reduce the amount of time it takes to read and write data to the drive.

Decompressing a drive means that the previously compressed information is expanded to its original size. If you decompress a drive, make sure you have enough free space to accommodate the expansion. (DriveSpace 3 will automatically alert you if you don't have enough free disk space to decompress the selected drive.)

To decompress your disk:

1. Click the Start button, select Programs, select Accessories, select System Tools, and then select DriveSpace.

2. Select the drive you want to decompress, and then pull down the Drive menu and select Uncompress. Click the Start button.

3. If you haven't backed up your files, click the Back Up Files button. After your files are backed up, click the Uncompress Now button.

CAUTION

Decompressing a drive can take several hours, during which time you cannot use your computer.

Scheduling Regular Maintenance with the Windows Tune-Up Wizard

The Windows Tune-Up Wizard is a scheduling utility that lets you automatically run other Windows utilities. This lets you automatically run various system maintenance tasks—including ScanDisk and Disk Defragmenter—while you're away from your computer.

To use the Windows Tune-Up Wizard:

1. Click the Start button, select Programs, select Accessories, select System Tools, and then select Windows Tune-Up Wizard.

2. When the Windows Tune-Up Scheduler Wizard appears, click the Next button.

3. When the Speed Up Programs dialog box appears, check the Yes option, and then click the Reschedule button. When the Reschedule dialog box appears (see Figure 9.5), select when you want to schedule the regular maintenance activities. You can select to run the tasks daily, weekly, monthly, when your system first starts, or when your system is idle. Click OK when done, and then click Next when you return to the Speed Up Programs dialog box.

FIG. 9.5
Select when—and how often—you want to run your tune-up tasks.

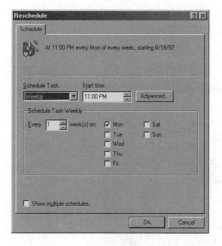

4. When the Scan Hard Disk for Errors dialog box appears, click the Yes option and then click the Reschedule button. Follow the instructions in step 4 to set when ScanDisk will run, and then click Next to proceed.

5. When the Delete Unnecessary Files dialog box appears, click the Yes option and then click the Reschedule button. Follow the instructions in step 4 to set when files will be removed, and then click the Settings button. When the Disk Cleanup Manager Settings dialog box appears, select which types of files you want to delete (such as temporary files

or files in the Recycle Bin). Click OK to return to the Delete Unnecessary Files dialog box, and then click <u>N</u>ext to proceed.

6. When the final dialog box in the Wizard appears, confirm your selections and click the Finish button.

The tasks you selected will now be run automatically at the times you selected.

Deleting Unused Files with Disk Cleanup Manager

Windows 98 includes a "hidden" utility (at least it's hidden in beta 2.1) that helps you identify and delete unused files on your hard disk. Use Disk Cleanup Manager when you want to free up extra hard disk space for more frequently used files.

1. Click the Start button and select <u>R</u>un.

2. When the Run dialog box appears, enter **c:\windows\cleanmgr.exe** in the Open box, and then click OK.

3. Disk Cleanup Manager will now start and automatically analyze the contents of your hard disk drive. When it is finished analyzing, it presents the dialog box shown in Figure 9.6.

FIG. 9.6

Use Disk Cleanup Manager to identify and delete unused files from your hard disk; select the files types you wish to delete, then click OK.

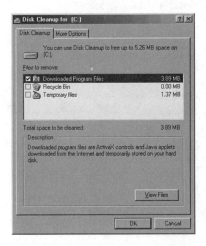

4. Click the Disk Cleanup tab and observe the types of files Disk Cleanup Manager has targeted for deletion. Select those file types you want to remove.

TIP You can view a list of all targeted files within a file type (except for Temporary files) by selecting the file type and clicking the <u>V</u>iew Files button.

5. Click the More Options tab. If you want to delete any unused components of Windows, click the Clean Up button in the Windows Setup section. If you want to delete any other unused applications on your hard disk, click the Clean Up button in the Installed Programs section. If you want to convert a non-FAT32 hard disk to the FAT32 file system, click the Convert button.

CAUTION

The operations on the More Options tab should be attempted by advanced users only. System malfunction could result from "cleaning up" some operating system and application files.

Part

III

Ch

9

6. Click OK to delete the selected files.

Updating Important Files with Windows Update

Windows is constantly changing. Microsoft often releases updated versions of critical system files to improve performance or fix bugs; peripheral manufacturers often issue updated versions of their driver files.

How do you make sure your system has the latest versions of these critical files? Windows 98's new Windows System Update utility compares the files on your computer system with a database of files on Microsoft's Web site—and automatically downloads and installs any new or updated files your system needs for best operation.

To update your system with Windows Update:

1. Click the Start button, select Settings, and then select Windows Update.
2. Windows 98 starts Internet Explorer and navigates to the Windows Update Web page.
3. When the Windows Update Web page displays, click the Update Wizard link.
4. The Update Wizard launches and runs a special program that scans your hard disk for files that might need updating. It may take several minutes for the Update Wizard to completely scan your hard disk.
5. As shown in Figure 9.7, Windows Update lists those items on your computer that need updating. To update each item, select it and then click the Install link. Follow any on-screen instructions to complete the updates. Close Internet Explorer when finished.

Monitoring the Performance of Your System

Windows 98 lets you monitor the performance of your computer's system components. This can be useful if you're evaluating new hardware or software and you want to know how much of the system resources the new items use.

FIG. 9.7

Use the Windows Update Manager to keep key files and drivers up-to-date on your computer system; select the item to update, and then click Install.

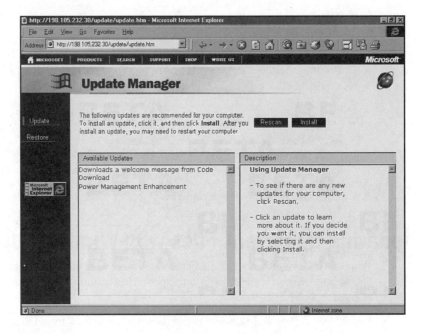

You can also use the System Monitor at any time to check your computer's current performance. If you are having problems with your system locking up or slowing down, you can use the monitor to tell you which device is using resources when the problems occur.

To start the System Monitor:

1. Click the Start button, select Programs, select Accessories, select System Tools, and then select System Monitor.

2. As shown in Figure 9.8, System Monitor automatically shows your processor usage.

3. If you want to monitor other system items, pull down the Edit menu and select Add Item. Select the category you want to monitor from the Category list, and then select the specific item to monitor from the Item list. Click the OK button.

4. If you want to remove an item from the Monitor list, pull down the Edit menu and select Remove Item. Select the item you want removed and click OK.

Windows 98 also lets you monitor and check the performance of major system components through the System Properties dialog box. Just click the System icon in Control Panel, and then select the Performance tab when the System Properties dialog box appears. The System Properties dialog box now displays the status of various system components, including memory, system resources, file system, and disk compression.

FIG. 9.8

Use System Monitor to monitor the performance of your system's processor and other devices.

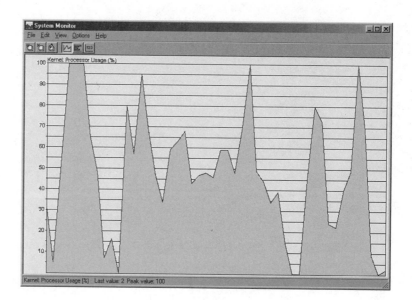

Part

III

Ch

9

Installing and Using Software Programs

Installing New Software

New Software Features of Windows 98

The software installation features of Windows 98 are basically unchanged from those of Windows 95. All programs that ran on Windows 95 should run on Windows 98 without problems.

Installing Windows Applications

Installing a new Windows application is as easy as running the automated Setup program included with most programs. When you insert the installation CD for a new program in your CD-ROM drive, the Setup program should start automatically; just follow the instructions on-screen to complete the installation. If it doesn't start automatically, you'll have to launch the Setup program manually; just click the Start button, select Run, type *x*:\setup in the Run dialog box (where *x* is the letter of your CD-ROM drive), and then click OK.

If you're installing from 3.5-inch floppy disks, you launch the Setup program by inserting the first disk into your floppy disk drive, clicking the Start button, selecting Run, typing **a:\setup** in the Run dialog box, and then clicking OK.

If the program you're installing doesn't have an automated Setup program, or if you prefer to install a new program manually, you can run Windows 98's Install Programs Wizard:

1. Click the Start button, select Settings, and then select Control Panel to open the Control Panel.

2. Click the Add/Remove Programs icon.

3. When the Add/Remove Programs Properties dialog box appears, choose the Install/ Uninstall tab and click Install.

4. Insert the program's disk or CD in the appropriate drive and choose Next. The Install Programs Wizard searches for an installation program (usually SETUP.EXE or INSTALL.EXE) and displays the command line in the Run Installation Program dialog box (see Figure 10.1). If the Wizard did not find a program, you must choose Browse to locate it. Locate the file in the Browse dialog box, select it, and then click the Open button to insert the selected file name in the Wizard.

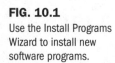

FIG. 10.1
Use the Install Programs Wizard to install new software programs.

5. Choose Finish to run the program's installation program; follow all on-screen instructions to complete the software installation.

N O T E   Not all older programs will run successfully on Windows 98. For a current list of programs with known incompatibility problems with Windows 98, refer to the PROGRAMS.TXT file in the Windows folder. ▪

Installing MS-DOS Applications

Although most new applications programs are Windows 98 compatible, many games programs are still DOS-based. Windows 98 lets you install MS-DOS applications by running the installation program for the application—assuming the program has an installation program. (Most do, fortunately.)

1. Start an MS-DOS session by clicking the Start button, selecting Programs, and then selecting MS-DOS Prompt. Your screen will change to an MS-DOS screen, complete with a command-line prompt.

2. At the DOS prompt, enter the command to start the installation program—generally something similar to **a:\install.exe** if you're installing from a floppy disk—and then press Enter.

3. Follow the on-screen directions for the installation program.

4. When the installation program is complete, you should be returned to the DOS prompt. Type **exit** and press Enter to close the MS-DOS session.

N O T E   If the MS-DOS application does not have an installation program, you can manually install it to your hard disk by creating a new folder and copying the files to the folder. ▪

You probably want to create a Start menu item for the new application; Windows doesn't do that automatically for DOS programs. (It does for Windows programs.)

▶ **See** "Adding Items to the Start Menu," **p. 57**

Uninstalling Windows Applications

Removing a Windows application can be easy—or it can be complicated. Most newer Windows programs include their own utilities to uninstall the program automatically. You should use this publisher-supplied utility, if it exists, to uninstall the program. You can generally find the program's uninstall utility in the folder where the program's other files reside.

If you want to remove a Windows application that doesn't include its own uninstall utility, the process has been simplified with the addition of the Add/Remove Programs Wizard. This built-in utility identifies every component of the application you want to remove and deletes them from your hard disk automatically. Only applications that provide uninstall programs designed to run in Windows 98 appear in the list for removal.

> **CAUTION**
>
> An uninstall program should *not* remove your personal files, even if they are stored in the application's folders. The files deleted during the automatic uninstall are not moved to the Recycle Bin. Just to be safe, however, you should move files you want to keep to a new folder before removing the application.

To remove an application from your system:

1. Click the Start button, select Settings, and then select Control Panel to open the Control Panel.

2. Click the Add/Remove Programs icon.

3. When the Add/Remove Programs Properties dialog box appears (see Figure 10.2), click the Install/Uninstall tab.

FIG. 10.2

You can remove a program automatically with the Add/Remove Programs utility.

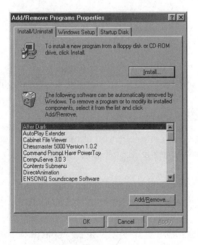

4. Select the program's name from the list of installed programs, and click the Add/Remove button. If prompted, confirm that you want to continue to uninstall the application.

5. Answer any other prompts the uninstall utility presents for removing the program. Some programs, such as Microsoft Word, may require you to insert the original installation disks or CD to perform the uninstall.

6. After the uninstall routine is completed, choose Cancel to close the Add/Remove Programs Properties dialog box, and then close the Control Panel.

When you remove Windows applications by following the preceding steps, the applications should no longer appear on the Start menu or as a desktop shortcut icon. If they were not removed, you'll need to remove them manually.

▶ **See** "Removing Items from the Start Menu," **p. 59**

N O T E If the Windows program you want to remove does not have an automatic uninstall utility, you have to delete the files for the program manually, using My Computer. (See the next section for instructions.) The problem with this method is that miscellaneous files associated with the program are often scattered throughout various folders on your hard disk; you may want to purchase a third-party uninstall program to find and remove all program remnants from your system. ■

Uninstalling MS-DOS Applications

You can remove MS-DOS applications from your computer by using My Computer to delete files from your hard disk.

1. Click the My Computer icon on your desktop to open My Computer.
2. Find the application's folder and click its icon.
3. Right-click the folder icon and select Delete from the pop-up menu.
4. Windows asks you to confirm that you want to remove the folder and move all its contents to the Recycle Bin. Choose Yes to remove the folder.

CAUTION

Before deleting the folder containing the DOS application, check for files and subfolders that contain your personal data. If you want to keep these files, move them before removing the application or they may be lost. Also, be sure the folder was created just for this application and does not contain other critical files used by other applications.

N O T E If the MS-DOS application you removed has a shortcut on the Start menu or desktop, you should remove it. ■

▶ **See** "Removing Items from the Start Menu," **p. 59**

Part

IV

Ch

10

Using Windows Software

The New Software-Related Features of Windows 98

All programs that ran on Windows 95 should run on Windows 98 without problems. Programs will work exactly the same way in Windows 98 as they did in Windows 95. Because there are no new system-level features in Windows 98 that require updating software programs, don't expect a lot of new "Windows 98-compatible" upgrades to your favorite software applications.

Understanding the Parts of an Application Window

All Windows applications look fairly much alike. Most of the time the same buttons are in the same places, so if you learn how one program works, other Windows programs will be familiar to you.

Figure 11.1 shows you a typical Windows application (with a document open) and the parts of the application window.

FIG. 11.1

The parts of an application window are the same no matter which application you're using.

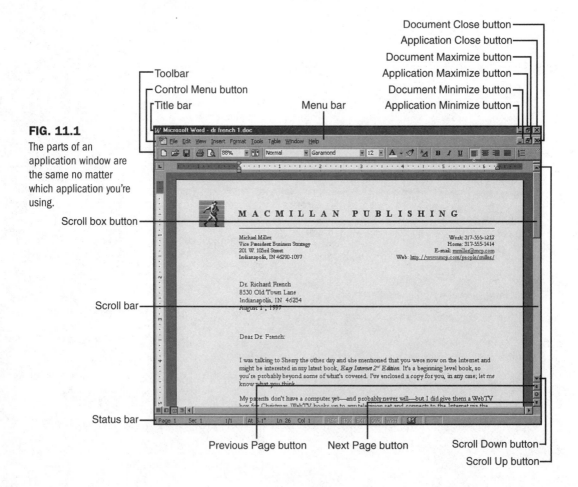

The following list explains the parts of an application window:

■ *Title bar.* The name of the program and the name of the open document is displayed here.

■ *Control Menu button.* Click here for a menu that lets you resize or close the application.

■ *Menu bar.* Click a menu item to see a drop-down menu of commands.

■ *Toolbar.* Comprised of buttons for common tasks; many applications let you right-click the toolbar to customize the buttons displayed.

■ *Scroll bar.* Use the scroll bar to scroll through long documents; the placement of the scroll box button indicates where you are in the document.

■ *Scroll box button.* Drag this button up to scroll up through a document; drag it down to scroll down.

■ *Scroll Up button.* Click this button to scroll up through a document.

■ *Scroll Down button.* Click this button to scroll down through a document.

■ *Previous Page button.* Click this button to move to the previous page.

■ *Next Page button.* Click this button to move to the next page.

■ *Status bar.* Information about the current document is displayed here.

■ *Document Minimize button.* Click this button to minimize the current document within the application.

■ *Document Maximize button.* Click this button to display the current document full-size within the application.

■ *Document Close button.* Click this button to close the current document (while leaving the application open).

■ *Application Minimize button.* Click this button to minimize the application within Windows.

■ *Application Maximize button.* Click this button to maximize the application within Windows.

■ *Application Close button.* Click this button to close the application.

TIP Without clicking, position your cursor over an item—like a toolbar button—to display a *ToolTip* (also called a *ScreenTip* in Office 97) that tells you what that item does.

Launching an Application from the Start Menu

Using the Start menu's Programs menu is probably the simplest way to launch an application. The Programs menu is always accessible and organized, and groups and folders are listed alphabetically, for easy reference.

Part
IV

Ch
11

N O T E   Generally, when you install an application, its group, folder, or application name is added
to the Programs menu for you. Some programs, however, install directly on the Start menu
instead of one level down on the Programs menu. ■

To launch an application from the Start menu:

1. Click the Start menu and select Programs. The Programs menu appears next to the Start
menu, as shown in Figure 11.2.

FIG. 11.2

Launching an applica-
tion from the Programs
menu; click the Start
button to get started.

2. Point to the application's folder or name on the menu. Applications in folders are listed
with an arrow, indicating that there are more folders within. When you point to a
program item with an arrow, a submenu opens. If the item you want is on that submenu,
point to it. The item you point to is highlighted.

3. Click the highlighted item to launch the application.

Launching an Application from My Computer

Another way to launch applications is to click the application file from My Computer.

1. Click the My Computer icon on your desktop to launch My Computer.

2. Navigate to the folder that contains the program you want to start. Click the folder icon
to display the files stored within that folder.

3. Click the icon for the application file that you want to open. The application starts
automatically.

Launching an Application from a Desktop Shortcut Icon

In addition to using the Start menu or My Computer to launch your programs, you can also create and use a desktop shortcut for any program you want to launch. Using a desktop shortcut is perhaps the fastest way to launch those programs you use all the time; it's a lot quicker to click an icon than it is to wade through layers of menus and folders.

To launch a program from a shortcut, simply click the shortcut icon on your desktop. Before you can launch a program from a desktop icon, however, follow these steps to create an icon on your desktop:

1. Click the My Computer icon on your desktop to launch My Computer.
2. Navigate to the folder that contains the program for which you want to create a shortcut. Click the folder icon to display the files stored within that folder.
3. Right-drag the selected file's icon onto the desktop, and then release the right mouse button. (Right-dragging is dragging while holding down the right mouse button.) A pop-up menu appears.
4. From the pop-up menu, select Create Shortcut(s) Here. The shortcut icon is placed on your desktop.
5. When the shortcut is created, Windows gives it a name that starts with "Shortcut to." If you want to rename the shortcut, single-click the shortcut to highlight the current name, and then edit the name or type in a new name.

 TIP You can also create a desktop shortcut by highlighting the file in My Computer, right-clicking the mouse, selecting Send To from the pop-up menu, and then selecting Desktop as Shortcut.

Part

IV

Ch

11

Switching Between Applications

When an application is open, it's easy to switch between that application and other open applications.

When multiple applications are open, you can determine which is the currently active window by the color of its title bar—the title bar for the active application is usually brighter than that of an inactive application. If applications are overlapped on your desktop, the active one is on top. Also, the active window's Taskbar button appears lighter and looks like it is pressed in.

There are many ways to switch between applications:

- Click the application's Taskbar button.
- Click the application's title bar.

■ Click almost any other part of the window that is visible.

■ Hold down the Alt key and then press the Tab key repeatedly until the application window you want is selected. (This cycles through all open windows.) When you're at the window you want, release the Alt key.

Closing an Application

After you've finished using an application, there are several ways you can close the application:

■ Click the x button in the window's upper-right corner.

■ Double-click the icon in the window's upper-left corner (the Control Menu button).

■ Pull down the File menu and select Exit.

■ Right-click the window's Taskbar button and choose Close.

■ Press Alt+F4.

> **CAUTION**
>
> If you attempt to close an application window without saving a document, the application will warn you and give you an opportunity to save the document. You must choose to save or not save the document before the application window will close.

Navigating Application Menus and Commands

Finding your way around menus and commands in Windows applications is easy, and is done the same way in almost every Windows program. You can navigate menus and commands by using the mouse or keyboard.

1. Move the mouse pointer left or right along the menu bar to select a menu item, such as File.

2. Click a menu item with your mouse. The commands for that menu drop down, as shown in Figure 11.3.

3. To choose a command on a menu, click it.

You will notice the following features on the menu:

■ If the command appears gray on the menu, it is disabled and not currently available. For example, the Edit menu's Copy command is grayed unless you have selected something to copy.

■ If the command has a right-arrow next to it, a submenu drops down automatically when you point to that command.

FIG. 11.3

Pull down the File menu to display file-related commands.

- If the command name is followed by three dots (...), selecting the command displays a dialog box with a selection of options.

- If the command name is followed by a shortcut, you can alternatively use the keyboard shortcut for the command. For example, Ctrl+V is the shortcut shown for the Paste command on the Edit menu.

- All commands have an underlined letter. You can press F10 or Alt on your keyboard to access the menu bar, and then press the underlined letter to choose the command. For example, Pressing F10 then F then S will pull down the File menu and Save the current document.

Part
IV

Ch
11

Common Windows Application Menus

Many Windows applications use similar menus to perform similar functions. The following table details some of the more common Windows menus:

Menu	Functions
File	Select various file commands, including Create a New document, Open an existing document, Save a document, Save As a new file name, Print a document.
Edit	Select various editing commands, including Undo Paste commands, Cut data, Copy data, Paste data, Select All data, Find specific data.
View	Select various document views.
Format	Select various formatting commands.
Window	Select various window configurations, including open a New window, Arrange All windows, and Split the current window.
Help	Select various help options.

Creating a New Document

Creating a new document is similar in most applications.

1. Pull down the File menu.
2. Select New.
3. If a dialog box appears prompting you to choose from various preselected document types, select one from the list and click OK.

Opening an Existing Document from Within an Application

There are many ways to open an existing document. If you already have the corresponding application open, follow these steps:

1. Pull down the File menu.
2. Select Open.
3. When the Open dialog box appears (see Figure 11.4), browse through the folders to select the document you want, and then click OK.

FIG. 11.4
Choose a document to open from the Open dialog box.

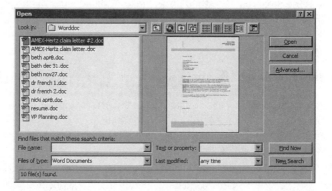

Opening an Existing Document from My Computer

You can also use My Computer to find and open any document—even if you don't currently have the associated application open. When you click a document file from My Computer, the associated application is automatically launched, with the selected document open. If the associated application is already running, the document you selected opens in that application.

To open an application from My Computer, follow these steps:

1. Click the My Computer icon on your desktop to launch My Computer.

2. Navigate to the folder that contains the program you want to start. Click the folder icon to display the files stored within that folder.

3. Click the icon for the document that you want to open. The document opens in the associated application.

Opening an Existing Document from a Desktop Shortcut

You can also create desktop shortcuts for your most frequently used documents. To open a document from a desktop shortcut, just double-click the shortcut icon; the associated application will launch and display the selected document.

To create a desktop shortcut for a document, follow these steps:

1. Click the My Computer icon on your desktop to launch My Computer.

2. Navigate to the folder that contains the document for which you want to create a shortcut. Click the folder icon to display the files stored within that folder.

3. Right-drag the selected file's icon onto the desktop, and then release the right mouse button. (Right-dragging is dragging while holding down the right mouse button.) A pop-up menu appears.

4. From the pop-up menu, select Create Shortcut(s) Here. The shortcut icon is placed on your desktop.

Part

IV

Ch

11

 You can also create a desktop shortcut by highlighting the file in My Computer, right-clicking the mouse, selecting Send To from the pop-up menu, and then selecting Desktop as Shortcut.

Opening a Recently Used Document from the Start Menu

Windows stores your most recently opened documents for display on the Start menu's Documents menu. If your document is on the menu, you can open it quickly using this method.

1. Click the Start button and select Documents.

2. Click the document's name or icon on the menu. The document opens in the associated application.

 To clear the list of documents on the Documents menu, click the Start button, select Settings, and then select Taskbar. When the Taskbar Properties dialog box appears, click the Start Menu Programs tab, click the Clear button, and then click OK.

Scrolling Through a Document

Most Windows applications include a vertical scroll bar on the right side of the screen and a horizontal scroll bar on the bottom of the screen. You use the scroll bars to view a part of the document window that is not currently visible.

- To scroll a short distance through your document, click the arrow at either end of the scroll bar to move in the direction the arrow points. Use the vertical scroll bar to scroll up and down. Use the horizontal scroll bar to scroll left and right.

- To scroll a longer distance through your document, click in the gray area next to the arrow or drag the scroll box button to a new location.

 When you scroll a document using the scroll bars, the insertion point remains at the same place in the document and can scroll out of view. If you want to move the insertion point, click a new position.

Arranging Document Windows

When you have multiple documents open within an application, you can use Windows commands to arrange the individual document windows.

1. Pull down the Window menu.

2. Select Arrange All to tile all the open document windows within the main application window (see Figure 11.5).

FIG. 11.5
Four open documents tiled in Microsoft Word; just pull down the Window menu and select Arrange All.

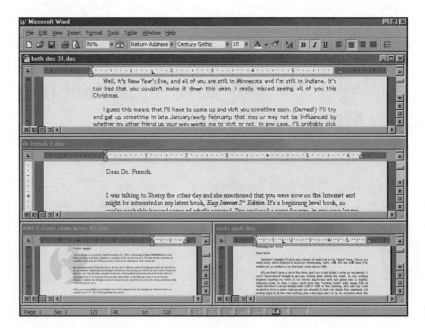

Switching Between Documents

Use the Window menu to select from all the open documents within your application.

1. Pull down the Window menu.
2. Choose the document's file name from the Window menu.

 TIP You can also switch between document windows by pressing Ctrl+F6.

Saving a Document

When you have finished creating or making changes to a document, you want to save that document to disk.

1. Pull down the File menu.
2. Select Save.
3. If the document has already been named and saved previously, it is resaved but remains open. If the document has not previously been saved, the Save As dialog box appears (see Figure 11.6).

Part
IV

Ch
11

FIG. 11.6

Saving a newly created file; pull down the File menu and select Save.

4. If the Save As dialog box appears, choose a drive and folder from the Save In list. Enter a File Name, and then click Save to save the file.

> **CAUTION**
>
> If you save a file as a type different from the application in which it was created, you may lose some formatting changes and any other features not available in the application type you choose.

Saving a File in a Different Format

Many Windows applications include built-in file converters that are designed to open or save files created in other programs. For example, you may want to convert a WordPerfect file to

Word. Ideally, file converters preserve as much as possible the document's text formatting and special elements. Whatever is not converted cleanly, you may need to edit after the conversion.

To save a file in a different format:

1. Pull down the File menu.

2. Select Save As.

3. When the Save As dialog box appears, choose a drive and folder from the Save In list, and enter a File Name. Pull down the Save as Type list to view a list of available file types; choose a file type from this list and click Save to save the file.

N O T E   File converters are sometimes a custom option in a program's setup. If a desired file type is not displayed in the Save As dialog box, you may have to run the application's setup program again to install the specific file converter needed for the conversion. ■

Closing a Document

When you've finished using a specific document, you can close the document while leaving the application open.

1. To close the current document, click the Close button in the upper-right corner of the document window, or pull down the File menu and select Close.

2. If you have not already saved the document, a message appears asking whether you want to save the document. Choose Yes to save the document.

> **CAUTION**
>
> Do not confuse the document's Close button with the application's Close button, or you'll close your entire application instead of just the document. Also, do not confuse the Close command in the File menu (which closes the current document) with the Exit command (which closes the entire application).

Selecting Text in a Document

When you're working within a document, you sometimes want to select a range of text to cut, copy, or delete. There are several ways to select text or other data:

■ Use your mouse to position the pointer at the start of the text you want to select. Hold down the left mouse button and highlight the entire range of text; release the button when the range is completely highlighted.

■ Double-click your mouse on a specific word to highlight that entire word.

■ Move your pointer to the left of a line of text and click the mouse to highlight the entire line.

- Move your pointer to the left of a paragraph and double-click the mouse to highlight the entire paragraph.
- Use your keyboard to position the cursor at the start of the text you want to select. Hold down the Shift key and use the appropriate arrow key to highlight the entire range of text; release both keys when the range is completely highlighted.
- Press Shift+Ctrl+Right Arrow to highlight to the end of a word.
- Press Shift+Ctrl+Down Arrow to highlight to the end of a paragraph.
- Press Shift+Ctrl+End to highlight to the end of the document.

Copying Data

Windows makes it easy to copy data to use in another part of your document—or even in a different document.

1. Select the text or data you want to copy.
2. Pull down the Edit menu and select Copy.
3. Place the insertion point where you want to paste the data.
4. Pull down the Edit menu and select Paste.

You can paste the same data repeatedly if needed; just continue to use the Paste command at different insertion points.

Part
IV

Ch
11

Moving Data with Cut and Paste

Moving data is different from copying data. When you copy data, the original data remains in the original position; when you move data, the original data is cut from its original position.

1. Select the text or data you want to move.
2. Pull down the Edit menu and select Cut.
3. Place the insertion point where you want to move the data.
4. Pull down the Edit menu and select Paste.

Mastering Drag and Drop to Move and Copy Data

Most Windows applications support a technique called *drag and drop*, which lets you move or copy items using the mouse instead of menu commands.

1. Select the text or object you want to copy or move.
2. To move the selection, place the mouse pointer on the selected text or object, click and hold down the left mouse button. (To copy the selection, you must also hold down the Ctrl key.)

3. Use the mouse to drag the selection to a new location. A gray vertical line indicates the exact location.

4. Release the mouse button (and the Ctrl key) to drop the cut or copied selection at the new location.

Linking Data from Different Programs

OLE (object linking and embedding) technology was designed by Microsoft to allow creation of compound documents that use data created in multiple applications. A compound document is created in one application; objects from other applications are linked or embedded in a single document.

To *embed* an object, simply copy from one document and paste it into another. The embedded object can be edited within the application where it is placed, without leaving the application. When you *link* an object from another document, the object is updated in the compound document whenever the object's main document changes.

To create a link between documents:

1. Open the document that contains the information you want to link, and select the object to be linked.

2. Pull down the Edit menu and select Copy.

3. Open the document where you want the information to appear (the compound document) and then click where you want to place the information.

4. Pull down the Edit menu and select Paste Special.

5. When the Paste Special dialog box appears, select the proper format and click OK.

N O T E   Paste Link may be disabled in some applications that do not support this feature.

The linked object is now embedded in your compound document, therefore allowing you to access the original application within the compound document. It also is linked, meaning that whenever the original object is changed—by whatever method—the document to which it is linked will automatically be updated with the new version of the object.

 To edit an embedded or linked object, double-click it. The original application opens within the compound document.

Using Windows 98's Built-In Applications

In this chapter

The New Applications in Windows 98

The only new utility application in Windows 98 is Imaging, a graphic viewer supplied by Kodak. Use Imaging to view graphics files, including files created by scanners and digital cameras.

Using the Windows Calculator

The Windows Calculator looks and operates just like any other calculator—except that you use it on-screen instead of in your hand.

1. Open the Calculator by clicking the Start button, selecting Programs, selecting Accessories, and then selecting Calculator (see Figure 12.1).

Deletes last number

FIG. 12.1
Use the Windows
Calculator just like a
normal handheld
model.

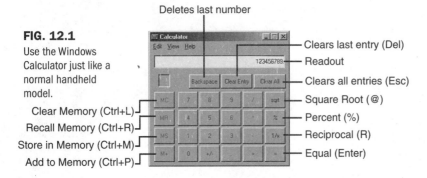

Clears last entry (Del)
Readout
Clears all entries (Esc)
Square Root (@)
Percent (%)
Reciprocal (R)
Equal (Enter)

Clear Memory (Ctrl+L)
Recall Memory (Ctrl+R)
Store in Memory (Ctrl+M)
Add to Memory (Ctrl+P)

2. Using the mouse or keyboard numeric keypad, enter numbers and operators. End by pressing the = button to display the result of the calculation in the Calculator display window.

TIP Windows 98 also includes a Scientific Calculator that lets you perform statistical calculations, such as standard deviations and averages, and scientific functions such as sines, cosines, tangents, powers, and logarithms. Switch to the Scientific Calculator by pulling down the View menu and selecting Scientific. Return to the standard Calculator by pulling down the View menu and selecting Standard.

Using Character Map to Insert Special Characters

The Character Map accessory is used to insert special symbols and characters into a document. For example, you can insert the registered trademark symbol directly into a Microsoft Word document.

1. Open Character Map by clicking the Start button, selecting Programs, selecting Accessories, and then selecting Character Map (see Figure 12.2).
2. Choose the font you want to use from the Font list.

FIG. 12.2
Use Character Map to insert special characters in your documents.

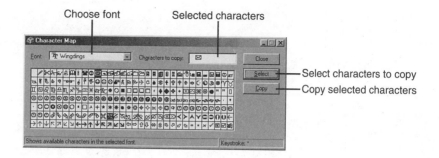

Choose font Selected characters

Select characters to copy
Copy selected characters

3. Select a character by double-clicking it, which places it in the Characters to Copy box. Select additional characters by double-clicking them.

4. Click the Copy button, which places the selected characters in the Windows Clipboard.

5. Switch to your main application and position the insertion point where you want to copy the characters. Pull down the application's Edit menu and select Paste.

TIP To view an enlarged image of a character before selecting it, click and hold down the mouse button on the character. You can also use the arrow keys to move the selection box around to view an enlarged image of each character.

Using the Clock

The Windows 98 clock is automatically displayed in the Taskbar tray. When you place the mouse pointer on the clock, the date is displayed in a ToolTip. If you need to change the date or time or correct the time zone, display the Properties dialog box.

1. Double-click the time in the Taskbar tray.

2. When the Date/Time Properties dialog box appears, select the Date & Time tab to change any of the following options: month, year, day, hour, minute, second, or AM/PM. Use the arrows to adjust to the correct setting.

3. If the Current Time Zone display is incorrect, select the Time Zone tab and choose the correct time zone from the drop-down list.

4. Choose OK to save the changes to the date, time, and time zone.

NOTE If the clock is not displayed in the Taskbar tray, right-click the Taskbar, select Properties from the pop-up menu, select Show Clock, and then click OK. ■

Using Notepad

Notepad is used for viewing or editing unformatted text files, such as small HTML or "read me" files. Because Notepad stores files in text format, almost all word processing programs can open Notepad's files.

Part
IV

Ch
12

> **CAUTION**
> Notepad presents a warning message if you try to open a file that is too large for Notepad to hold. In that case, you can open the file in WordPad.

1. Open Notepad by clicking the Start button, selecting Programs, selecting Accessories, and then selecting Notepad (see Figure 12.3).

┌─Pull down the Edit menu to cut, copy, or paste text
 └─Pull down the Search menu to search for specific text

FIG. 12.3
Use Notepad to edit
small text files.

Pull down the
File menu to open,─
close, or save files

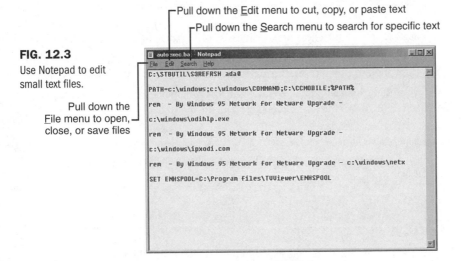

```
C:\STBUTIL\S3REFRSH ada8

PATH=c:\windows;c:\windows\COMMAND;C:\CCMOBILE;%PATH%

rem  - By Windows 95 Network For Netware Upgrade -
c:\windows\odihlp.exe

rem  - By Windows 95 Network For Netware Upgrade -
c:\windows\ipxodi.com

rem  - By Windows 95 Network For Netware Upgrade - c:\windows\netx

SET ENHSPOOL=C:\Program files\TVViewer\ENHSPOOL
```

2. Type and edit text as desired. You must press Enter at the end of each line.
3. Pull down the File menu and select Save to name and save the file.

Using WordPad

WordPad is the accessory word processor that comes with Windows. It has more features than Notepad, including some rudimentary text formatting features. It also allows you to open larger documents than does Notepad.

1. Open WordPad by clicking the Start button, selecting Programs, selecting Accessories, and then selecting WordPad (see Figure 12.4).
2. WordPad opens with a new document. You can begin typing in the new document or open an existing document by pulling down the File menu and selecting Open.
3. Type and edit text as desired. You can use the formatting tools on the toolbar to boldface, italicize, underline, and align your text.
4. Pull down the File menu and select Save to name and save the file.

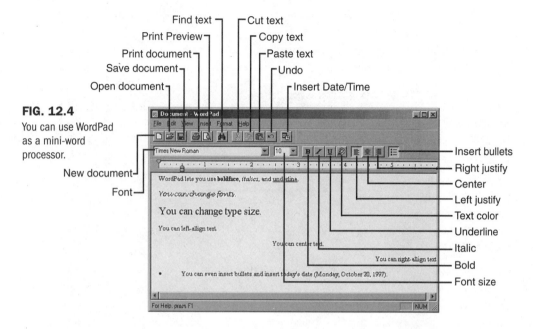

FIG. 12.4
You can use WordPad as a mini-word processor.

You can work on only one document at a time in WordPad. If you open another document, the displayed document closes. If you haven't saved changes, WordPad prompts you to save the changes.

Using Paint

Use Windows Paint to create, edit, and save bitmapped image files. The Paint toolbox contains the tools you need to create and modify a picture.

1. Open Paint by clicking the Start button, selecting Programs, selecting Accessories, and then selecting Paint (see Figure 12.5).

2. Paint opens with a new image file. You can begin painting in the new file or open an existing image by pulling down the File menu and selecting Open.

3. At the left side of the Paint window, click to select the tool you want to use.

4. Position the tool's pointer where you want to begin the drawing.

5. Press and hold down the mouse button and drag to create the shape you want. Release the mouse to stop drawing.

6. Pull down the File menu and select Save to name and save the file.

Part
IV

Ch
12

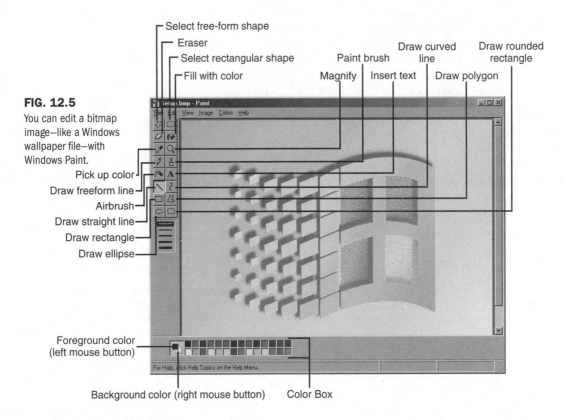

FIG. 12.5

You can edit a bitmap image—like a Windows wallpaper file—with Windows Paint.

Select free-form shape
Eraser
Select rectangular shape
Fill with color
Paint brush
Magnify
Draw curved line
Insert text
Draw polygon
Draw rounded rectangle

Pick up color
Draw freeform line
Airbrush
Draw straight line
Draw rectangle
Draw ellipse

Foreground color (left mouse button)
Background color (right mouse button)
Color Box

Using Imaging by Kodak

Imaging is a new application in Windows 98. Developed by Kodak, Imaging lets you view all types of graphics files. You can also use Imaging to view and manipulate images scanned into your system by a scanning device or digital camera.

1. Click the Start button, select Programs, select Accessories, and then select Imaging. The Imaging window appears, as shown in Figure 12.6

2. To load an existing image, pull down the File menu and select Open.

3. To scan a new image, pull down the File menu and select Scan New. Follow the on-screen instructions to complete the scan.

4. To change the size of the image displayed, pull down the Zoom menu and choose the desired display scale.

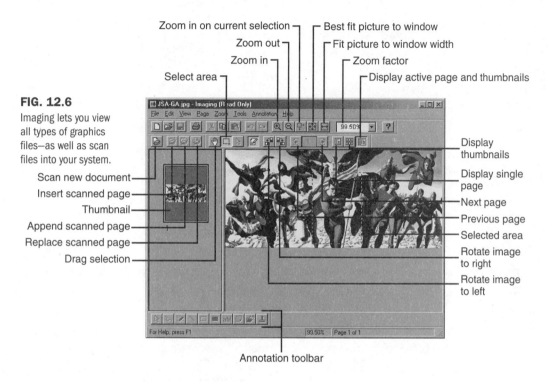

FIG. 12.6

Imaging lets you view all types of graphics files—as well as scan files into your system.

Zoom in on current selection

Zoom out

Zoom in

Select area

Best fit picture to window

Fit picture to window width

Zoom factor

Display active page and thumbnails

Scan new document

Insert scanned page

Thumbnail

Append scanned page

Replace scanned page

Drag selection

Display thumbnails

Display single page

Next page

Previous page

Selected area

Rotate image to right

Rotate image to left

Annotation toolbar

Using the Phone Dialer

The phone dialer is an automatic dialing application. Use it to dial common numbers or just to avoid the hassle of holding the phone while you dial and wait for someone to answer.

1. Start Phone Dialer by clicking Start, selecting Programs, selecting Accessories, and then selecting Phone Dialer (see Figure 12.7).

Pull-down list of previously dialed numbers

FIG. 12.7

Computerized dialing with Phone Dialer can free your hands for other tasks.

Click to dial current number

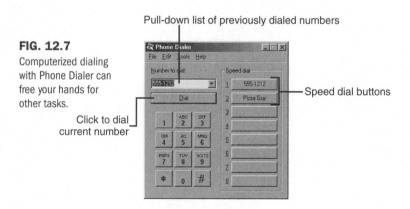

Speed dial buttons

2. If you haven't dialed the number with Phone Dialer before, enter it in the Number to Dial box. If you have dialed the number before, you can select it from the drop-down list.

3. Click the Dial button to make the call.

 If you have a number you call often, you can enter it into one of the speed dial buttons. Simply click the button you want to set, enter the name and number, then click Save or Save and Dial. The next time you want to call that number, you need only click its speed dial button.

Using HyperTerminal

HyperTerminal is a communications accessory that enables you to connect to and communicate with a variety of different online services—including online bulletin board systems (BBSs). Unlike dial-up networking, which only dials the connection, HyperTerminal dials the connection and then provides an interface for you to interact with the selected online service.

To establish a connection with HyperTerminal, follow these steps:

1. Open HyperTerminal by clicking the Start button, selecting Programs, selecting Accessories, and then selecting HyperTerminal.

2. When HyperTerminal first launches, it displays the Connection Description dialog box. Enter a Name and choose an Icon for the new connection, and then click OK.

3. HyperTerminal now displays the Connect To dialog box. Enter the phone number and modem information, and then click OK.

4. You now see the Connect dialog box. Verify the information presented, and then click Dial. HyperTerminal will now connect to the service indicated.

CHAPTER 13

Using DOS Software

In this chapter

The New Software-Related Features of Windows 98

All DOS programs that run on Windows 95 should run on Windows 98 without problems. DOS programs will work exactly the same way in Windows 98 as they do in Windows 95. As with Windows 95, you can run most DOS programs in either full-screen or windowed modes.

Launching a DOS Application from My Computer

Because DOS applications do not automatically install on the Windows Start menu, you need to launch most DOS programs manually from My Computer.

1. Click the My Computer icon on your desktop to launch My Computer.
2. Navigate to the folder that contains the program you want to start. Click the folder icon to display the files stored within that folder.
3. Click the icon for the application file that you want to open. The application starts in a special DOS window, normally displayed maximized to full-screen size.

 TIP You may want to add a DOS program to your Start menu, or create a desktop shortcut for the program.

▶ **See** "Creating New Shortcuts on the Desktop," **p. 54**

Closing a DOS Application

To close a DOS application, follow these steps:

1. Use the normal program commands to close the program.
2. If, after the program closes, the DOS window or a DOS prompt remains on-screen, type **exit** and press Enter to close the DOS session.

Switching Between DOS and Windows Applications

Most DOS applications will open in full-screen mode, thus obscuring your normal Windows desktop. It is helpful, then, to know how to switch between DOS and Windows applications without having to close the DOS application.

- If your DOS application is running in full-screen mode, press Alt+Tab to return to your normal Windows desktop.
- If your DOS application is minimized in Windows, click its Taskbar button to return to the DOS program.

Switching Between Full-Screen and Windowed Modes

Many DOS applications don't have to run in full-screen mode; they can run in a window on your Windows desktop.

- If your DOS application is running in full-screen mode, press Alt+Enter to display the program in a window on your desktop.

- If your DOS application is running in windowed mode, click the Full Screen button (in the middle of the toolbar) or press Alt+Enter to return to full-screen mode.

 TIP To configure your DOS program to always run in windowed mode, switch to windowed mode and click the Properties button on the toolbar. When the Properties dialog box appears, click the Screen tab and select <u>W</u>indow in the Usage section.

Copying Data from DOS to Windows Applications

Windows 98 lets you exchange data between most DOS and Windows applications.

1. Open the DOS application in a window and display the data you want to copy. (You may need to press Alt+Enter to display the DOS application in a window.)

2. Click the Mark toolbar button. A blinking cursor appears in the DOS window, indicating that you are in marking mode.

3. Click and drag with the mouse to select the data you want to copy, and then release the mouse button.

4. Click the Copy button in the toolbar.

5. Press Alt+Tab to switch to the Windows application.

6. Place the cursor where you want the data to be copied, and then click the Paste button in the toolbar of the Windows application.

Personalizing How Your DOS Application Runs Within Windows

When you display your DOS application in a window, a toolbar appears that lets you configure several different display and editing options.

1. If your DOS application is displayed full-screen, press Alt+Enter to switch to windowed mode. When your DOS application is running in a window, a special DOS toolbar is displayed (see Figure 13.1).

Part
IV

Ch
13

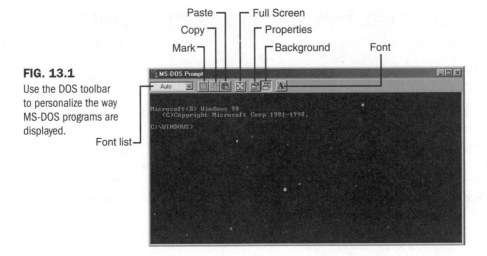

FIG. 13.1
Use the DOS toolbar to personalize the way MS-DOS programs are displayed.

The DOS toolbar contains the following buttons:

- *Font list.* Pull down this list to choose a new display scheme.
- *Mark button.* Select data in your DOS application.
- *Copy button.* Copy selected data.
- *Paste button.* Paste data into your DOS application.
- *Full Screen button.* Switch to full-screen mode.
- *Properties button.* Display the Properties dialog box.
- *Background button.* Continue running your DOS program in the background.
- *Font button.* Select from various font types and schemes.

2. Click the Properties button to display the Properties dialog box (see Figure 13.2).

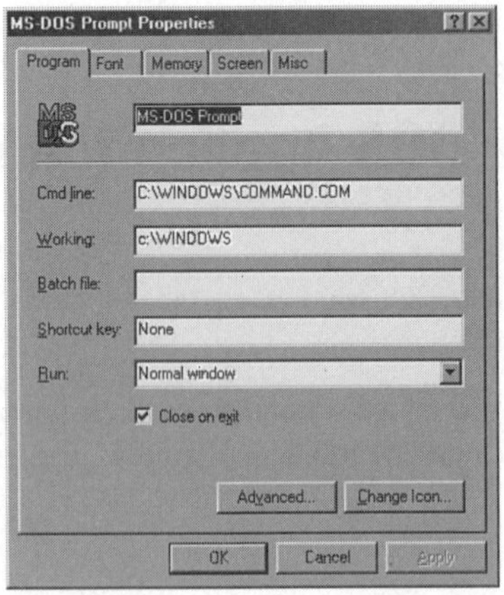

FIG 13.2
You can adjust display and operating properties for your DOS applications.

3. Adjust the settings as described in Table 13.1. (In most cases, it's best to accept the default settings in this dialog box. You only need to alter these settings if you're having trouble running your DOS program within Windows.)

4. Click OK when finished.

Table 13.1 DOS Program Properties

Tab	Functions
Program	Enables you to rename the program, edit the command line used to start the application, set a working directory, select a batch file to run when you start the program, assign a shortcut key to the program, select the kind of window in which the program should run, and choose whether or not the associated DOS window should close when you exit the program.
Font	Allows you to choose the types of fonts used to display text in the DOS window, as well as what size fonts to use. Temporary settings are displayed in small preview windows in the dialog box.
Memory	Selects what type of conventional, expanded, extended, and protected-mode memory will be used by the DOS program.
Screen	Selects whether the screen should run in full-screen or windowed mode; the initial size of the window; and whether or not to display the DOS toolbar, to restore these settings when you next start the DOS program, to use fast ROM emulation, or to use dynamic memory allocation.
Misc	Selects whether to have the program work with your Windows screen saver; to allow the DOS program to work in the background while other Windows programs operate; to enable various mouse options; to warn if you try to terminate the program while it's still running; to allow fast pasting; and to enable various shortcut keys.

Working from the MS-DOS Prompt

If you choose, you can also work directly from the MS-DOS Prompt.

CAUTION

Don't run anything in a Windows MS-DOS session that alters system-critical files, such as the File Allocation Table. For example, don't run disk defragmenters, undelete, or unerase utilities. Use Windows versions of these utilities instead.

1. Click the Start button, select Programs, and then select MS-DOS Prompt.

2. At the command prompt, type DOS commands or start a DOS application.

Part
IV

Ch
13

3. To close the MS-DOS session, close all DOS applications and then type **exit** at the DOS prompt. Press Enter to register the command and close the session.

Running a Troublesome Application in MS-DOS Mode

To run MS-DOS applications that don't seem to run correctly in Windows, you may be able to reconfigure the program's properties; or you may need to switch to MS-DOS mode, which shuts down normal Windows operations while you run the DOS application.

> **CAUTION**
>
> Many of these options are rather technical and are best tried by more experienced users.

If you have trouble running a DOS program, follow these steps to enter MS-DOS mode:

1. Create a shortcut icon for the DOS application.

   ▶ **See** "Creating New Shortcuts on the Desktop," **p. 54**

2. Right-click the shortcut icon and choose Properties from the pop-up menu.

3. When the Properties dialog box appears, select the Program tab and then click the Advanced button.

4. When the Advanced Program Settings dialog box appears (see Figure 13.3), select Prevent MS-DOS-Based Programs from Detecting Windows, and click OK.

FIG. 13.3

You can try to get your DOS program to work by configuring the program's advanced settings.

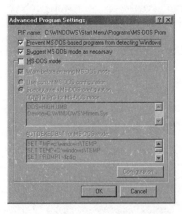

5. Start the program by clicking the shortcut icon. If the program still doesn't work properly, close the program and proceed to the next step.

6. Repeat steps 2 and 3 to reopen the Advanced Program Settings dialog box.

7. Select MS-DOS mode and click OK.

8. Start the program by clicking the shortcut icon. If the program still doesn't work properly, close the program and proceed to the next step.

9. Repeat steps 2 and 3 to reopen the Advanced Program Settings dialog box.

10. With MS-DOS mode selected, select Specify a New MS-DOS Configuration. Compare the current settings in the CONFIG.SYS section to the settings specified in the DOS program's manual, making any changes as needed. Then compare the current settings in the AUTOEXEC.BAT section to the settings in the manual, again making any changes as needed. (If you make changes to the AUTOEXEC.BAT file, you'll need to restart your computer for the changes to take place.)

11. If necessary, click the Configuration button and choose from the options in the Configuration Options dialog box. (See a computer technician well-versed in DOS applications before making changes to this section.)

12. Click OK and try running the program again.

Setting Up Your System to Run DOS Games

Games written for any recent version of windows—Windows 98, Windows 95, or Windows 3.x—are easily played under Windows 98. They are designed to use all the memory and resources that you have installed in your system. If you intend to play DOS-based games, however, you may need to reconfigure certain settings to run the games properly.

N O T E   Open the file PROGRAMS.TXT (in the WINDOWS folder) for more information about running MS-DOS programs—as well as specific compatibility information for certain software. ■

1. From My Computer, locate the file for your game program. Right-click the program icon and select Properties from the pop-up menu to open the program's Properties dialog box.

2. Click the Program tab and click the Advanced button.

3. When the Advanced Program Settings dialog box appears (refer to Figure 13.3), select MS-DOS mode, and select Specify a New MS-DOS Configuration.

4. Compare the current settings in the CONFIG.SYS section to the settings specified in the game program manual, making any changes as needed. Then compare the current settings in the AUTOEXEC.BAT section to the settings in the manual, making any changes as needed. (If you make changes to the AUTOEXEC.BAT file, you'll need to restart your computer for the changes to take place.)

5. Click the Configuration button to open the Select MS-DOS Configuration Options dialog box (see Figure 13.4). Click the check box to the left of each of the possible options: Expanded Memory (EMS), Disk Cache, MS-DOS Command Line Editor (Doskey), and Direct Disk Access. Click OK in each dialog box to accept the changes and finally return to the desktop.

Part

IV

Ch

13

FIG. 13.4

You can select more MS-DOS configuration options in this dialog box.

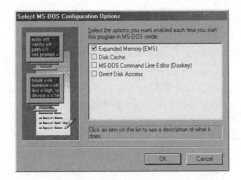

The next time you run the game from Windows 98, the game will use these settings. ●

P A R T

V

Installing and Using Hardware Devices

CHAPTER 14

Installing and Configuring Peripheral Devices

In this chapter

The New Hardware Features of Windows 98

The big hardware-related change in Windows 98 is that it's now much easier to install new hardware than it was with Windows 95. The entire installation process is totally automated by the Add New Hardware Wizard. All you have to do is follow the on-screen instructions, and Windows does the rest.

In most cases, you don't even have to launch the Wizard manually. Windows 98 does a good job of sensing any newly installed hardware when it first launches. You'll be greeted by a message informing you that Windows is configuring itself for your new hardware the next time you boot up after installing the hardware.

The other new hardware-related feature for Windows 98 is Windows Update. This new utility automatically searches for new or updated drivers for your installed hardware. On your command, Windows Update will automatically open an Internet connection and connect to Microsoft's Web site to search for, download, and install upgraded device drivers.

Checking Performance Settings

It's a good idea to check the performance of your system before you add new hardware. The performance of your system can be reviewed and modified through the System Properties program found in the Control Panel.

1. Click the Start button, select Settings, and then select Control Panel to open the Control Panel.

2. Click the System icon to open the System Properties dialog box, and then click the Performance tab (see Figure 14.1).

FIG. 14.1

Check your system's performance from the System Properties dialog box.

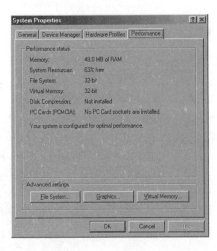

3. The Performance Status group displays the current Memory, System Resources, File System, Virtual Memory, Disk Compression, and PC Cards (PCMCIA) status. See Table 14.1 for explanations of these settings.

4. To see additional information, or to change the File System, Graphics, or Virtual Memory settings, click the appropriate button in the Advanced Settings group at the bottom of the dialog box.

Table 14.1   System Properties Settings

Setting	Explanation
Memory	The amount of random access memory (RAM) on your system.
System Resources	The percentage of resources (combination actual and virtual memory) currently available for use. (The higher the number, the better.)
File System	Specifies whether you are using the Windows true 32-bit file system (FAT32) or the DOS-compatible 16-bit file system.
Virtual Memory	Specifies whether you are using 32-bit or 16-bit disk-based virtual memory.
Disk Compression	Specifies whether or not you have enabled disk compression.
PC Cards (PCMCIA)	Specifies whether or not you have any PCMCIA PC Card sockets installed on your system.

Creating a System Hardware Report

Windows 98's Device Manager can provide you with various reports that detail the devices installed on your system and which resources they're using. It is a good practice to know what your settings are before installing new equipment.

1. Click the Start button, select Settings, and then select Control Panel to open Control Panel.

2. Click the System icon to open the System Properties dialog box, and then click the Device Manager tab.

3. Select View Devices by Type to list all devices by class.

4. To print a report for a specific class or device, select the name in the devices list box, and click Print to open the Print dialog box.

5. When the Print dialog box appears, select the type of report to print, as described in Table 14.2.

6. Click OK in the Print dialog box to print the report on the selected output device.

Part

V

Ch

14

Table 14.2 System Hardware Reports	
Report	**Description**
System Summary	Lists the resources on your system, as well as which hardware is using each resource.
Selected Class or Device	Lists the resources and device drivers used by the device selected in the device list.
All Devices and System Summary	Lists all the hardware on your system, including a list of all resources used by the hardware.

 Use the All Devices And System Summary report to determine whether you have a potential conflict with new hardware that you are preparing to install in the computer. Print the report, highlight all IRQ, I/O, and MEM settings, and then compare these to the settings that the new device(s) can be set to.

Installing New Hardware

Windows 98 works with both *Plug and Play* and older *legacy* (non-Plug and Play) hardware. Plug and Play hardware is automatically identified by Windows 98; older hardware sometimes needs to be manually identified before it can be installed in your system.

Windows 98 provides the Add New Hardware Wizard to aid in the configuration of drivers for new hardware devices. The Wizard detects both Plug and Play and legacy devices, checks the results against the list of previously installed hardware, and installs drivers for the new found devices.

1. Click the Start button, select Settings, and then select Control Panel to open Control Panel.

2. Click the Add New Hardware icon to open the Add New Hardware Wizard. When the first screen of the Wizard appears, click the Next button.

3. When the second screen appears, click Next and Windows will search for any new Plug and Play devices installed on your system.

4. The Wizard will now prepare to search for any hardware that is not Plug and Play. In most cases, you'll want to have Windows identify your hardware automatically; select Yes and click the Next button.

5. The next screen in the Wizard tells you that it is now going to look for new hardware. Choose Next to start the search. When your new hardware has been identified, the Wizard displays a message that it is ready to begin installing the device(s). Click the Details button to view the device(s) Windows has identified; click Finish to complete the installation.

6. If the Add New Hardware Wizard cannot locate the required files on your hard drive, you are prompted to identify the type of hardware you're installing and then to choose the

manufacturer and model of your hardware. If your specific model isn't listed, click the Have Disk button and place the CD-ROM or floppy disk(s) containing the driver files into the appropriate drive. When the necessary files have been loaded, follow the on-screen instructions to complete the installation.

If you experience trouble while adding new hardware, turn to Chapter 31, "Troubleshooting Hardware Installations."

Upgrading Device Drivers

The most appropriate drivers for your hardware are installed when Windows 98 is first installed. You can, however, upgrade your drivers at any time—if new drivers are available.

To upgrade a specific device driver:

1. Click the Start button, select Settings, and then select Control Panel to open Control Panel.

2. Click the System icon to open the System Properties dialog box, and then click the Device Manager tab.

3. Select View Devices by Type and click the "+" next to the type of adapter you want to upgrade.

4. Highlight the installed driver and click the Properties button to open the Properties dialog box.

5. When the Properties dialog box appears, click the Driver tab, and then click the Upgrade Driver button.

6. When the Upgrade Device Driver Wizard appears, click the Next button.

7. When asked what you want to do, select Search for a Better Driver, and then click Next.

8. As shown in Figure 14.2, you are now prompted as to *where* you want to search for an upgraded driver. If you have new driver software from your hardware's manufacturer, select either Floppy Disk Drives or CD-ROM Drive, as appropriate. Insert the disk or CD-ROM and click Next, and then follow the on-screen instructions to install your specific driver.

FIG. 14.2

You can choose to install a driver supplied by your hardware's manufacturer, or to search Microsoft's Web site for an updated driver.

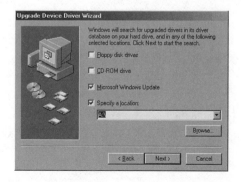

9. If you prefer to search Microsoft's Web site for an upgraded driver, select Microsoft Windows Update On-Line, and then click Next. Windows will connect to the Internet and retrieve any updated drivers that exist. The Wizard tells you whether or not it found an updated driver. If no better driver was found, click Next to keep your current driver. If an updated driver is available, click Next to install the new driver, following the appropriate on-screen instructions.

Creating New Hardware Profiles

You can create additional hardware profiles, each with a different configuration, for the changing equipment you use. A laptop used with and without a docking bay is a prime system for creating additional profiles—the original for the Undocked configuration and the copy named for the Docked setup.

You create a new profile by copying and renaming an existing profile. When a hardware profile is highlighted and copied, its exact configuration is assumed by the new copy. Change the name to reflect the type of configuration or usage the profile is used in, such as Undocked and Docked for a laptop. The name of a profile can be changed at any time and all hardware setups will be updated with the new name.

1. Click the Start button, select Settings, and then select Control Panel to open Control Panel.

2. Click the System icon to open the System Properties dialog box, and then choose the Hardware Profiles tab (see Figure 14.3).

FIG. 14.3

Create a new hardware profile in the System Properties dialog box.

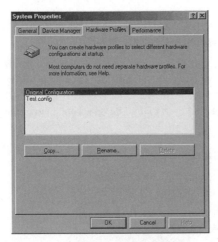

3. Select the hardware profile in the list box and click Copy.

4. When the Copy Profile dialog box appears, type a new name for the profile over the original name in the To field. Click OK when done.

Customizing Hardware Profiles

After copying and naming a new profile (as described in the previous section), you may want to customize your new configuration by selecting which devices are used by that profile.

N O T E Check with your system administrator before making changes to any hardware profiles files concerning network connections. ■

1. Click the Start button, select Settings, and then select Control Panel to open Control Panel.

2. Click the System icon to open the System Properties dialog box, and then choose the Hardware Profiles tab. Select the profile you want to edit, and then click the Device Manager tab.

3. Open a class by clicking the "+" to the left of the class name. Select a device in the list below the class name and click the Properties button. When the Properties dialog box appears, select the General tab.

4. If you want to delete this device from this hardware profile, select Disable in This Hardware Profile. Otherwise, select Exists in All Hardware Profiles.

5. When you have made the desired changes, click OK in each of the dialog boxes to close the boxes, apply the changes, and return to the desktop. Choose Cancel in any of the dialog boxes to cancel the changes and close the box.

Repeat these steps for any device(s) you want to add or remove from a specific hardware profile.

N O T E Devices that are *not* loaded by the hardware profile used for startup are shown in the Device Manager with a red X on the device icon. ■

Configuring and Using Printers

The New Printer Features of Windows 98

Microsoft pretty much had printing figured out in Windows 95. The only new feature related to printing in Windows 98 is the ease in which new printers can be added to your system, described in Chapter 14, "Installing and Configuring Peripheral Devices."

Adding a New Printer

If you have a Plug and Play-compatible printer, Windows 98 will recognize your new printer the next time you start Windows. If your printer is not Plug and Play-compatible, Windows 98 uses the Add Printer Wizard to assist you with installation. If your printer is not already installed, run the Wizard to add the printer.

> **N O T E** The following steps show you how to install a printer that is connected directly to your
> computer. If you need to install a printer that you print to over a network, read the section
> "Installing a Network Printer" in Chapter 28. ■

To run the Add Printer Wizard:

1. On your desktop, click the My Computer icon. When the My Computer window opens, click the Printers folder icon. When the Printers window appears, click the Add Printer icon to start the Add Printer Wizard. Choose Next when the first screen of the Wizard appears.

2. If your computer is connected to a network, you'll be asked whether you're installing a local or network printer. Select local if this printer is for your personal use.

   ▶ **See** "Installing a Network Printer," **p. 298**

3. When the next screen of the Wizard appears, select the printer's manufacturer in the Manufacturers list box (see Figure 15.1). Select the specific model of the printer in the Printers list box, and then click Next.

   If your printer is not on the list, either choose the Generic Manufacturer and Generic/Text Only printer or click the Have Disk button and follow instructions to install a vendor-supplied driver.

 T I P If your specific printer model isn't on the list but you know it's compatible with some standard printer that is on the list (such as a LaserJet II), choose the printer it is compatible with.

4. When the next screen of the Wizard appears, select the port to which the printer is connected, and then click Next.

5. In the Printer Name text box, type a name for the printer or keep the name that is displayed. Select the Yes option button if you want Windows-based programs to use this printer as the default printer. (If a different printer is the default printer, choose No.) Choose Next.

FIG. 15.1

To install a new local printer, just pick the right make and model from the list.

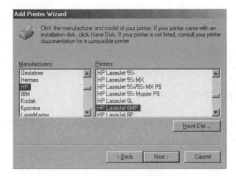

6. Select Yes if you want to print a test page, and then choose Finish. The test page prints (if you selected Yes). The Wizard copies the printer drivers to your system, prompting for the Windows 98 CD if needed.

> **CAUTION**
>
> If the test page does not print correctly, you can work through any potential problems with Windows 98's Print Troubleshooter. Click the Start button and select Help. When the Help window appears, select the Contents tab, double-click the Troubleshooting icon, and then select Print. When the Print Troubleshooter appears, follow the steps on-screen to track down and fix your specific problem.

Deleting an Existing Printer

If you no longer need a printer installed in Windows 98, you can delete it from the Printers folder window:

1. Click My Computer and then click the Printers folder icon.

2. Right-click the icon for the printer you want to delete. When the pop-up menu appears, select Delete.

3. Windows asks if you are sure that you want to delete the printer. Choose Yes. The printer icon is deleted.

4. Windows then asks if it can remove files that were used only for this printer. Choose Yes. (If you plan to reattach this printer in the future, choose No.)

Renaming an Existing Printer

The Add Printer Wizard gives you an option to name the printer when you install it. You can rename the printer later without reinstalling it. The name is changed throughout Windows after you rename the printer.

1. Click My Computer and then click the Printers folder icon.

2. Right-click the icon for the printer you want to rename. When the pop-up menu appears, select Rename.

3. Type a new name to replace the highlighted name and press Enter.

Setting Printer Properties

After you install a printer in Windows, you can make changes to the configuration to customize it for different printing requirements. You make these changes in the printer's Properties sheet.

1. Click My Computer and then click the Printers folder icon.

2. Right-click the icon for the printer you want to reconfigure. When the pop-up menu appears, select Properties to open the Properties dialog box (see Figure 15.2).

FIG. 15.2

Use the Properties dialog box to configure your printer.

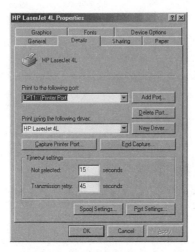

3. The Properties dialog box contains several tabs. Select each tab to view the various settings, as explained in Table 15.1. Properties vary according to each printer's capabilities.

4. Change settings as desired, and then choose OK to save the new settings. Choose Cancel if you prefer to abandon all changes.

Table 15.1 Printer Properties

Tab	Properties
General	Enter comments about this printer, and select whether or not to insert separator pages between each printed page. Click the Print Test Page button to test your printer's output.

Tab	Properties
Details	Select which port and driver to use; select timeout settings (how long your printer will wait for data from your computer before displaying an error message); click the Spool Settings button to determine how your printer handles multiple print jobs.
Sharing	Determine whether your printer will be shared by other users on your network.
Paper	Select the default paper size, paper orientation (portrait or landscape), paper source, media choice, and number of copies.
Graphics	Select how your printer will display graphics; the higher the resolution (and the finer the dithering), the more memory is required inside your printer.
Fonts	Determine how to handle TrueType fonts; the default is to download TrueType fonts as bitmap soft fonts.
Device Options	Determine settings specific to your model printer, such as print density, print quality, and printer memory tracking.

Setting Up a Color Printer

Windows uses Kodak's Image Color Matching (ICM) technology to provide consistent color from the screen to the printed page. If you're using a color printer, you can define graphics and color settings in the printer's Properties dialog box:

1. Click My Computer and then click the Printers folder icon.

2. Right-click the icon for the printer you want to reconfigure. When the pop-up menu appears, choose Properties to open the Properties dialog box. Select the Graphics tab.

3. Click the Color button. If your printer does not have color, this button is not available. Select from the following color settings:

Color Control	Print in black and white or color, with or without ICM technology.
Color Rendering Intent	Choose the best setting as indicated for presentation graphics, photographs, or color matching.

4. Choose OK twice to keep changes to settings. Notice there is a Restore Defaults button on each page of the Properties sheet to return to the defaults for the selected printer.

Selecting the Default Printer

The *default* printer is the printer that your applications will automatically use when you choose to print a document. If you have multiple printers hooked up to your computer (via a network, say), you'll need to select one of them as your default printer.

1. Click My Computer and then click the Printers folder icon.
2. Right-click the icon for the printer you want as your default printer. When the pop-up menu appears, select Set as Default.

 The default printer appears with a check mark next to its icon in the Printers window.

Creating a Desktop Shortcut for Your Printer

Windows 98 permits printing from the desktop, which requires that you first create a shortcut icon for the printer on the desktop.

1. Click My Computer and then click the Printers folder icon.
2. When the Printers window appears, select the printer, right-drag it onto the desktop, and drop it.
3. Click Yes when Windows asks if you want to create a shortcut.

Printing from the Desktop

You can print a document in Windows 98 without first starting the application for the document you want to print. Just drag the document from My Computer or Windows Explorer onto the printer's shortcut icon.

1. In My Computer or Windows Explorer, open a folder that contains a printable document and select that document.
2. Drag the document's icon to the printer shortcut icon on your desktop.
3. Release the mouse button to drop the file onto the printer icon. Windows starts the application associated with the document, places the document on the print queue, closes the application, and background prints the spooled files.

 You can select multiple documents to print and then drag them to the desktop printer icon. The documents can be associated with different applications. Windows will start and close each application sequentially.

Printing from Windows Applications

Printing a document is similar in most Windows applications. You can pull down the application's File menu and select Print to select options in a Print dialog box. The dialog box allows you to change the page range to print, number of copies, collating, default tray, resolution, and many more options that vary with the specific printer and application.

CAUTION

Pressing the Print button on an application's toolbar prints the current document using the current defaults— without prompting you for any specific options. Until you know the action of the Print button, don't choose it unless you want to print the entire document to the default printer. Instead, follow the steps listed in this section to open the Print dialog box.

1. Open a document to print and then choose the application's print command by pulling down the File menu and selecting Print.

2. When the Print dialog box appears (see Figure 15.3), the default printer will be selected as the printer to print to. To print to a different printer, select the desired printer from the Name drop-down list. Select the number of copies you want to print in the Number of Copies input box.

FIG. 15.3

Pull down the File menu and select Print to print a document in Microsoft Word.

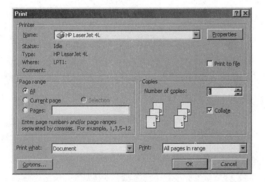

3. Specify the print range. The default is All. Alternatively, you can usually enter a range of pages. If you have selected text, you can usually choose the Selection option to print only the selected text.

4. Choose from the other available options, which will vary depending on the application from which you're printing. The application's documentation may be helpful in explaining its more complex printing options.

5. Make sure the printer is powered up and online, and then choose OK.

The Print dialog box closes during printing. You may see a printing status window appear, or notice the Print Manager icon in the Taskbar.

Printing from MS-DOS Applications

Windows 98 supports printing from MS-DOS applications, even in the same print stream with print jobs from Windows applications. You can use the Print Manager to queue your MS-DOS print jobs:

1. From within your DOS application, open the document you want to print.

2. In the MS-DOS application, choose the print command.

A short print job may seem to go directly to the local printer, but it is actually spooled by Windows. (*Spooling* means that the print job is stored in a special area of your computer's memory until printing is complete, allowing you to return immediately to your program.) If you print a larger file, you should see the job appear in Print Manager. There you can pause or cancel the job as needed.

Managing Print Jobs from Print Manager

Print Manager is used to control print jobs sent to a printer. There is a separate manager for each printer installed on your system. If the jobs you have sent to a printer are not so small that they go quickly to the printer's buffer, you will have time to double-click the printer icon that appears in the Taskbar, near the clock. After the printer icon disappears from the Taskbar, you can only control your job at the printer itself.

There are several ways to open Print Manager:

■ Click the My Computer icon and then click the Printers folder icon. Click the printer icon for the printer you want to manage.

■ Click the Start button, select Settings, and then select Printers. Click the printer icon for the printer you want to manage.

■ If a print job is in progress, double-click the printer icon in the Taskbar.

Checking the Status of a Print Job

A quick way to check the status of print jobs is to double-click the printer icon in the Taskbar to open the Print Manager.

1. Double-click the printer icon in the Taskbar to open the Print Manager. This icon is displayed only when there are print jobs.

2. Look at the jobs in the queue and view their status (such as printing, paused, or spooling) in the Status column (see Figure 15.4).

3. View the status bar to see the number of jobs remaining to be printed. Pull down the View menu and select Status Bar to turn the status bar on and off.

Pausing a Print Job

If you have multiple print jobs on a single printer, you can choose to pause specific print jobs—and continue printing all non-paused jobs.

To pause a print job:

1. Double-click the printer icon in the Taskbar to open the Print Manager.

2. Select one or more documents from the print queue list.

FIG. 15.4
Use Print Manager to view the status of all current print jobs.

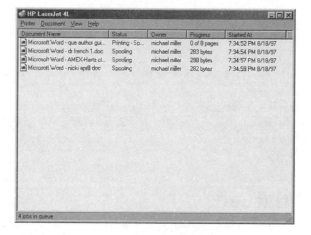

3. Pull down the Document menu and select Pause Printing.

TIP To pause a document quickly, right-click its entry in the print queue and then choose Pause Printing from the pop-up menu.

NOTE Pausing a specific print job is not the same as pausing all printing. To pause all current print jobs from Print Manager, pull down the Printer menu (**not** the Document menu) and select Pause Printing. ■

Resuming a Paused Print Job

Usually you pause a print job so that you can restart it later. Maybe you want to change to a different paper stock or change the toner. The job remains paused in Print Manager until you restart it or cancel it.

To continue printing a paused print job:

1. Double-click the printer icon in the Taskbar to open the Print Manager.
2. Select the paused document.
3. Pull down the Document menu and select Pause Printing. The selected document no longer displays a Paused status and will begin printing in its place in queue.

Canceling a Print Job

You can cancel a print job in the print queue even if it has started to print.

1. Open the Print Manager by double-clicking the printer icon on the Taskbar.
2. Select one or more documents from the print queue list.
3. Pull down the Document menu and select Cancel Printing.

To cancel printing a document quickly, right-click its entry in the print queue and then choose Cancel Printing from the pop-up menu.

CAUTION

When you cancel a print job, it disappears immediately from the print queue (although any pages already sent to the printer will continue to print until finished). You may want to try pausing the job first to be sure you are canceling the right job.

Purging All Print Jobs

Purging removes all of the queued print jobs. You can purge all of the jobs that have not started to print.

1. Double-click the printer icon in the Taskbar to open the Print Manager.
2. Pull down the Printer menu and select Purge Print Jobs.
3. Close the Print Manager by clicking its Close button.

CHAPTER 16

Configuring and Using Modems

In this chapter

The New Modem Features of Windows 98

The most important news regarding modems in Windows 98 is that Windows is now automatically configured for ISDN modems. In Windows 95, this capability was not built in, and you had to install a separate ISDN pack (downloadable from Microsoft's Web site at **www.microsoft.com/windows/getisdn/**) before you could connect an ISDN modem to your system. In Windows 98, you simply install your ISDN modem as you would any other conventional modem; there is nothing extra to install or configure.

Configuring Your Modem

When you install a new modem in your system, Windows 98 installs the drivers for your modem by using a series of default settings that work best for most computer systems. When you need to make changes, possibly because an online service provider or Bulletin Board Service (BBS) that you want to connect to requires different settings, use the Modem Properties program in the Control Panel to make the necessary changes. Check your modem's instruction manual for details on which of these settings to enable in specific circumstances.

To change your modem settings:

1. Click the Start button, select Settings, and then select Control Panel. Click the Modems icon to open the Modems Properties dialog box.

2. Click the General tab, highlight the modem to be configured, and click the Properties button.

3. When the Properties dialog box for your modem displays, click the General tab, and then click the Port drop-down list box to select from the available communications ports. Click the horizontal bar of the Speaker Volume control to adjust the loudness of the modem speaker. To change the maximum connect speed of the modem, click the Maximum Speed drop-down list box and select from the speed options.

 TIP If your modem is Plug and Play, you may not have the option to change port or speaker volume settings.

4. Click the Connection tab (see Figure 16.1). Set the Data Bits, Parity, and Stop Bits values in the drop-down list boxes in the Connection Preferences section.

5. Click the Port Settings button to open the Advanced Port Settings dialog box and modify the Receive Buffer and Transmit Buffer settings as appropriate. The settings can be returned to the Windows default by clicking the Defaults button. Return to the Modems Properties dialog box by clicking OK or Cancel.

6. Click the Advanced button to open the Advanced Connection Settings dialog box. Check Use Flow Control and select either Hardware(RTS/CTS) or Software(XON/XOFF) to enable flow control and indicate the type of control. Return to the Modems Properties dialog box by clicking OK or Cancel.

7. When you have made the desired changes, click the OK buttons in each of the dialog boxes to close the boxes, apply the changes, and return to the desktop. Click the Cancel button in any of the dialog boxes to cancel the changes and close the box.

FIG. 16.1

Reconfiguring your modem's connection properties could solve some connection problems.

Part

V

Ch

16

Using Drivers Provided by Your Modem Manufacturer

Windows 98 ships with a wealth of drivers for a great variety of modems. But as time passes, new modems are manufactured that are not included in the Windows drivers database, and new drivers are developed by the manufacturers.

To install a new modem driver:

1. Click the Start button, select Settings, and then select Control Panel. When Control Panel launches, click the Modem icon.

2. When the Modems Properties dialog box appears, click the Add button to open the Install New Modem Wizard.

3. When the New Modem Wizard appears, select Don't Detect My Modem; I Will Select It From a List and click the Next button. If your new modem is not in the Manufacturers and Models list boxes and you have the drivers from the manufacturer, click the Have Disk button.

4. Insert the disk that has the appropriate installation (.INF) file in drive A: and click OK. If you have downloaded new drivers from an online service to your computer, instead of inserting a floppy disk, click the Browse button to select the folder that the drivers were downloaded into. Click the OK buttons to return to the Install New Modem Wizard and then click Next.

5. Select the communications port the modem is set for or connected to (if it is external) and click Next.

6. Click the Finish button in the last screen of the Wizard to return to the desktop.

> **N O T E**   Windows 98 is automatically configured for use with ISDN (Integrated Services Digital
> Network), a digital alternative to standard phone service—and an ultra-fast way to connect
> to the Internet. ISDN offers connect speeds of up to 128,000 bps, more than four times that of
> standard 28,800 bps modems. For more information about using ISDN, go to Microsoft's ISDN Web
> page at the following address: **www.microsoft.com/windows/getisdn/**. ■

Setting Your Modem to Dial

You need to configure Windows 98's dialing properties to connect to all types of online services. Just provide Windows with your home and office information, and determine how you
want to handle your Call Waiting and calling card requirements.

To configure your modem's dialing properties:

1. Click the Start button, select Settings, and then select Control Panel. Click the Modems
   icon to open the Modems Properties dialog box.

2. When the Modems Properties dialog box appears, select the General tab and click the
   Dialing Properties button.

3. When the Dialing Properties dialog box appears (see Figure 16.2), enter your area code
   in the Area Code field and select the country or region you are setting up in the I Am In
   This Country field to define the default location.

FIG. 16.2

Use the Dialing
Properties dialog box to
configure your system
for all modem-based
calls.

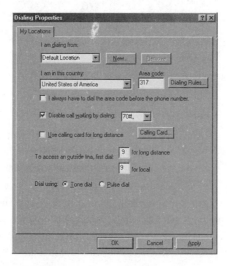

4. If you have to dial the code before the phone number, select the I Always Have to Dial
   the Area Code box.

5. If you want to disable call waiting while you're using your modem (a good idea), select
   the Disable Call Waiting box and select the necessary dialing code.

6. If you want to use a calling card for your modem calls, select the Use Calling Card for Long Distance box, and then click the Calling Card button and enter the appropriate information.

7. If you have to dial a number to access an outside line, enter the appropriate numbers in the For Long Distance and For Local fields.

 TIP You may want to insert a comma between the number you dial to get an outside line and the actual number; this instructs Windows to pause slightly between numbers, thus allowing a smooth transfer to the outside line.

Part

V

Ch

16

8. Click OK when done. Windows will use this information for all your modem calls.

The information you enter in the Dialing Properties dialog box is used by all Windows 98 telecommunications programs, such as Microsoft Fax, Phone Dialer, and Dial-Up Networking.

Diagnosing Modem Problems

Windows 98 provides a useful tool for diagnosing problems with your modem:

1. Click the Start button, select Settings, and then select Control Panel. Click the Modem icon to open the Modems Properties dialog box, and then click the Diagnostics tab (see Figure 16.3).

FIG. 16.3
If your modem isn't working properly, use the Diagnostics tool to examine and correct your modem settings.

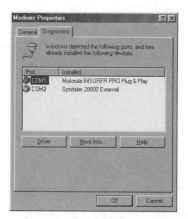

2. Highlight the communications port that the modem is attached to in the Port list. Click the More Info button to open the More Info information box.

3. Review the information in the Port Information group at the top and in the modem Response code group at the bottom of the dialog box. Click OK to return to the Modem Properties dialog box.

4. Click the Driver button to view the communications driver currently used by Windows 98. Compare this data with that provided by your modem manufacturer. Click OK to return to the Modems Properties dialog box.

5. Click the OK or Cancel buttons to close the Modems Properties dialog box.

Configuring and Using Video Options

The New Video Options in Windows 98

There are several new options that positively affect playback of full-motion video in Windows 98. These include:

- *Windows Broadcast Architecture*. This future technology will allow Windows 98 to receive special Internet-related content embedded as part of special Enhanced Television signals. Windows 98 users will be able to link Web content with specific television programs and receive normal Web pages without tying up their existing phone lines.

- *TV Viewer*. Part of the Windows Broadcast Architecture technology, but with immediate application. TV Viewer lets you use Windows 98 to receive and display broadcast and cable programs—as long as you have a special TV tuner card in your computer system.

- *Program Guide*. Linked to TV Viewer, this is an on-screen guide to television programming transmitted by DirecTV over a direct broadcast satellite (DBS).

- *NetShow*. This is a built-in component of Internet Explorer 4.0 that lets you receive streaming audio and video broadcasts over the Web—without waiting for large file downloads.

- *DirectShow*. Formerly known as ActiveMovie, NetShow is a streaming-video technology built into Windows 98 that delivers high-quality video playback of a variety of popular media file types, including MPEG, WAV, AVI, and QuickTime.

Configuring Video Playback Properties

You can adjust the manner in which Windows 98 displays video clips by using the Multimedia Properties dialog box. Video clips can be displayed either in a window or by using your entire screen.

1. Click the Start button, select Settings, and select Control Panel to open Control Panel.

2. Click the Multimedia icon to open the Multimedia Properties dialog box, and then click the Video tab (see Figure 17.1).

3. To show videos in an appropriately sized window, check the Window option and select Original Size from the pull-down list. To show videos full-screen, check the Full Screen option. The preview screen above the group box will display a sample of how the video will look on your monitor.

4. Click the Apply button in the bottom-right corner of the dialog box to apply the change, and then click OK.

 TIP Choosing to display moving video in a larger window will often result in a choppier, lower-resolution picture. Better performance often results from using a smaller window for video display.

FIG. 17.1
Use the Multimedia
Properties dialog box to
select how you view
video clips—either full-
screen or in a window
on your desktop.

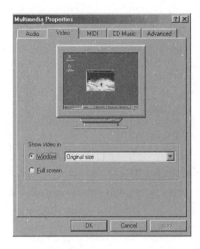

Playing a Video Clip

Use Windows 98's Media Player to play full-motion video clips.

1. Click the Start button, select Programs, select Accessories, select Multimedia, and then select Media Player to open the Media Player program window.

2. To select a video clip, pull down the Device menu, select Video for Windows, and then locate the file you want to open.

3. A window for this video file appears on your desktop (see Figure 17.2). Click the Play button in the Media Player program window to start playing the video clip.

FIG. 17.2
Use the controls in the
Media Player program
window to start and
stop playback of video
clips (displayed in a
separate window).

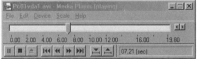

NOTE You can also select Sound, MIDI Sequencer, CD Audio, and ActiveMovie files from the Device menu. If you've installed other media types on your system—such as QuickTime for Windows—these will also appear on the Devices menu. ■

Part
V

Ch
17

Installing TV Viewer

If you have the proper hardware installed in your computer system, Windows 98 lets you watch TV broadcasts on your PC, download TV listings from the Web, and—in the future—display Enhanced Television broadcasts that include embedded Web pages. You use Windows 98's TV Viewer utility to view television and cable broadcasts. To install TV Viewer:

1. Click the Start menu, select Settings, and then select Control Panel. When Control Panel opens, click the Add/Remove Programs icon.

2. When the Add/Remove Programs Properties dialog box appears, click the Windows Setup tab. Scroll through the Components list and select TV Viewer.

3. Insert your Windows 98 CD and click OK to begin the installation.

Using TV Viewer

When you install TV Viewer (and hook up your system to a television or cable feed), you use your PC to view television and cable programs. If you hook your system up to a direct broadcast satellite (DBS) with a DirecTV subscription, you also have access to an online program guide.

1. All TV Viewer functions are accessed from the TV Toolbar. Display the TV Toolbar by pressing the F10 key on your keyboard.

2. When you first start TV Viewer, you'll need to sign on. Click Sign On to display the Sign On dialog box; select your user name and click OK.

3. To select a program to view from an on-screen Program Guide, click Guide on the TV Toolbar, click the program you want to watch, and then click the Watch button.

4. You can place up to five of your favorite channels on the TV Toolbar. Just tune to the channel you want to add, press F10 to display the TV Toolbar, and then click the Add button.

Capturing Full-Motion Video

Full-motion videos are just about the most system-intensive process that you can put your computer through. And the most system-intensive full-motion videos are those you capture from a live video source, like a VCR or camcorder.

If you want to capture real video—meaning flicker-free motion—the most important component to have on your system is a big, fast hard drive. Hard drives that use a SCSI (Small Computer Systems Interface) interface are the fastest type of drive possible, making for even transfer of video data during capture and playback. Look for a hard drive that lists a high rotation speed, such as 7200 RPM, and uses at least a SCSI-2 interface.

The other component that can affect the recording and playback of full-motion video is the sound card. When considering which sound card to use, look for a card that uses true 16-bit DMA (Dynamic Memory Addressing) rather than 8-bit DMA, which is sometimes found in a 16-bit sound card. The memory addressing uses processor time, thereby affecting the video capture.

If you intend to use your system to capture video from a VCR or camcorder, keep these tips in mind:

- Always defragment the hard drive that you intend to capture video to before starting the capture.
- Update your video card drivers to the most current version of Windows 98. (Many drivers were written before Windows 98 came on the market and are not necessarily as well tuned to the Windows 98 system as is possible.)
- Use the highest quality cables possible between the video capture board and the video input device—whether a VCR, video camera, and so on—to ensure the highest quality image.
- Use a disk utility to order your files on the hard drive, with the video data files located closer to the outside of the drive where access is faster because the data is not compressed (whereas data on inner tracks is compressed).

Part

V

Ch

17

Configuring and Using Sound Options

The New Audio Features of Windows 98

The sound-related features in Windows 98 are largely duplicative of those in Windows 95. The primary new feature related to audio in Windows 98 is the ease in which new sound cards can be added to your system, described in Chapter 14, "Installing and Configuring Peripheral Devices."

Configuring Audio Properties

After you install a new sound card, you may want to tweak its basic configuration. You do this in the Multimedia Properties dialog box.

1. Click the Start button, select Settings, and then select Control Panel to open the Control Panel.

2. Click the Multimedia icon to open the Multimedia Properties dialog box.

3. Click the Audio tab to view the audio options, as shown in Figure 18.1.

FIG. 18.1

You can configure basic audio options in the Multimedia Properties dialog box.

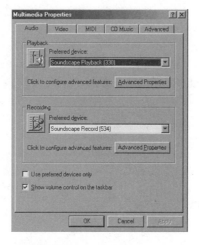

4. To change the playback volume, click the Playback button to display the Volume Control dialog box. Click and drag the volume slider to the desired level.

5. To display a volume control icon in the Taskbar tray, select Show Volume Control On The Taskbar.

6. To change the preferred playback device, select a new device from the Preferred Device list in the Playback section. To change the preferred recording device, select a new device from the Preferred Device list in the Recording section.

7. To change the quality of sounds recorded on your system, select CD Quality, Radio Quality, or Telephone Quality from the Preferred Quality list in the Recording section. This selection affects both the quality of the recording and the amount of hard disk space used by the recording. The better the quality, the more space used to record.

8. When you have made the desired changes, click the OK button in each dialog box to close the boxes, apply the changes, and return to the desktop. Click the Apply button in the bottom-right corner of the dialog box to apply interim changes without closing the dialog box.

Adjusting the Volume

After you've installed the volume control icon in the Taskbar tray (see previous section), changing your system's volume is as easy as clicking and dragging your mouse.

1. Click the volume control icon in the Taskbar tray.

2. A Volume slider pops up; drag the slider up to increase the volume or down to decrease the volume.

3. To completely mute the sound, select Mute on the Volume slider.

The Volume slider adjusts the volume of all devices on your system simultaneously. To adjust the volume of individual devices, right-click the volume control icon and select Open Volume Controls from the pop-up menu. This displays the Volume Control dialog box shown in Figure 18.2 (your dialog box may appear slightly different, depending on the capabilities of your specific sound card). This dialog box enables you to adjust the volume and left/right balance for all the sound devices installed on your system.

Part
V

Ch
18

FIG. 18.2
Use the Volume Control dialog box to fine-tune the volume and balance for your system's audio devices.

 T I P To turn off the sound for all devices, select Mute All in the Volume Control dialog box. To mute only specific devices, select Mute for each specific device control.

Changing Windows Sounds

Windows assigns certain sounds to system events, such as starting and exiting Windows, and emptying the Recycle Bin. If you want, you can change Windows default sounds.

1. Click the Start button, select Settings, and then select Control Panel to open the Control Panel.

2. Click the Sounds icon to display the Sounds Properties dialog box.

3. In the Events list, select a sound event for which you want to assign or change the sound.

4. In the Name drop-down list, select a .WAV file for the selected event. If the file you want is not in the list, click Browse, find the file, and then click OK. Click the Play button to the right of the Preview icon to hear the sound.

5. If you prefer to select a uniform sound *scheme* instead of selecting individual sounds, choose a scheme from the Schemes list.

6. Click Apply to make the changes and keep the Sounds Properties dialog box open to make additional changes, or choose OK to accept the changes and close the dialog box.

Setting Up MIDI Output

MIDI (Musical Instrument Digital Interface) is a specification for high-quality digital sound. MIDI devices are used to provide playback for PC games and Web site sound; musicians also use MIDI instruments to synthesize and sequence their music.

Windows 98 can output MIDI audio and accept input from MIDI instruments. To configure the MIDI output of your system, follow these steps:

1. Click the Start button, select Settings, and then select Control Panel to open the Control Panel.

2. Double-click the Multimedia icon to open the Multimedia Properties dialog box. Click the MIDI tab.

3. If you're using MIDI playback primarily for general computer or game uses, check Single Instrument and select a device from the list of installed MIDI instruments.

4. If you're using multiple MIDI devices (something musicians often do), check Custom Configuration and pick a definition from the MIDI Scheme list. To create a new scheme or configure an existing scheme, click the Configure button to configure the instrument according to the instructions included with your MIDI devices. Click OK to return to the Multimedia Properties dialog box.

5. Click OK when finished, or click Apply to apply the changes without closing the dialog box.

Installing a New MIDI Instrument

MIDI was originally developed for and by musicians, although all computer users can benefit from MIDI sound today. MIDI instruments are now standard equipment for most musicians, whether you're just learning how to play piano from a MIDI keyboard or whether you're programming complex musical scores into a MIDI sequencer.

To add a new MIDI instrument to your computer system:

1. Plug your instrument into one of the MIDI ports on your sound card, and turn on the instrument's power.

2. Click the Start button, select Settings, and then select Control Panel to open the Control Panel.

3. Click the Multimedia icon to open the Multimedia Properties dialog box. Click the MIDI tab.

4. Click Add New Instrument to display the MIDI Instrument Installation Wizard.

5. On the first screen of the Wizard, select the MIDI port that this instrument is connected to, and then click Next.

6. Select the instrument definition for your new instrument, and then click Next.

7. Enter a name for your new MIDI instrument and click Finish.

8. When the Wizard is finished, select Single Instrument on the MIDI tab, select the device you just installed, and click OK.

Playing Audio CDs with CD Player

Part
V

Ch

18

Playing a music or audio CD in your computer's CD player is just as easy as using a regular audio CD player. Windows 98 even includes a special program, CD Player, which functions just like the CD player you have in your home audio system.

1. Click the Start button, select Programs, select Accessories, select Multimedia, and then select CD Player to open the CD Player program (see Figure 18.3).

FIG. 18.3

Playing an audio CD with CD Player.

2. If you have not yet placed an audio CD in your CD-ROM drive, the message Please insert an audio compact disc is displayed in the Title field of the dialog box. To proceed, place an audio CD in your CD-ROM drive.

3. Click the Play icon on the player controls toolbar to start playing the CD.

 T I P Identify a button by hovering your cursor over the button; Windows displays a ToolTip identifying that specific button.

4. To stop playing the CD, click the Stop button. To pause play, click the Pause button.

5. To play the tracks of the CD in random order, pull down the Options menu and select Random Order.

6. To move to the next track on the CD, click the Fast Forward button. To move back to the previous track, click the Fast Reverse button.

N O T E   When you select Continuous Play from the Options menu of the CD Player, the CD will continue to play even when the CD Player is closed. ▪

Playing an Audio File

Windows 98's Media Player is designed to play any type of media file (audio, MIDI, or video). You can also use Media Player to select and cut portions of audio files to the Windows Clipboard; these clips can then be included in documents, spreadsheets, other files, or other media clips.

1. Click the Start button, select Programs, select Accessories, select Multimedia, and then select Media Player to open the Media Player program window (see Figure 18.4).

FIG. 18.4

Use Media Player to play audio clips.

2. To select an audio clip, pull down the Device menu, select Sound, and then locate the file you want to open.

N O T E   You can also select video, MIDI, and CD Audio files from the Device menu. If you've installed other media types on your system—such as QuickTime for Windows—these will also appear on the Devices menu. ▪

3. To play an audio clip, click the Play button on the controls toolbar at the bottom of the window. The elapsed time the clip has played is displayed in the small window to the right of the controls toolbar.

N O T E   You can set the media file to continually repeat—as well as set other options—by pulling down the Edit menu, selecting Options, and then selecting the settings you want from the Options dialog box. ▪

Recording New Sounds with Sound Recorder

The Sound Recorder, installed with Windows 98, is your channel for creating the audio portion of your own multimedia clips. Although the Sound Recorder is not as full-featured as a commercial product, you can still do a very good job of creating your own clips.

Using the Sound Recorder, you can capture sound clips from any type of sound device connected to the sound card in your computer, including CDs, videotapes, or even a microphone.

> **CAUTION**
>
> It is very important to review the sound properties that you have selected for recording. If you have decided to record at CD quality by using 44,100-Hz, 16-Bit Stereo, the recording will use 172K of hard drive space for every second of recording. A 60-second recording, therefore, uses 10M of space.

To record audio with Sound Recorder:

1. Click the Start button, select Programs, select Accessories, select Multimedia, and then select Sound Recorder to open the Sound Recorder program window (see Figure 18.5).

FIG. 18.5
Get ready to make a recording with Sound Recorder.

Part

V

Ch

18

2. Pull down the File menu and select Properties to display the Properties for Sound dialog box.

3. In the Format Conversion section, select Recording Formats from the Choose From list.

4. Click the Convert Now button to display the Sound Selection dialog box. Review and change, if necessary, the recording quality settings in the Name list, Format list, and the Attributes list. Remember, the higher the quality recording, the more hard disk space required.

5. Click the OK buttons to close the Sound Selection and Properties for Sound dialog boxes and return to the Sound Recorder.

6. Using a microphone attached to the appropriate jack on your sound card, begin recording by clicking the red Record button at the bottom-right corner of the recorder. As the recording begins, you will notice that a green bar is displayed and will continually expand and contract in the window at the center of the recorder window. This visual wave display reflects the volume and intensity of the recording.

7. To stop recording, click the Stop button.

8. To return to the start of your recording, click the Fast Rewind button. Click the Play button to replay your recording.

9. To change or add effects to your recording, pull down the Effects menu and select one of the menu options: Increase Volume (by 25%), Decrease Volume, Increase Speed (by 100%), Decrease Speed, Add Echo, or Reverse. Any changes you make can be undone by pulling down the File menu and selecting Revert.

10. To save your recording, pull down the File menu and select Save.

After you have recorded a sound clip, the ways you can use it are limited only by your imagination. ●

Configuring and Using Disk Drives

The New Disk Drive Features of Windows 98

There are two important new disk drive-related features in Windows 98:

- *FAT32 support*. FAT32 is a new 32-bit file system that is much more efficient in dealing with large hard disks than the 16-bit file system in Windows 95. If you have a large hard disk—more than 2G—FAT32 lets you take advantage of every bit of available disk space, without special partitioning. FAT32 also squeezes additional space out of any drive larger than 512M.

- *DVD support*. DVDs are the latest storage media, the same size as CD-ROMs but with much larger capacity. Windows 98 lets your system read DVDs just as it would CDs.

Using CD-ROM and DVD Drives

Using your CD-ROM or DVD drive is just like using a floppy disk or hard disk drive. My Computer displays an icon for your CD-ROM/DVD drive, labeled with the next letter of the alphabet after the last installed hard drive on your system. If you have only one hard drive, labeled C:, the CD-ROM/DVD drive will be labeled D:.

To view the contents of the CD-ROM or DVD drive, make sure a disk is inserted in the drive, and then click the drive icon in My Computer. You can launch any program from your CD-ROM or DVD drive just as you do from any other drive. You can also copy files from the CD-ROM/DVD to your hard drive or to a floppy disk.

NOTE   CD-ROM and DVD drives are read-only devices; although you can copy files *from* the CD-ROM/DVD, you cannot copy or save files *to* the CD-ROM/DVD. ▓

Installing a New Hard Disk Drive

New, larger software programs—and the storage space necessary for Internet browsing—can quickly fill up older, smaller hard disks. To add more storage to your system, you may want to replace your old hard disk with a larger model, or add a second hard disk.

CAUTION
Installing a new hard disk should be attempted only by experienced computer users. Make sure you have backed up all the data on your existing hard disk before adding a new hard disk, and follow the specific instructions provided by the manufacturer of your new disk drive.

To add a new hard disk drive to your system, follow these general steps:

1. Exit Windows, turn off your PC, and disconnect your PC from the power outlet.
2. Set the jumper settings on your new hard disk as directed by your manufacturer.

3. Remove the system cover from your PC, locate an empty drive bay, and install the new drive.

4. Attach the IDE interface cable and the power supply cable to your new hard disk drive, as directed by your manufacturer.

5. Reassemble your system case, and plug your PC into a power outlet.

6. Insert your Windows 98 Startup disk in drive A: and turn on your PC.

▶ **See** "Creating a Startup Disk," **p. 107**

7. During the startup procedure, enter the CMOS settings area (as specified by your PC's manufacturer). Follow the on-screen instructions to configure your new drive; typically you want to select the "auto config" option. Save the new settings and continue to start up your system.

8. At the A: prompt, type **fdisk *x*:**, where *x* is the letter of your new hard drive. Press Enter and follow the instructions listed in the "Using FDISK to Partition a New Hard Disk Drive" section.

9. Format your new hard disk drive by typing the following at the A: prompt: **format *x*:**, where *x* is the letter of your new hard drive. Press Enter to begin formatting.

10. When formatting is complete, remove the Windows 98 Startup disk and press Ctrl+Alt+Del to restart your computer. Windows 98 should launch with your new hard disk automatically configured and visible in both My Computer and Windows Explorer.

Using FDISK to Partition a New Hard Disk Drive

Before you format or use a new hard disk drive, you first must create one or more partitions on the disk. In previous versions of Windows, drives larger than 2Gb had to have more than one partition (each partition could be no larger than 2Gb). With Windows 98's FAT32 file system—described in "Converting Your Existing Hard Drive to FAT32" later in this chapter—even the largest drives can use a single partition.

Part
V

Ch
19

> **CAUTION**
>
> Do not run FDISK on an existing hard disk drive; partitioning the drive will delete all data on the drive.

You use a special DOS command called FDISK to partition your hard disk:

1. Click the Start button and select Shut Down. When the Shut Down Windows dialog box appears, select Restart in MS-DOS Mode.

2. When your computer restarts, it will automatically launch in a special non-Windows mode called MS-DOS mode. You can run FDISK only in MS-DOS mode.

3. At the DOS prompt, type **fdisk** and press Enter.

4. A special FDISK menu is now displayed. Select the drive you want to partition, and then choose option 1 from the menu. When asked whether you want to use the entire drive for your DOS partition, answer yes.

5. After the partition is created, your computer will restart and you can format the new hard disk.

Formatting a New Hard Disk Drive

You shouldn't find yourself formatting a hard disk very often. If you purchased a new hard drive or an additional hard drive, however, you need to format the drive before you can store information on it. Sometimes, if a drive and an operating system become very corrupted, you may have to format your existing drive and start from scratch. Before formatting your existing drive, however, back up your files and make sure you have a Startup disk with the Format utility.

1. If you are formatting a new hard drive, insert the Windows 98 Startup disk into drive A: and turn on the computer. Windows will detect the new drive and ask whether you want to allocate all the unallocated space on your drive. Answer yes.

2. You can also format an existing drive from Windows. First, make sure you have backed up important files from the drive, and then make sure all applications are closed. Start My Computer by clicking the My Computer icon on your desktop. Right-click the drive you want to format and choose Format from the menu. Select the Quick format type, enter a label for the disk, and then click the Start button.

> **CAUTION**
>
> You cannot format the drive that contains Windows while Windows is running. If you need to format this drive, you need the Windows 98 Startup disk, a set of Windows 98 upgrade disks that contain a disk for formatting disks, or a disk copy of MS-DOS with the Format command. Formatting the drive that contains Windows will make your system unbootable without a boot floppy. Before proceeding with the format, make sure you can boot your system from the DOS disks or the upgrade disks.

N O T E   If your disk was previously compressed, you must decompress it before you can format it. ▧

Naming a Hard Disk Drive

A volume label is simply a name for a disk. Having labels on your hard drive(s) can be useful because these labels will be shown when you use My Computer. You can change an existing label or give a new disk its first name:

1. Start My Computer by clicking the My Computer icon.

2. Right-click the drive icon and choose Properties from the pop-up menu.

3. When the Properties dialog box appears (see Figure 19.1), select the General tab and type the desired volume name into the Label text box. Click the OK button.

FIG. 19.1
Change the name of a disk with the Properties dialog box.

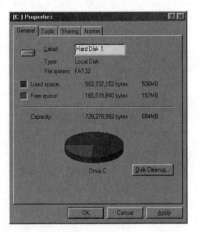

Transferring the Contents of Your Old Hard Disk to Your New Drive

If you want to use your new hard disk as your system's primary disk, you first need to transfer all your old files to your new hard disk—including Windows 98's system files. To copy all your files and make your new hard disk your primary boot drive, follow these steps:

Part
V

Ch
19

> **CAUTION**
>
> This procedure should be attempted only by experienced computer users. Make a complete backup of your hard disk before attempting this procedure, in case of accidental data loss.

▶ See "Backing Up Data," **p. 110**

1. Following the manufacturer's instructions, install your new drive as your system's *secondary* or "slave" drive.

2. After the new drive is installed and formatted, restart your computer and copy the Windows system files to the new disk by clicking the Start button, selecting Programs, and then selecting MS-DOS Prompt. When the DOS window appears, type **sys** *x***:** (where *x* is the letter of your new hard disk drive), and press Enter. Type **exit** to close the DOS window.

3. Disable your system's virtual memory by clicking the Start button, selecting Settings, and then selecting Control Panel. When Control Panel opens, click the System icon. When the System dialog box appears, select the Performance tab and click the Virtual

Memory button. Check Let Me Specify My Own System Memory Setting, and then click OK. When prompted, opt to restart Windows.

4. After Windows restarts, copy the contents of your old hard disk by clicking the Start button, selecting Run, and typing the following into the Run dialog box: **xcopy** *x***:*.* /** **e/h/k/r/c** *y***:** where *x* is the letter of your old hard disk drive and *y* is the letter of your new drive. Click OK to begin copying.

5. All your files will now be copied to your new hard disk drive. This may take several minutes, depending on the amount of data on your old hard disk.

6. After all the files are copied, shut down Windows 98, turn off your PC, and change the jumper settings on your drives so that your new drive is now selected as the *primary* or "master" drive. (See your manufacturer's instructions for precise details.)

7. Place your Windows 98 Startup disk in the floppy drive and turn on your PC. During the startup procedure, enter the CMOS settings area (as specified by your PC's manufacturer) and edit the CMOS settings to reflect the change in primary/secondary drives. Save the new settings and continue to start up your system.

8. At the A: prompt, type **fdisk** and select option **2** to make your new hard disk drive the active drive. Exit FDISK, remove the Windows 98 Startup disk, and press Ctrl+Alt+Del to restart your system.

9. Windows 98 should now launch with your new hard disk selected as your primary drive. Reset your virtual memory settings by clicking the Start button, selecting Settings, and then selecting Control Panel. When Control Panel opens, click the System icon. When the System dialog box appears, select the Performance tab and click the Virtual Memory button. Check Let Windows Manage My Virtual Memory Settings, and then click OK. When prompted, opt to restart Windows.

Converting Your Existing Hard Drive to FAT32

Windows' file system uses a special section on each hard disk, called the File Allocation Table (FAT), to store the data needed to track the location of all your files. The 16-bit FAT used in previous operating systems was effective in managing data on smaller hard disks, but was inefficient in managing larger hard disks. In addition, it could track data on disks only under 2Gb in size; for that reason, larger hard disks had to have multiple partitions of 2Gb or less.

Windows 98 includes a new 32-bit file system called FAT32 that is much more efficient in dealing with large hard disks—and can recognize disks larger than 2Gb. If you buy a new PC with Windows 98 preinstalled, chances are it will already have FAT32 enabled. If you're upgrading from an earlier version of Windows, however, you may want to convert from the existing 16-bit FAT system to FAT32.

> **CAUTION**
>
> FAT32, while more efficient in using disk space than earlier versions of FAT, is also slightly slower. If you're using a smaller hard disk, you may not want to upgrade to FAT32—your disk access will actually be slower than with the existing 16-bit FAT.

To convert your hard disk to FAT32 operation:

1. Click the Start button, select Programs, select Accessories, select System Tools, and then select FAT32 Converter.
2. When the FAT32 converter launches, follow the on-screen instructions to begin the conversion process.
3. After your drive has been converted to FAT32 operation, Windows will automatically launch Disk Defragmenter. Defragmenting your drive after it has been converted is necessary for optimal operation, although it may take several hours.

▶ **See** "Make Your Hard Disk Run Better by Defragmenting," **p. 113**

> **CAUTION**
>
> Many older, third-party disk utilities are designed for the 16-bit FAT system and will not work with FAT32. You may need to update your disk utilities if you have an earlier version. The disk utilities included with Windows—ScanDisk, Disk Defragmenter, and so on—have already been revised to support FAT32.

Installing Portable Zip and Jaz Drives

Zip™ and Jaz® drives are portable storage media manufactured by Iomega Corporation. Each Zip disk can hold up to 100M of data (compare this to the 1.44M of storage on a typical 3.5-inch floppy disk). Each Jaz disk can hold up to 1 *gigabyte* of data. It's easy to move *portable* Zip and Jaz drives from one computer to another, thus making it more convenient to transport large amounts of data.

N O T E These instructions apply to portable Zip and Jaz drives connecting through a parallel port. If you have a permanent drive that connects through an IDE or SCSI interface, follow the manufacturer's installation instructions. ■

To install a portable Zip or Jaz drive on your system:

1. Shut down your computer.
2. Connect the Zip/Jaz drive to your system using the supplied cable. Connect the Zip/Jaz drive's power cable.

3. Restart your computer and launch Windows 98.

4. Insert the supplied Tools disk into the Zip/Jaz drive.

5. Insert the Install floppy disk into your computer's floppy disk drive.

6. Click the My Computer icon on your desktop to launch My Computer.

7. Click the icon for your floppy disk drive (normally the A: drive). When the contents for this disk are displayed, click the Guest95 file. This launches the setup program for your Zip/Jaz drive. Follow the instructions on-screen to complete the installation.

The Zip or Jaz drive will now appear as a new drive in My Computer and Windows Explorer. Normally the Zip/Jaz drive carries a letter label after your last hard drive, but before your first CD-ROM drive. For example, if you have one hard disk drive and one CD-ROM drive, your hard disk will be labeled C:, your Zip/Jaz drive will be labeled D:, and your CD-ROM will be labeled E:.

N O T E Get more information about Zip and Jaz drives on Iomega's Web site at **http:// www.Iomega.com**. ■

Using Zip and Jaz Drives

You use your Zip or Jaz drive just like you would any disk drive. Given the large storage capabilities of these disks, here are some suggested uses above and beyond the norm:

■ *Use the Zip/Jaz drive to transfer large files from one computer to another.* When you have a program or document file that is larger than the 1.44M capacity of a normal 3.5-inch floppy disk, use a Zip or Jaz disk to move the file from one machine to another.

■ *Use the Zip/Jaz drive as a second hard disk.* If you're running low on hard disk space, use the Zip/Jaz drive to hold overflowing files or less frequently used programs.

■ *Use the Zip/Jaz drive to back up files from your hard disk.* Protect the data on your hard drive by backing it up frequently. (See Chapter 9, "Basic System Maintenance," for more information on backups.) Zip and Jaz disks are large enough to function as backup disks for your hard disk data.

CHAPTER 20

Configuring and Using Keyboards, Mice, and Joysticks

The New Input Device Features of Windows 98

There are only a handful of new features in Windows 98 that relate to input devices:

- Support for keyboards with special Windows keys
- Support for the Microsoft IntelliMouse
- Simplified calibration for game joysticks

Personalizing Your Keyboard

You can change keyboard properties to set the character repeat rate, cursor blink rate, the language, and the keyboard type. You can also select multiple languages for your keyboard and switch between them. To change keyboard properties:

1. Click the Start button, select Settings, and then select Control Panel to open the Control Panel.
2. Click the Keyboard icon.
3. When the Keyboard Properties dialog box opens (see Figure 20.1), click one of the tabs described in the Table 20.1 to make changes.

FIG. 20.1
Use the Keyboard Properties dialog box to change various keyboard options, such as repeat rate and delay.

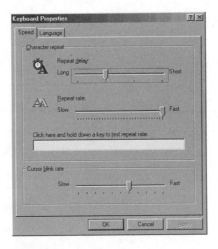

4. Click Apply to accept changes as you go, or click OK to accept the changes and close the Keyboard Properties dialog box. You may be prompted to restart the computer for the changes to take effect.

Table 20.1   Keyboard Properties

Tab	Description
Speed	Drag the sliders to set Repeat Delay (how long you hold down a key without it repeating), Repeat Rate (how fast a key repeats when depressed), and Cursor Blink Rate (how rapidly your cursor blinks on-screen). You can use the text box to test the repeat rate before accepting the change.
Language	Select a language in the Language list box to change languages. Click Add to add another language to the list. Choose Properties to select an alternative keyboard layout—such as the Dvorak layout, which is an alternative configuration that rearranges the keys on your keyboard in a manner some users prefer to the traditional keyboard layout. Click Remove to delete a language from the list.

N O T E   Changing the keyboard language does not change the language used by Windows. To do that, you must purchase a different language version of Windows. ∎

Changing Your Mouse's Buttons

Use the Mouse Properties program to customize your mouse for left-handed use and to adjust the mouse driver to recognize how you double-click with the mouse.

1. Click the Start button, select Settings, and then select Control Panel to open the Control Panel.

2. Click the Mouse icon to open the Mouse Properties dialog box.

3. Click the Buttons tab (see Figure 20.2). Click either the Right-handed or the Left-handed option button, changing the functions performed when you click the left and right mouse buttons.

4. If Windows does not seem to always respond when you double-click, adjust the Double-click Speed indicator at the bottom of the Buttons property sheet and test the new setting in the Test Area of the property sheet.

5. When you have made the desired changes, click OK in each dialog box to close the box, apply the changes, and return to the desktop. Click the Cancel button in any dialog box to cancel the changes and close the box.

Part
V

Ch
20

Configuring Mouse Motion

In Windows 98, you can customize the way that the mouse moves and appears on-screen. By using settings on the Motion tab in the Mouse Properties dialog box, you can set the pointer speed and pointer trail.

FIG. 20.2

Changing the properties of your pointing device in the Mouse Properties dialog box.

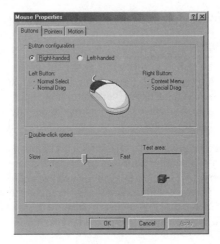

1. Click the Start button, select Settings, and then select Control Panel to open the Control Panel.

2. Click the mouse icon to open the Mouse Properties dialog box.

3. Click the Motion tab. Click and drag the speed indicator in the Pointer Speed field to speed up or slow down how fast the mouse pointer follows mouse movement. Click the Apply button to apply the change and to experience how the change affects the mouse pointer movement.

4. To display pointer trails (an echo of the pointer) as the mouse moves, check Show Pointer Trails. Click and drag the indicator in the field below to control the appearance of the mouse pointer trail as it follows mouse movement. Click the Apply button to apply the change.

5. When you have made the desired changes, click the OK button to close the dialog box, apply the changes, and return to the desktop. Click the Cancel button to cancel the changes and close the box.

 Turning on pointer trails is helpful when you are using a laptop. Many times, the mouse cursor is lost on the LCD screen, and the pointer trail allows you to track the movement of the mouse in less than optimal lighting conditions where LCD screens have problems.

Using an IntelliMouse

Microsoft's IntelliMouse looks just like a normal mouse, with one difference—it has a little wheel between the two normal mouse buttons. This wheel can be used to scroll through many Windows applications. This is particularly useful when you're browsing through large documents, or surfing World Wide Web sites.

The IntelliMouse installs just like any normal mouse—and, except for the wheel, operates like any other mouse. You can start using the wheel to scroll through documents from the moment it is installed.

Installing and Calibrating a Joystick

There are many brands and types of joysticks and game controllers available for use with Windows and DOS games. Windows 98 provides the Joystick control panel program to define and configure your joystick for the best action possible.

1. Click the Start button, select Settings, and then select Control Panel to open the Control Panel.

2. Click the Game Controllers icon to open the Game Controllers dialog box.

3. Click the General tab, select the controller to be calibrated from the Game Controllers list, and then click the Properties button.

4. When the Game Controller Properties dialog box appears, click the Settings tab. Click the Calibrate button to configure the game controller/joystick. Follow the instructions on-screen, clicking Next to proceed to each subsequent step. Click OK when you are satisfied with the calibration of the joystick.

5. Click the Test tab to test the various controls on your game controller. Click OK to return to the Joystick Properties dialog box.

Communications and the Internet

CHAPTER 21

Connecting to the Internet and Online Services

In this chapter

The New Connection Features of Windows 98

In Windows 95, you used the Dial-Up Networking utility to connect to the Internet. The problem was, Dial-Up Networking was somewhat less than user-friendly. Microsoft fixes this annoyance in Windows 98, with the following new features that help you easily establish an Internet connection:

- *Online Services folder.* As part of an agreement with several commercial online services and Internet Service Providers, Windows 98 includes a special folder on the desktop that contains one-click access to the following services: America Online, AT&T WorldNet, CompuServe, the Microsoft Network, and Prodigy Internet. When you click one of the icons in this folder, you're led step-by-step through the membership process for that service.

- *Internet Connection Wizard.* This Wizard leads you step-by-step through the otherwise complicated process of creating a Dial-Up Networking connection to your Internet Service Provider. (You can still create a new connection manually, but the Wizard is a much easier way to do it.)

- *Automatic connecting.* After you have your Internet connection established, Windows 98 will automatically connect your computer to your ISP any time you launch Internet Explorer or Outlook Express—you don't have to manually establish the connection first.

Understanding the Internet

The Internet is a giant network of computers, spanning the globe and connecting millions of computers just like yours. This network enables you to communicate with computer users in other countries and to search for information that may reside on different computers in different areas of the world. Furthermore, you get to cruise around the world from the safety of your own PC, using normal phone lines—and without paying long-distance phone charges.

After you're connected to the Internet, you can perform a variety of tasks—you can send and receive e-mail, exchange messages in topic-specific newsgroups, upload and download files, and search for all sorts of information on the World Wide Web. All you have to do is establish an Internet connection, launch the right software, and you're ready to cruise the Net!

Finding an Internet Service Provider

Before you connect to the Internet, you need to establish an account with a firm that provides Internet service—an *Internet Service Provider*, or ISP. The U.S. alone has thousands of ISPs, many of which are locally based. In addition, several large national ISPs exist (see Table 21.1), most of which provide local numbers for you to dial into. You can also connect to the Internet via one of the major commercial online services, such as America Online or the Microsoft Network. These services provide Internet access in addition to their normal proprietary content.

Table 21.1   Major Internet Service Providers

ISP	Contact	Web site
GTE Internet Solutions	800-363-8483	**http://www.gte.net**
MCI Internet Dial Access	800-550-0927	**http://www.mci.com**
Netcom	800-353-6600	**http://www.netcom.com**
Sprint Internet Passport	800-359-3900	**http://www.sprint.com/sip**

When you call an ISP to set up an account, you need only your phone number and credit card number. (Most ISPs charge in the neighborhood of $20/month for unlimited access.) In return, many ISPs will provide you with a package of Internet software and utilities, as well as the information you need to configure Windows to connect to their service.

Choosing an Internet Service Provider from the Online Services Folder

Microsoft provides almost instant access to five major ISPs and online services directly from a folder placed on the Windows 98 desktop. As shown in Figure 21.1, the Online Services folder contains icons for America Online, AT&T WorldNet, CompuServe, the Microsoft Network, and Prodigy Internet. Just open the Online Services folder and click the icon for the service of your choice, and you'll be led through a series of steps to sign you up as a paid subscriber.

FIG. 21.1
Open the Online Services folder to subscribe to any or all of these five major service providers.

Table 21.2 provides more details about each service in the Online Services folder.

Part
VI

Ch
21

Table 21.2   Services in the Online Services Folder

Service	Contact	Description
America Online	800-827-3338	The largest commercial online service in the world, with more than eight million subscribers in the U.S. alone. Because of its size, it also is able to offer the most proprietary content—content that you won't find on the Web.
AT&T WorldNet	800-967-5363	A traditional Internet Service Provider. AT&T provides access to the Internet only, without any propriety content of their own.
CompuServe	800-336-6823	The world's oldest existing commercial online service, predating AOL and MSN by several years. Although AOL has more subscribers and MSN has a newer interface, CompuServe offers more features of interest to businesses—including a variety of information-packed databases. It was recently announced that America Online is purchasing CompuServe; the word is that for now AOL and CompuServe will be kept as separate services.
The Microsoft Network	800-386-5550	Created by the same company that created Windows 98, MSN is the newest commercial online service. Designed specifically for Windows users, MSN has the most state-of-the-art user interface, plenty of proprietary content, and seamless access to all aspects of the Internet.
Prodigy Internet	800-213-0992	Prodigy Internet is a blend of a traditional ISP and a commercial online service. The focus is on Internet access, but much Internet-based proprietary content is available.

N O T E   *Using CompuServe, Third Edition* is a book by Que that helps you use the latest version of CompuServe. ■

Gathering the Information You Need to Connect

Before you create your new Internet connection, you need to gather various pieces of information from your Internet Service Provider:

■ Area code and telephone number of your Internet Service Provider (*not* their voice number, their dial-up number)

■ Your user name and password as assigned by your ISP

- Your e-mail address (in the form of *xxx@xxx.x*) as assigned by your ISP
- The names of your ISP's incoming and outgoing e-mail servers (may be the same)
- Your e-mail POP account name and password as assigned by your ISP
- The name of your ISP's news server
- If your ISP offers LDAP "white pages" service (not all do), the name of your ISP's LDAP server

If you do not yet have an Internet Service Provider, don't worry; you can let the Internet Connection Wizard find an ISP for you, or you can choose one from Windows 98's Online Services folder.

Creating a New Connection with the Internet Connection Wizard

Windows 98 includes the Internet Connection Wizard, a special utility used to automate the creation of a new Internet connection. The Wizard makes it easy to establish a new connection; all you need to do is input some connection information provided by your Internet Service Provider, and the Wizard does the rest of the setup—including setting up your e-mail and USENET newsgroup accounts.

To create a new connection with the Internet Connection Wizard:

1. Click the Start button, select Programs, select Internet Explorer, and then select Connection Wizard.

2. When the first screen of the Wizard appears, click Next to display the Setup Options screen (as shown in Figure 21.2).

FIG. 21.2

Use the Internet Connection Wizard to create a new Internet connection.

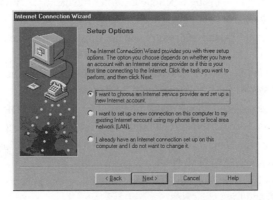

3. If you haven't chosen an ISP yet, select the first option, I Want To Choose An Internet Service Provider and Set Up a New Internet Account. The Wizard will then present a list of ISPs from which you can choose to establish an account.

4. If you already have established an account with an ISP, choose the second option, I Want to Set Up a New Connection to My Existing Internet Account Using My Phone Line or Local Area Network, and then click the Next button.

TIP If you realize you made a mistake when providing information to the Wizard, you can use the Back button to return to a previous screen.

5. When the Set Up Your Internet Connection dialog box appears, select Connect Using My Phone Line if you're connecting via a normal dial-up connection, and then click Next.

6. When the Choose Modem dialog box appears, select your modem from the pull-down list, and then click Next.

7. When the Dial-Up Connection dialog box appears, select Create a New Dial-Up Connection and click Next.

8. When the Phone Number dialog box appears, enter the area code, phone number, and country of your Internet Service Provider, and then click Next.

9. When the User Name and Password dialog box appears, enter the user name and password provided by your Internet Service Provider, and then click Next.

10. When the Advanced Settings dialog box appears, click No (unless your ISP instructs you to reconfigure Windows advanced connection settings) and click Next.

11. When the Dial-Up Connection Name dialog box appears, provide a name for this connection and click Next.

12. When the Set Up Your Internet Mail Account dialog box appears, click Yes to set up the mail account at your ISP, and then click Next.

13. When the Internet Mail Account dialog box appears, click Create a New Internet Mail Account, and then click Next.

14. When the Your Name dialog box appears, enter the name you want to use with this account and click Next.

15. When the Internet E-Mail Address dialog box appears, enter the e-mail address (in the form *xxx@xxx.xxx*) given you by your ISP, and then click Next.

16. When the E-Mail Server Names dialog box appears, enter the incoming and outgoing server names provided by your ISP, and then click Next.

17. When the Internet Mail Logon dialog box appears, enter the POP account name and password given you by your ISP, and then click Next.

18. When the Friendly Name dialog box appears, enter a name for this e-mail account (for your own use), and then click Next.

19. When the Set Up Your Internet News Account dialog box appears, click Yes to set up a new account, and then click Next.

20. When the Internet News Account dialog box appears, click Create a New Internet News Account, and then click Next.

21. When the Your Name dialog box appears, enter the name you'd like displayed on outgoing messages, and then click Next.

22. When the Internet News E-Mail Address dialog box appears, enter the e-mail address given you by your ISP, and then click Next.

23. When the Internet News Server Name dialog box appears, enter the name of your ISP's news server (should be provided by your ISP), and then click Next.

24. When the Friendly Name dialog box appears, enter the name you want to give this account, and then click Next.

25. When the Set Up Your Internet Directory Service dialog box appears, click Yes if your ISP offers LDAP "white pages" service, and then click Next.

N O T E   Not all ISPs offer LDAP directory services. ■

26. When the Internet Directory Service dialog box appears, click Set Up a New Directory Service and click Next.

27. When the Internet Directory Server Name dialog box appears, enter the name of your ISP's LDAP server and click Next.

28. When the Check E-Mail Addresses dialog box appears, click Yes and then click Next.

29. When the Friendly Name dialog box appears, enter the name you want to give this directory service, and then click Next.

30. When the Complete Configuration dialog box appears, click Finish to finalize your new connection.

Setting Up a Dial-Up Connection Manually

Although most users will prefer to use the Internet Connection Wizard to automate their Internet setup, circumstances may arise in which you want to create a connection manually— for a nonstandard online service, for example, such as a local bulletin board. Windows 98 uses Dial-Up Networking to create new online connections.

1. Click the Start button, select Programs, select Accessories, and then select Dial-Up Networking.

2. When the Dial-Up Networking window appears, click the Make New Connection icon.

3. When the first screen of the Make New Connection Wizard appears (see Figure 21.3), give the new connection a name, select the modem you want to use, and click Next.

4. Enter the area code and the telephone number of the service to which you want to connect, and then click Next.

5. When the last Wizard screen is displayed, click Finish to complete the dial-up networking connection setup.

Part
VI

Ch
21

FIG. 21.3
Use the Make New
Connection Wizard to
create a new Dial-Up
Networking connection.

Connecting to Your Internet Service Provider with Dial-Up Networking

After you've created your Internet connection, all it takes to get online is a click of your mouse:

1. Click the Start button, select Programs, select Accessories, and then select Dial-Up Networking.

2. When the Dial-Up Networking window appears, click the icon for your Internet Service Provider.

3. When the Connect To dialog box appears (see Figure 21.4), enter your user name and password and click the Connect button.

FIG. 21.4
Getting ready to connect
to your ISP—don't forget
your password!

4. Windows now will dial your ISP and automatically establish a connection. When the connection is established, an icon, indicating the nature of your connection, will appear in the Taskbar tray.

5. Now you can launch the appropriate Internet software, such as Internet Explorer or Outlook Express.

N O T E   If you launch Internet Explorer or Outlook Express before you establish your dial-up connection, they will automatically launch Dial-Up Networking so that you can establish a connection to the Internet. ■

6. To close the connection, right-click the connection icon in the Taskbar tray and choose <u>D</u>isconnect from the pop-up menu.

Connecting to the Internet from a Network

The Internet runs on a networking protocol called TCP/IP. This same protocol also supports most local area networks (LANs). If your company provides Internet access through its LAN, then you can configure Windows to access the Internet over your company's network—at much faster speeds than when you connect over normal phone lines.

To configure your computer to connect to the Internet from your company's LAN

1. Click the Start button, select <u>S</u>ettings, and then select <u>C</u>ontrol Panel.
2. When Control Panel launches, click the Internet icon.
3. When the Internet Properties dialog box appears, select the Connection tab and select <u>C</u>onnect to the Internet using a Local Area Network (see Figure 21.5). This will prevent Windows 98 from trying to use dial-up networking to make your Internet connection, and instead, it will use your current LAN access.

FIG. 21.5

Select whether to connect via phone line or via your local area network in the Internet Properties dialog box.

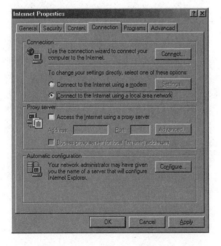

4. If your company uses a proxy server to access the Internet (your network administrator can tell you if this is the case), check Access the Internet using a Proxy Server and enter the appropriate information. (If you are not sure if your company uses a proxy server—most don't—leave this option unchecked.)
5. Click OK to save your settings.

The next time you launch Internet Explorer or Outlook Express, you will be connected via your company's network, direct to the Internet—no phone lines involved. ●

Part
VI

Ch
21

CHAPTER 22

Surfing the Internet with Internet Explorer

In this chapter

The New Browser Features of Windows 98

Windows 95 didn't include a Web browser; Windows 98 does. In fact, most of the new interface features of Windows 98 are built around Internet Explorer 4.0 (IE4), the latest version of Microsoft's Web browser—now included as part of Windows 95. If you're using Windows 95, you can download Internet Explorer 4.0 (from **www.microsoft.com/ie/ie40**) and get most of the interface functionality of Windows 98 today.

Internet Explorer 4.0 has many features not found in previous versions of the browser:

- *Favorites pane*. When you click the Favorites button, a new pane appears displaying your favorite Web sites. You can also rearrange items on the Favorites list by using drag and drop.

- *History pane*. Your most recently visited Web pages are listed in a separate pane when you click the History button. Sites are sorted by day visited, then by site, then by individual page.

- *Search pane*. When you click the Search button, a new pane appears that lets you search the Web using a variety of popular search engines.

- *Full-screen mode*. When you click the Full Screen button, Internet Explorer enlarges to fill the entire screen (including the Windows Taskbar area) with a special minimized menu bar.

- *Subscriptions and offline browsing*. With Internet Explorer 4.0, you don't have to manually retrieve updated versions of your favorite Web pages. All you have to do is tell IE4 you want to *subscribe* to a page, and any time that page is updated the new version will automatically be downloaded to your computer. You can then use IE4 *offline* (without connecting to the Internet) to view your subscription pages.

- *Microsoft Wallet*. With older browsers, any time you wanted to purchase an item over the Internet, you had to manually fill in your personal and charge card information. Microsoft Wallet lets you enter this information once, stores it, and then automatically transmits it (in secure mode) the next time you make an online purchase.

- *Security Zones*. To protect your system from rogue files and programs on the Internet that can wreak havoc with your computer system, IE4's new *security zones* let you assign different levels of security to different types of sites.

- *Content Advisor*. If you want to keep family members from accessing inappropriate Web sites, enable the new *Content Advisor* feature that classifies Web sites by type of content—and enables you to limit access to unsuitable sites.

- *PowerToys*. The gang at Microsoft have come up with a set of unofficial add-on utilities—called *PowerToys*—that enhance and extend the power of IE4.

- *Browse your desktop like the Web*. IE4 can also be used to browse your desktop—your disks, folders, and files—just as My Computer can also be used to browse the Web.

Understanding the World Wide Web

The Internet has many components, including e-mail post offices, USENET newsgroups, FTP downloading sites, and a really big component called the World Wide Web.

The Web is the "cool" part of the Internet. Web pages are colorful and include graphics, sound, and even moving video images. Web pages are connected via *hyperlinks*; clicking a hyperlink automatically connects you to another linked Web page. The Web contains millions of pages, covering hundreds of thousands of topics.

You view Web pages with a software program called a *Web browser*. Microsoft's Web browser—included with Windows 98—is called Internet Explorer.

Launching Internet Explorer

When Windows installs Internet Explorer (IE), it creates an icon for IE on the Quick Launch toolbar. Clicking this icon launches Internet Explorer and opens your dial-up connection to your Internet service provider (ISP).

▶ **See** "Adding Toolbars to the Taskbar," **p. 68**

To launch Internet Explorer and connect to the Internet

1. Click the Internet Explorer icon on the Quick Launch toolbar. This launches Dial-Up Networking, which dials your ISP and automatically establishes a connection. When the connection is established, an icon indicating the nature of your connection appears in the Taskbar's tray. (See Chapter 21, "Connecting to the Internet and Online Services," for more information on establishing a connection to an ISP.)

2. After the connection is established, Internet Explorer launches and connects to your default start page.

3. To close Internet Explorer, pull down the File menu and select Close. You'll be asked if you want to close the connection to your ISP. Click Yes to end your Internet session.

Configuring Internet Explorer

You can change many options in Internet Explorer to make it better suit your personal needs. For example, you may want to change the color of links you have visited; or if you are concerned about security, you may want to turn on warnings when entering an unsecured site. You can change the options at any time—whether you are currently connected to the Internet or not.

To change Internet Explorer's default configuration:

1. Start Internet Explorer by clicking the Internet Explorer icon on the Quick Launch toolbar.

2. Pull down the View menu and select Internet Options.

3. When the Internet Options dialog box appears, configure the appropriate options as described in Table 22.1.

4. After you have Internet Explorer configured as you like, click the OK button.

Table 22.1   Internet Explorer Configuration Options

Tab	Options
General	Select the home page you want to view when IE first launches and determine how much disk space is devoted to keeping temporary and history files. Click the Colors, Fonts, Languages, and Accessibility buttons to set various display options.
Security	Set up different "zones" of content, each of which can be set for different levels of security.
Content	Enable Ratings to help you control the content your children can view on the Internet; enable the use of Certificates to verify content from specific Web sites; and create a personal profile to automatically send information to selected Web sites.
Connection	Use the Connection Wizard to set up your Internet connection; adjust individual settings specific to your current connection.
Programs	Select which programs to use for Internet Mail and News (Outlook Express is the default for both); select programs to use for other Internet-related activities.
Advanced	Turn on or off various advanced options related to browsing, multimedia, security, Java, printing, searching, the IE Toolbar, and HTTP settings.

 You can also configure Internet Explorer's toolbars, just like you can the toolbars in My Computer or Windows Explorer.

▶ **See** "Resizing and Rearranging Toolbars," **p. 90**

Understanding How Internet Explorer Works

Internet Explorer functions like any Windows program, using a series of pull-down menus and toolbar buttons. Because a browser is a bit different from a word processor, however, use Figure 22.1 and the list that follows to learn the parts of the IE interface.

Toolbar—click these
buttons to perform
common functions

Address box—enter Web
addresses here

FIG. 22.1

Use Internet Explorer to
browse the World Wide
Web; enter new URLs in
the Address box.

Links bar—quick
links to common
Web sites

Status bar—displays
current URL when
loading, or the URL for
any highlighted link

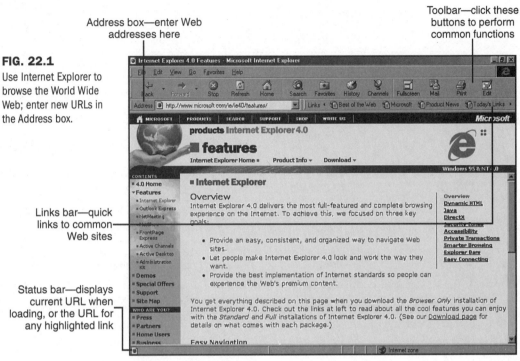

Table 22.2 describes the operation of each button on the default IE toolbar:

Table 22.2   Internet Explorer Toolbar Buttons

Button	Button Name	Operation
Back	Back	Return to the previously viewed page
Forward	Forward	View the next page
Stop	Stop	Stop loading of current page
Refresh	Refresh	Reload the current page
Home	Home	Return to your designated start page
Search	Search	Display the Search pane and initiate a Web search

continues

Table 22.2   Continued

Button	Button Name	Operation
Favorites	Favorites	Display the Favorites pane
History	History	Display the History pane to see a list of recently viewed pages
Channels	Channels	View a list of Active Channels with specific content "pushed" to your desktop
Fullscreen	Fullscreen	View Web pages in full-screen mode
Mail	Mail	Launch Outlook Express to read e-mail and newsgroup articles
Print	Print	Print the current page
Edit	Edit	Display the HTML code for the current page

Browsing the Web with Internet Explorer

Internet Explorer enables you to quickly and easily browse the World Wide Web—just by clicking your mouse.

1. Start Internet Explorer by clicking the Internet Explorer icon on the Quick Launch toolbar or the Internet Explorer shortcut on your desktop. Internet Explorer will load your predefined start page.

2. Enter a new Web address in the Address box and press Enter. IE will load the new page.

3. Click any link on the current Web page. IE will load the new page.

4. To return to the previous page, click the Back button. If you've backed up several pages and want to return to the page you were at last, click the Forward button.

 TIP Click the down arrow next to the Back or Forward button to display a drop-down list of recently visited pages in either direction.

5. To return to your start page, click the Home button.

N O T E A Web page address is called an URL (for Uniform Resource Locator). All Web addresses start with **http://**—you can leave out this part of the address, and IE will enter it automatically for you. ■

Stopping and Refreshing Web Pages

Sometimes Web pages will take a long time to load—if they contain a lot of graphics, for example. If you get tired of waiting for a Web page to load, you can click a button to stop the process. If you want to reload a partially loaded page, IE lets you do that, as well.

1. To stop the loading of the current page, click the Stop button.

2. To reload the current page, click the Refresh button.

Adding a Web Address to Your Favorites List

When you find a Web page you like, add it to a list of Favorites within IE. With this feature, you can access any of your favorite sites just by choosing it from the list.

To add a page to your Favorites list

1. Go to the page you would like to add to your Favorites list.

2. Pull down the Favorites menu and select Add to Favorites.

3. When the Add Favorite dialog box appears, click No Subscription and confirm the page's Name, and then click the Create In button.

4. Select the folder where you want to place this link, and then click OK.

Viewing Your Favorites List

Use the Favorites list to quickly access your favorite Web pages. To view a page in your Favorites list

1. Click the Favorites button. The browser window will automatically split into two panes, with your favorites displayed in the left pane (see Figure 22.2).

2. Click any folder in the Favorites pane to display the contents of that folder.

3. Click a favorite and that page will be displayed in the right pane.

4. Click the Favorites button again to hide the Favorites pane.

Organizing Your Favorites List

If you add a lot of pages to your Favorites list, it can become unwieldy. IE enables you to organize your favorite pages into folders, thus maintaining a neat and orderly Favorites list.

1. Pull down the Favorites menu and select Organize Favorites.

2. When the Organize Favorites dialog box appears, double-click the folder containing the links you want to change.

3. To move a link to another folder, select the link, click the Move button, and then select where you want to move the link.

4. To rename a link, select the link, click the Rename button, and enter a new name.

5. To delete a link from your Favorites list, select the link and click the Delete button.

6. To create a new folder, click the Create New Folder button on the toolbar.

FIG. 22.2
Click the Favorites button to display the Favorites pane; click any link to display that page in the right pane.

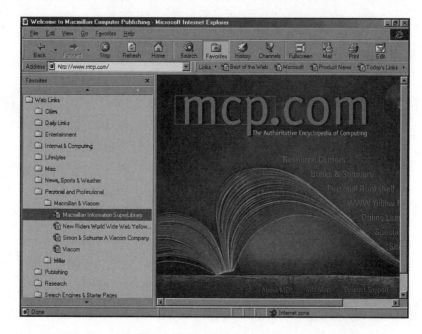

 T I P You can also move items on the Favorites list by opening the Folders pane and using your mouse to drag items from one location to another.

Revisiting Web Pages with the History List

Internet Explorer keeps track of all the Web pages you visit; returning to a previously viewed page is as easy as accessing IE's History list.

1. To display IE's History list, click the History button.

2. The browser window is automatically split into two panes. A list of previously visited sites, organized by day, is displayed in the left pane.

3. Click the folder for the day you want to revisit; the contents of that folder (the sites visited that day) will be displayed.

4. Click the link for any site, and that site will be displayed in the right pane.

5. To hide the History pane, click the History button again.

T I P By default, IE keeps five days' worth of pages in the History list. To change the number of days that IE keeps pages in the History list, pull down the View menu and select Internet Options. When the Internet Options dialog box appears, select the General tab, and choose the number of Days to Keep Pages in History in the History section. Click OK when finished.

Part

VI

Ch

22

Searching the Web

With millions of pages on the Web, how do you find any single page? You find things on the Web by using *search engines,* special sites designed to catalog and organize pages by topic. Internet Explorer includes a built-in function that enables you to access a variety of popular search engines (such as Yahoo!, Excite, Lycos, and Alta Vista) with the click of a button—and display the results right in your browser window.

1. Click the Search button.

2. The browser window is automatically split into two panes, as shown in Figure 22.3.

FIG. 22.3

Click the Search button to display the Search pane—and begin searching the Web.

3. In the Search pane, select a search engine from the Select Provider pull-down list. By default, IE rotates a variety of popular search sites as a "pick of the day."

4. Enter the word(s) you're searching for in the search box and press Enter.

5. The results of your search are displayed in the Search pane. Click any link to go directly to that page in the right pane of the browser.

6. To hide the Search pane, click the Search button again.

TIP You can also initiate a search of a special Microsoft/Yahoo! search page directly from the Address box. Just enter a **?** followed by the term you want to search for (for example, **? miller** to search for "miller") in the Address box, and then press Enter. The results will be displayed in the browser window.

Choosing a Search Site

Internet Explorer enables you to choose from a number of search sites when you click the Search button. Which is the best search site for your needs? Table 22.3 provides details about the major search sites on the Web.

Table 22.3   Popular Internet Search Engines

Search Site	Information
AltaVista	Possibly the largest collection of Web pages—plenty of raw data with little organization. Not for the easily intimidated.
AOL NetFind	A rather limited list of sites, hand-picked for relevancy.
Excite	An "intelligent" search engine that tries to interpret your search to include the most relevant responses. The main Excite site (**www.excite.com**) is actually a small community, with news feeds, classified ads, and free e-mail.
HotBot	Another "intelligent" search engine, associated with HotWired, the online site of *Wired* magazine.
InfoSeek	Handpicked directory of sites, well organized. The main InfoSeek site (**www.infoseek.com**) also includes the Ultraseek search engine for more inclusive searches.
Lycos	Basic search engine with little organization. The main Lycos site (**www.lycos.com**) also includes a hand-picked directory of the most popular sites on the Web.
Yahoo!	The most popular site on the Web, this is a hand-picked directory of sites, very well organized. The main Yahoo! site (**www.yahoo.com**) is a huge community with numerous features, including Yahooligans! (a directory for kids), My Yahoo! (a personalized start page), Yahoo! Get Local (news and features for your region), and a variety of news feeds and links.

These are just a few of the more popular general search sites on the Web. There are also dozens of more specialized search sites, including

- DejaNews (**www.dejanews.com**), lists articles posted in USENET newsgroups.
- Download.com (**www.download.com**), from cInet, lists files available for downloading across the Internet.

- PersonalSeek (**www.personalseek.com**), lists personal Web pages from other users.
- Search.com (**www.search.com**), from clnet, lists numerous general and specialized search sites available on the Web.
- Switchboard (**www.switchboard.com**), lists street addresses and phone numbers for people and businesses nationwide.
- WhoWhere (**www.whowhere.com**), lists e-mail addresses from other users.

Viewing Web Pages in Full-Screen Mode

Internet Explorer includes a special full-screen mode that displays Web pages using your entire desktop (see Figure 22.4 for an example). To use full-screen mode, follow these steps:

FIG. 22.4
A Web page viewed in full-screen mode; click the Full screen button again to return to the normal Internet Explorer window.

1. To switch to full-screen mode, click the Fullscreen button on IE's toolbar.
2. To return to normal windowed mode, either click the Fullscreen button again, or click the Minimize button in the upper-right corner of the screen.

Subscribing to Web Pages

Normally you have to manually revisit a Web site to see if the content has changed. Internet Explorer, however, enables you to "subscribe" to individual pages, and then notifies you when those pages have changed.

To subscribe to a Web page:

1. Go to the page to which you would like to subscribe.
2. Pull down the Favorites menu and select Add to Favorites.
3. When the Add Favorite dialog box appears, select Partial Subscription and click the Customize button.

 T I P If you'd prefer to read your subscribed pages offline, select Full Subscription and any time that page changes, the entire page will be downloaded to your hard disk. (See "Using Internet Explorer to Work Offline," later in this chapter.)

4. When the Web Site Subscription Wizard appears, click No, Just Notify Me When the Page Changes, and then click Next.
5. When the next page of the Wizard appears, click No (unless you'd prefer to be notified of any page changes by e-mail), and then click Next.
6. If the site requires a password, enter that information; otherwise, click No. Click Finish to register the subscription.

To view subscribed pages, pull down the Favorites menu and select Manage Subscriptions. When the Subscriptions dialog box appears, click the subscription you want to view; the updated page will appear in the Internet Explorer browser window.

Saving Web Page Graphics and Backgrounds

The World Wide Web is full of interesting graphics. Internet Explorer enables you to save these graphics for your own use with a few simple mouse clicks.

If you see a graphic on a Web page you'd like to save, follow these steps:

1. Go to the page that contains the graphic or background that you'd like to save.
2. To save the graphic to a file, right-click the graphic and choose Save Picture As from the pop-up menu. When the Save Picture dialog box appears, select a name and location for the file and click Save.
3. To make the graphic a background wallpaper for your desktop, right-click the graphic and select Set as Wallpaper from the pop-up menu.

Viewing HTML Source Code

If you want to create your own Web pages, it's useful to study the HTML code used to create existing pages on the Web. IE lets you view and save the code for any Web page you visit.

N O T E The code used to create Web pages is called HTML, for Hypertext Markup Language. Use a program such as FrontPage Express to automatically generate and edit HTML code and create Web pages.

▶ **See** "Creating Your Own Web Pages with FrontPage Express," **p. 276** ▪

To view the HTML code for a specific page:

1. Go to the page that you'd like to review.

2. Pull down the View menu and select Source.

3. This will open the HTML text file. You can then edit the source code or save it to your hard disk.

Making It Easy to Purchase Online with Microsoft Wallet

If you've ever purchased anything online, you know you have to manually enter your personal and charge card information at every site from which you purchase Internet Explorer 4.0 enables you to enter this information *once*—in the secure Microsoft Wallet—and then transmit this information automatically to online retailers when you want to make a purchase.

1. From within Internet Explorer, pull down the View menu and select Internet Options.

2. When the Internet Options dialog box appears, select the Content tab.

3. Click the Addresses button to display the Address Options dialog box. Click the Add button to display the Add a New Address dialog box. Enter your first, last, and middle names, your full address, your e-mail address, and your phone number; then click OK. When you return to the Address Options dialog box, click Close.

4. From the Internet Options dialog box, click the Payments button. The Installing Payment Extensions dialog box appears. After you see the message Digital Signature Verified, click the Install button.

5. When the Payment Options dialog box appears, click the Add button and select a credit card type from the drop-down list.

6. When the Add a New Credit Card Wizard appears, click Next to proceed to the second screen.

7. On the second screen of the Wizard, enter the appropriate credit card information, and then click Next.

8. Select a Billing Address from the drop-down list, or click New Address to enter a new billing address. Click Next to proceed.

9. Enter a password for this credit card, and then click Finish.

10. When you return to the Internet Options dialog box, click OK to complete the configuration.

When you visit an online retailer that supports the Microsoft Wallet standard, follow the on-screen instructions to automatically transmit your previously entered information.

Protecting Your System with Security Zones

You don't know what's waiting for you on the Internet. Some Web sites contain files and applications that can download viruses to your computer—or even tamper with your hard disk's files. IE4 helps to protect you from dangers lurking on unknown sites by letting you enable different *security zones*.

Each security zone is assigned one of three levels of security—Low, Medium, or High. Low security provides no warning if you're about to run potentially damaging content; Medium security prompts you before running questionable items; High security simply won't let you run anything potentially dangerous.

The security zone for the current Web page is shown on the right side of the Internet Explorer status bar. You can assign sites to four security zones:

- *Local Intranet Zone*. This zone is dedicated to pages on your company's local intranet. The default security level is Medium.
- *Trusted Sites Zone*. This zone contains sites that you know are completely safe. The default security level is Low.
- *Restricted Sites Zone*. This zone contains sites you don't trust. The default security level is High.
- *Internet Zone*. This is IE's default zone; any site not previously visited falls into this zone. The default security level is Medium.

By default, new sites you visit are assigned to the Internet Zone. To assign a site to a different security zone

1. From within Internet Explorer, pull down the View menu and select Internet Options.
2. When the Internet Options dialog box appears, select the Security tab.
3. Select a different type of Zone from the pull-down list.
4. Click the Add Sites button.
5. When the Zone dialog box appears, type the URL for the new site in the Add This Web Site to the Zone box, and then click the Add button. Click OK when done.
6. When you return to the Internet Options dialog box, click OK.

Avoiding Inappropriate Web Sites with Content Advisor

Some Web sites contain content that is not suitable for all family members. To limit access to unsuitable sites, use Internet Explorer's new Content Advisor features.

1. From within Internet Explorer, pull down the View menu and select Internet Options.
2. When the Internet Options dialog box appears, select the Content tab.

3. To adjust the tolerance level for different types of questionable content (such as language, nudity, sex, and violence), click the Settings button in the Content Advisor section.

4. When prompted for your Supervisor Password, enter your Windows password and click OK.

5. When the Content Advisor dialog box appears, click the Ratings tab and select a category. When a category is selected, a Rating slider appears (as shown in Figure 22.5). Adjust the slider to the right to increase the tolerance for this type of content; leaving the slider all the way to the left is the least tolerant level. Click OK when done.

FIG. 22.5
Use the Content Advisor to adjust your tolerance for different types of questionable content.

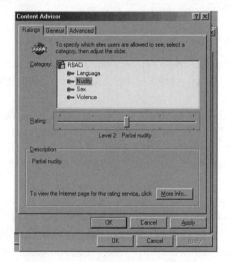

6. To enable Content Advisor, return to the Internet Options dialog box and click the Enable button. (You'll be prompted for your Supervisor Password; enter your Windows password and click OK.)

7. To disable Content Advisor, return to the Internet Options dialog box and click the Disable button. (You'll again be prompted for your Supervisor Password; enter your Windows password and click OK.)

8. Click OK to close the Internet Options dialog box.

With Content Advisor enabled, when you visit a site that does not pass your tolerance levels for specific content (or a page that has not been rated), you're alerted by a message saying that Content Advisor will now allow you to see this site. You can override this block by entering your Windows password and clicking OK. Other users with other passwords cannot gain access.

Enhancing Internet Explorer with PowerToys

Microsoft has created several add-on utilities to enhance the way Internet Explorer operates. These utilities are collectively called PowerToys, and you can download them from a special Microsoft Web site (**www.microsoft.com/ie/ie40/powertoys/**).

CAUTION

Although PowerToys were created by Microsoft employees, they are not official Microsoft software—and as such are not endorsed or supported by Microsoft. Because PowerToys come with no official technical support, they should be used only by experienced users.

Among the Internet Explorer PowerToys available are

- *Zoom In/Zoom Out*. When this PowerToy is installed, you can zoom in and zoom out of any Web page image. Just right-click the image and select Zoom In or Zoom Out from the pop-up menu.

- *Quick Search*. This PowerToy enables you to quickly search the Web from the IE Address Box by using a specific search engine of your choice. Just type the abbreviation for the search engine in the Address Box, followed by your search term. (For example, *av* is the abbreviation for Alta Vista; you'd type **av miller** to search for the word *miller* on Alta Vista.)

- *Image Toggler*. This PowerToy installs a new Toggle Images button on the IE Links bar. Just click this button to turn off the loading of images for faster speed.

- *Text Highlighter*. With this PowerToy installed, you can easily highlight text on a Web page. Just select the text, right-click the selected text, and choose Highlight from the pop-up menu.

- *Open Frame in New Window*. This PowerToy enables you to expand the contents of a frame into its own separate browser window. Just right-click anywhere in the frame and select Open Frame in New Window from the pop-up menu.

- *Web Search*. This PowerToy enables you to search on selected words on a Web page. Just right-click the selected the word or words and select Web Search from the pop-up menu. The selected words are then used as the search term in your default search engine.

- *Links List*. When installed, this PowerToy enables you to see a list of all the links on the current Web page. Just right-click anywhere on the current page and select Links List from the pop-up menu.

Using Internet Explorer to Work Offline

Internet Explorer enables you to browse Web pages without being connected to the Web. This is called offline browsing and is especially useful if you choose to download subscribed pages for later viewing.

To use Internet Explorer offline

1. Start Internet Explorer by clicking the Internet Explorer icon on the Quick Launch toolbar.

2. Pull down the File menu and select Work Offline.

3. Now you can browse any Web pages recently visited (which are automatically stored for at least at day) by clicking the History button and selecting a page from the History list. In addition, you can view any pages downloaded via subscription.

Using Internet Explorer to Browse Your Desktop

Internet Explorer not only can browse the World Wide Web, but it can also browse your desktop. This is part of the new desktop/Internet built into Windows 98.

You can use Internet Explorer to browse your desktop in a number of ways:

- Enter **c:** in IE's Address box to browse your main hard disk drive.

- Enter the precise location of a folder or file (drive letter and folder or subfolders) in IE's Address box to go directly to that location.

- Enter **My Computer** in IE's Address box to turn the Internet Explorer window into a My Computer window (see Figure 22.6).

FIG. 22.6
Use Internet Explorer to browse your desktop by entering **My Computer** in the Address box.

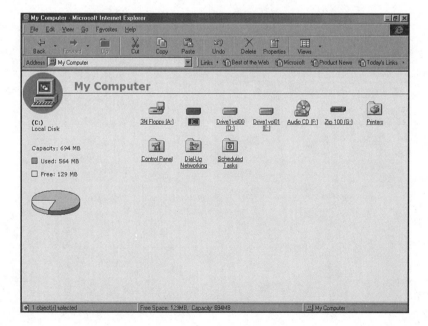

Using My Computer to Browse the Internet

Just as you can use Internet Explorer to browse your hard disk, you can also use My Computer to browse the Internet.

1. From My Computer, enter a Web address (URL) in the Address box and press Enter.

2. If you are not currently connected to the Internet, My Computer will connect to the Internet and automatically display the designated Web page.

3. From this point, you can continue to enter URLs in My Computer's Address box, click on links on the displayed page to jump to other Web pages, or enter **My Computer** in the Address box to return to normal My Computer operation.

Using Web Channels and Subscriptions

The New Active Channel Features of Windows 98

One exciting new feature of Windows 98 is the ability to display active *channels* of information "pushed" to your desktop over the Internet. Channels are Web sites that are automatically sent to your computer according to a schedule specified by the content provider; you can then view these channels offline, at your leisure.

Microsoft has partnered with numerous firms to provide channels with various types of content. Among the initial content providers are clnet, the *Wall Street Journal*, Quicken, ESPN, Warner Brothers, and MSNBC.

Displaying the Internet Explorer Channel Bar

When Windows is first installed, buttons for a variety of content channels are displayed in a new Channel Bar (shown in Figure 23.1), which resides directly on your desktop. If the Channel Bar is *not* displayed on your desktop, follow these steps to activate it:

1. Right-click the desktop and then choose Properties from the pop-up menu.
2. When the Display Properties dialog box appears, click the Web tab.
3. Select Internet Explorer Channel Bar from the Items on the Active Desktop list, and then click OK. The Channel Bar is now installed on your desktop; just click a channel button to connect to the Internet and view that channel's contents.

FIG. 23.1
Click any button in the
Channel Bar to view the
contents of that
particular channel.

 TIP Make sure Windows 98's Active Desktop is enabled before you try to display the Channel Bar.
▶ **See** "Activating the Active Desktop," **p. 74**

Subscribing to Active Channels

As initially configured, the Channel Bar contains a number of different types of content channels. When you subscribe to a channel, new content from that channel is automatically downloaded to your PC on a predetermined schedule.

To subscribe to a specific channel:

1. Click the button for a specific content channel in the Channel Bar.

2. Your normal Windows desktop is replaced by the Active Channel Viewer, described in "Viewing Active Channels with the Active Channel Viewer," later in this chapter.

3. When a channel is first displayed, you will be prompted to subscribe to that channel (or, in some cases, to "add active channel" or "add to channels"). Follow the on-screen instructions to subscribe; the instructions for each channel are different.

4. When the Add Active Channel Content dialog box appears (see Figure 23.2), you have the following options:

   - To add the channel to your channel bar *without* subscribing, select No Just add It To My Channel Bar.

   - To add the channel to your channel bar and receive notification when the content is updated, select Yes But Only Tell Me When Updates Occur.

   - To add the channel to your channel bar and automatically download all new content, select Yes Notify Me of Updates and Download the Channel for Offline Viewing.

FIG. 23.2

When you choose to subscribe to a channel, you must decide how you want to receive new content.

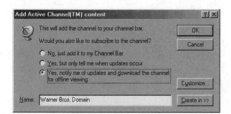

5. If you chose either Yes option, click the Customize button. When the Channel Subscription Wizard appears, confirm how you want the content downloaded, and then click Next. When the next screen appears, check No (unless you want to be notified of changes by e-mail) and click Next. When you're asked *when* the content should be updated, click AutoSchedule if you're connecting via a network; otherwise, click Manually and then click Next. You'll now be returned to the Add Active Channel Content dialog box.

6. Click OK to register your subscription.

Configuring Channel and Subscription Options

If, at a later date, you want to change your subscription information to a particular channel:

1. From Internet Explorer, pull down the Favorites menu and select Manage Subscriptions.
2. When the Subscriptions dialog box appears, right-click the subscription you want to reconfigure. When the pop-up menu appears, select Properties to display the Properties dialog box.
3. To cancel a subscription, select the Subscription tab and click Unsubscribe.
4. If you want to change how you're notified of content changes—or whether or not new content is automatically downloaded—click the Receiving tab and make the appropriate changes.
5. If you want to change the schedule for downloading new content for this channel, click the Schedule tab and make the appropriate changes.
6. Click OK when you're done making changes.

Viewing Active Channels with the Active Channel Viewer

Channels are viewed with the Active Channel Viewer, which is actually just Internet Explorer in full-screen mode. To view specific channels:

1. Click the button for a specific content channel in the Channel Bar.
2. Your normal Windows desktop is replaced by the Active Channel Viewer (see Figure 23.3).
3. Any new channel content since the last automatic download will be automatically downloaded to your computer. Each channel looks different; click the appropriate parts of the channel window to view specific channel information.
4. To switch to another channel, move your cursor to the left side of the screen. When the Channel Bar displays, click the new channel you want to view.
5. To minimize the Active Channel Viewer, click the Full Screen button in the toolbar.
6. To close the Active Channel Viewer, click the Close button at the top right corner of the screen.

 TIP You can also access content channels from within Internet Explorer; just click the Channels button on the IE Toolbar.

Finding New Content Channels

Windows 98 includes a limited number of preselected content channels in the Channel Bar. There are many more content channels available for your viewing pleasure.

1. Click the Channel Guide button in the Channel Bar.
2. You'll be connected to a special Microsoft Channel Guide Web page, displayed in the Active Channel Viewer (see Figure 23.4).

FIG. 23.3
Use the Active Channel Viewer to view channels you select from the Channel Bar—such as the Prevue Channel, shown here.

Part

VI

Ch

23

FIG. 23.4
Click the Channel Guide button to see even more content channels.

3. Click a heading to view available channels for any given topic, and then click any channel to subscribe; follow the on-screen instructions. The new channel will automatically appear on your Channel Bar.

Using Channel Content as a Screen Saver

You can also use your subscribed active content as a screen saver, to be displayed when your computer is inactive. To activate the Channel Screen Saver:

▶ **See** "Using Screen Savers," **p. 65**

1. Right-click the desktop and then choose Properties from the pop-up menu.

2. When the Display Properties dialog box appears, click the Screen Saver tab.

3. From the Screen Saver list, select Channel Screen Saver.

4. Click the Settings button to configure the display options for this screen saver.

5. When the Screen Saver Properties dialog box appears, select which channel(s) you want to display and how long you want to display each channel. Click OK to return to the Display Properties dialog box.

6. Click OK when finished.

CHAPTER 24

Sending and Receiving E-Mail with Outlook Express

The New E-Mail Features of Windows 98

Windows 95 included an e-mail program called Windows Messaging. (On some versions of Windows 95, Windows Messaging was also called Microsoft Exchange.) In Windows 98, Windows Messaging has been replaced with a much more functional e-mail program called Outlook Express.

The good thing about Outlook Express is that it includes many more options than Windows Messaging (including the capability to function as a USENET newsgroup reader—see Chapter 25 for more details). The bad thing is that by dumping Windows Messaging, Microsoft also had to dump Microsoft Fax (which depended on Windows Messaging to work). So Windows 98 (at least at the beta 2.1 stage) has a great e-mail program, but no fax program.

Among the new features in Outlook Express are:

- *HTML e-mail.* Outlook Express lets you send and receive e-mail messages that include HTML code. You can actually send and receive Web pages directly to your desktop using Outlook Express.

- *Stationery.* Because Outlook Express messages can include HTML code, you can spruce up your messages with fancy graphical backgrounds (called *stationery*).

- *Multiple configurations.* You can customize Outlook Express with various panes and menus and toolbars until it looks just the way you want.

- *Multiple accounts.* Outlook Express is easily configured for multiple e-mail accounts at multiple ISPs—it will put messages from multiple sources into a common inbox.

- *Universal Address Book.* The Address Book in Windows 98 is shared by all Windows 98 applications—and can be accessed independently of Outlook Express.

- *Automatic address searching.* Outlook Express includes a Find utility to search the Internet for specific e-mail addresses.

Understanding E-Mail

Electronic mail (e-mail) is a way to send messages—in electronic format—from one computer to another. E-mail messages look a lot like word processing documents and are delivered electronically using your computer's modem and a normal phone line.

When you send an e-mail message to another computer user, that message travels from your computer to your Internet service provider (ISP), to the Internet, to your recipient's Internet service provider, to your recipient's personal computer, and thus to your recipient. All you have to do is compose the message—using Windows 98's Outlook Express program—and click the Send button. Everything else happens automatically. It happens automatically, that is, providing you know the right address for your recipient. E-mail addresses are composed of three parts: The user's *log-in name*, the @ sign, and the user's *domain* (usually the name of their ISP). Using my address as an example, my log-in name is **mmiller**, my ISP's domain is **mcp.com**, so my full e-mail address is **mmiller@mcp.com**.

Configuring Outlook Express Manually

Before you can send and receive e-mail, you first have to configure Outlook Express, as well as establish an Internet access account, because your e-mail will be sent via the Internet. If you used the Internet Connection Wizard to create your Internet connection, Outlook Express was automatically configured at that time. If you didn't use the Internet Connection Wizard, you need to configure Outlook Express Manually.

▶ **See** "Creating a New Connection with the Internet Connection Wizard," **p. 221**

To configure Outlook Express for e-mail use:

1. Click the Launch Outlook Express icon on the Quick Launch toolbar to launch Outlook Express.

2. Pull down the Tools menu and select Accounts.

3. When the Internet Accounts dialog box appears (see Figure 24.1), click the Mail tab, and then click the Add button and select Mail.

FIG. 24.1

Pull down the Tools menu and select Accounts to use the Internet Accounts menu to add a new e-mail account.

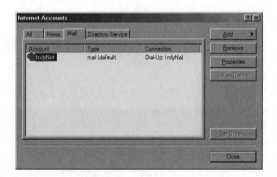

4. Outlook Express now launches a subset of the Internet Connection Wizard. When the Your Name dialog box appears, enter the name you want to use with this account and click Next.

5. When the Internet E-Mail Address dialog box appears, enter the e-mail address (in the form *xxx@xxx.x*) given you by your ISP, and then click Next.

6. When the E-Mail Server Names dialog box appears, enter the incoming and outgoing server names provided you by your ISP, and then click Next.

7. When the Internet Mail Logon dialog box appears, enter the POP account name and password given you by your ISP, and then click Next.

8. When the Friendly Name dialog box appears, enter a name for this e-mail account (for your own use), and then click Next.

9. When the Choose Connection Type dialog box appears, select Connect Using My Phone Line if you're using a dial-up connection; select Connect Using My Local Area Network if you're connecting via a company-wide network. Click Next to proceed.

Part
VI

Ch
24

10. When the Choose Modem dialog box appears, select your modem from the pull-down list and click <u>N</u>ext.

11. When the Dial-Up Connection dialog box appears, check <u>U</u>se an Existing Dial-Up Connection, select your connection from the list, and then click <u>N</u>ext.

12. When the Congratulations dialog box appears, click Finish to finalize your configuration.

 TIP If you have more than one e-mail account with multiple ISPs, repeat these steps to add your additional accounts.

Configuring the Outlook Express Window

The Outlook Express window can be configured for a number of different views. For example, you may want to display a preview pane to preview selected messages. You may also want to show the various Outlook Express options in a traditional tree structure or as icons in a sidebar.

Figure 24.2 shows the Outlook Express window in standard configuration. Figure 24.3 shows a different configuration, with the Outlook bar to the left, folder bar to the top, and preview pane underneath the message pane.

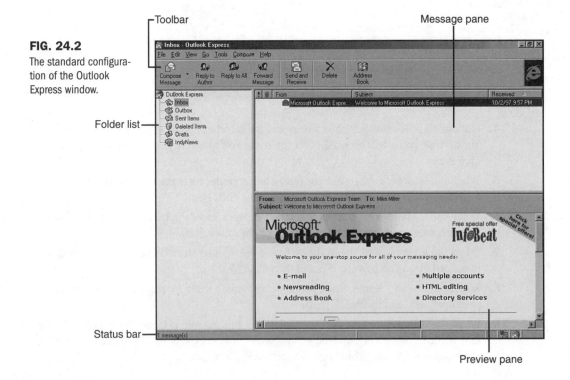

FIG. 24.2
The standard configuration of the Outlook Express window.

Toolbar

Folder bar (click to display
the folder tree)

Message pane

FIG. 24.3

Another configuration—
click an item in the
Out-look bar to display
its contents in the
message pane; click
a message in the mes-
sage pane to display its
contents in the preview
pane. Pull down the
folder bar to display
Outlook Express folders.

Outlook bar —

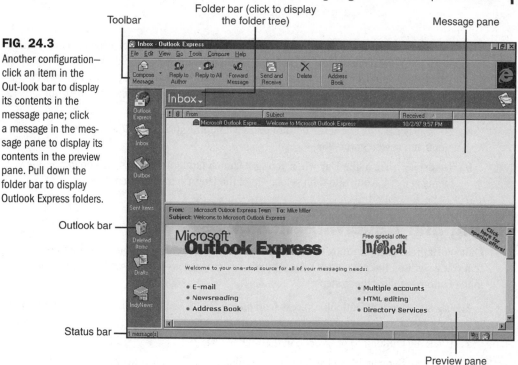

Part

VI

Ch

24

Status bar —

Preview pane

To configure the Outlook Express window:

1. Click the Launch Outlook Express icon on the Quick Launch toolbar to launch Outlook Express.

2. Pull down the Go menu and select Inbox to display the Outlook Express Inbox.

3. To display a preview pane, pull down the View menu and select Layout. In the Preview Pane section of the Window Layout Properties dialog box, select Use Preview Pane, and then select whether to display the pane Below Messages or Beside Messages. If you want to show a message header in the preview pane, select Show Preview Pane Header. Click OK when done.

4. To display an Outlook Bar—a pane in the far left of the main window containing icons for various Outlook Express options and items—pull down the View menu, select Layout, and select Outlook Bar. Click OK when done.

5. To display a Folder List—a traditional tree structure of Outlook Express folders—pull down the View menu, select Layout, and select Folder List. Click OK when done.

6. To display a Folder Bar—a pull-down bar at the top of the screen that displays Outlook Express folders in a traditional tree structure—pull down the View menu, select Layout, and select Folder Bar. Click OK when done.

7. To display a standard Toolbar, pull down the View menu and select Toolbar. Then pull down the View menu, select Layout, and select where you want to display the Toolbar—Top, Left, Bottom, or Right. You can also elect to show text on the toolbar buttons; click the Customize Toolbar button if you want to add or delete individual buttons from the toolbar. Click OK when done.

8. To display a status bar at the bottom of the Outlook Express window, pull down the View menu and select Status Bar.

9. To display a Tip of the Day when you first launch Outlook Express, pull down the View menu, select Layout, and then select Tip of the Day. Click OK when done.

Sending and Receiving Messages

Outlook Express uses an Inbox to store received messages and an Outbox to store messages that you've written but not yet sent. To retrieve new messages—and to send messages stored in the Outbox—follow these steps:

1. Click the Launch Outlook Express icon on the Quick Launch toolbar to launch Outlook Express.

2. Click the Outlook Express icon in the Folder List.

3. Click the Send and Receive icon on the toolbar. If you're not yet connected to the Internet, Outlook Express will automatically make a connection to your ISP, retrieve any waiting messages to the Inbox, and send all mail holding in the Outbox.

N O T E You must use the Send and Receive button to send e-mail messages. Just clicking Send within a message only sends the message to the Outbox; messages are not sent to the Internet until the Send and Receive command is issued. ▪

Reading an E-Mail Message

If you've received new e-mail messages, they will be stored in the Outlook Express Inbox. To read a new message:

1. Click the Launch Outlook Express icon on the Quick Launch toolbar to launch Outlook Express.

2. Click the Inbox icon in the Folder List (or pull down the Go menu and select Inbox).

3. All waiting messages will now appear in the message pane. Click the message header of the message you want to read to display the contents of the message in the preview pane (see Figure 24.4).

4. To display the message in a separate window, double-click the message in the message pane.

FIG. 24.4

To view a message in the Inbox, click the message header in the message pane; the contents are displayed in the preview pane.

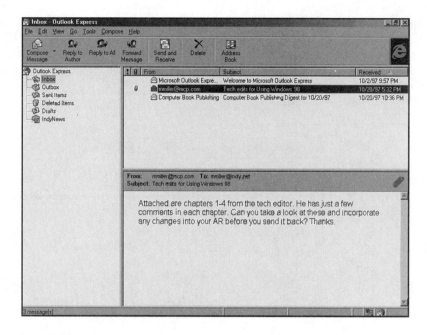

Replying to an E-Mail Message

Replying to an e-mail message is as easy as clicking a button.

1. In the message pane, click the message header you want to reply to.

2. Click the Reply to Author button on the toolbar.

3. A Re: window appears (see Figure 24.5). The original message sender is now listed in the To box, with the original message's subject referenced in the Subject box. The original message is quoted in the text area of the window, with > preceding the original text.

4. Type your reply in the text area above the quoted text.

5. Click the Send button to send this reply to your Outbox.

CAUTION

Remember that clicking the Send button really doesn't send the message over the Internet; it only sends the message to your Outbox. Click the Send and Receive button on the Outlook Express toolbar to send messages stored in the Outbox.

Part
VI

Ch
24

FIG. 24.5

Replying to an e-mail message; note that the original text is "quoted" in the text area of the message.

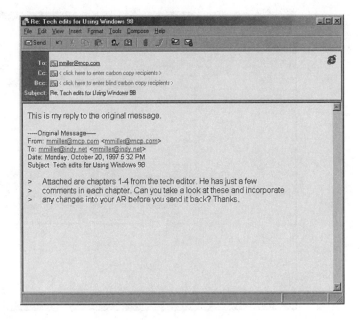

Opening and Saving an Attached File

Some e-mail messages have additional files attached to the mail message. Attaching files to an e-mail message is a way to send files from user to user over the Internet. When you receive a message with an attachment, you can open it or save it to your hard disk.

If a message contains an attachment, you'll see a paper clip icon in the message header. To open or save attached files to your hard disk:

1. From the message pane, double-click the message header that contains the attachment.

2. The message will be displayed in a new window, and the attached file will be displayed (as an icon) in a separate pane under the main message text.

3. To open the attached file, right-click the file icon and select Open.

4. To save the attached file to your hard disk, right-click the file icon and select Save As. When the Save Attachment As dialog box appears, select a location for the file and click Save.

Creating a New E-Mail Message

Use Outlook Express to create all your mail messages and take advantage of features like spell checking and formatting. To create a new e-mail message:

1. Click the Launch Outlook Express icon on the Quick Launch toolbar to launch Outlook Express.

2. Click the Outlook Express icon in the Folder List.

3. Click the Compose Message button on the toolbar.

4. When the New Message dialog box appears (see Figure 24.6), enter the e-mail address of the recipient(s) in the To: field and the address of anyone you want to receive a carbon copy into the Cc: box. Separate multiple addresses with a semicolon (;) like this: **mmiller@mcp.com; gjetson@sprockets.com**.

FIG. 24.6

Creating a new e-mail message; enter the recipient's address in the To: field, the topic of the message in the Subject field, and the text of the message in the big text area.

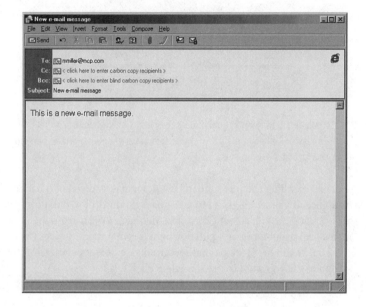

5. You can also select names from your Address Book by clicking the Address Book button on the toolbar. When the Select Recipients dialog box appears (see Figure 24.7), select the name(s) of whomever you want to send the message to and click the To: button. Select the name(s) of whomever you want to send a carbon copy of the message to and click the Cc: button. Click OK when done.

 TIP You learn to add individuals and groups to the address book later in this chapter.

6. Enter the subject of the message in the Subject field.

7. Move your cursor to the main message area and type your message.

8. You can choose to send your message in either plain text or HTML format. If you choose to send it in HTML format, you can use the formatting buttons on the toolbar to add boldface, italic, underline, or aligned text. To select HTML formatting, pull down the Format menu and select Rich Text (HTML).

FIG. 24.7
Use the Address Book to add stored names to your recipient list; just highlight the name in the left pane and click the To button.

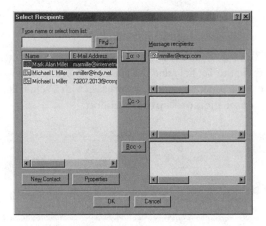

N O T E HTML text formatting in e-mail messages works only when your recipient is using Outlook Express or Exchange mail. If your recipient is using another e-mail program (such as cc:Mail), all text formatting will be lost. ■

9. If you're sending the message in HTML format, you can add background colors and graphics. If you simply want to use a background color, pull down the Format menu, select Background, select Color, and then pick a color from the color list. If you want to use a background picture, pull down the Format menu, select Background, and select Picture. When the Background Picture dialog box appears, enter the name of the graphics file you want to use, and then click OK.

10. When your message is complete, send it to the Outbox by clicking the Send button.

N O T E Your messages will stay in the Outbox until you click the Send and Receive button on the main Outlook Express toolbar. ■

Attaching a File to an E-Mail Message

If you want to send a file to someone over the Internet, the easiest way to do so is to attach that file to an e-mail message.

1. Create a new e-mail message, as described in the previous section.

2. Click the Attachment button (looks like a paper clip) on the toolbar.

3. When the Insert Attachment dialog box appears, locate the file you want to send and click Attach. The attached file appears as an icon in a new pane under the main text pane of your message.

4. Click the Send button to send the message with the attachment to the Outbox.

Adding Stationery and a Signature to Your Messages

Outlook Express lets you create custom backgrounds and text for your messages. When you create this *stationery*, it is used as the default background for all your new messages. An important part of your stationery is your "signature," a two- or three-line message attached to the end of your messages that describes the sender.

To create a default stationery for your new messages:

1. Click the Launch Outlook Express icon on the Outlook Bar.
2. Pull down the Tools menu and select Stationery.
3. When the Stationery dialog box appears, click the Mail tab.
4. To create a special background for your new messages, select This Stationery and then click the Select button. When the Select Stationery dialog box appears (see Figure 24.8), select a stationery from the Stationery list; see the background displayed in the Preview pane. Click OK to return to the Mail tab in the Stationery dialog box.

FIG. 24.8

Use the Outlook Express Stationery feature to add custom backgrounds to all your new e-mail messages.

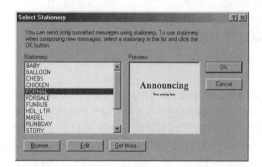

5. To add a custom signature to your e-mail messages, click the Signature button. Select Add This Signature to include the signature on all new messages, and then select Text and enter the text for your signature. If you'd prefer not to include your signature on replies to messages, select Don't Add Signature to Replies and Forwards. Click OK when done.
6. When you return to the Stationery dialog box, click OK.

Adding Names to Your Address Book

The Address Book is a handy way of keeping track of everyone's addresses and has the added benefit of being capable of assigning simple names in place of complicated e-mail addresses.

To add a new name to your Address Book:

1. Click the Outlook Express icon in the Folder List.
2. From the Inbox window, click the Address Book button, or pull down the Tools menu and choose Address Book.

Part
VI

Ch
24

3. When the Address Book window appears, click the New Contact button on the toolbar. This displays the Properties dialog box (see Figure 24.9).

FIG. 24.9
Use the Address Book to store complete information about your contacts—including personal, home, and business data.

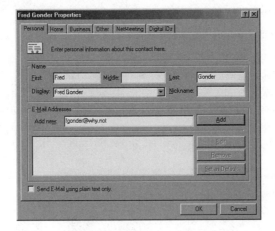

4. Select the Personal tab and enter the person's name, e-mail address, and other information. Click the Add button to register this as a new e-mail address. (If the person is not using Outlook Express or Exchange Mail, select Send E-Mail Using Plain Text Only.)

5. Select the Home tab and enter the person's home address and phone information.

6. Select the Business tab and enter the person's company and job-related information.

7. Click the Other tab and enter any additional information about this person.

8. Click OK to add this contact to your address book.

Adding Groups to Your Address Book

You can also create groups of frequently used names in your Address Book. This way, you can send messages to groups of people with a single click.

1. Click the Outlook Express icon in the Folder List.

2. From the Inbox window, click the Address Book button, or pull down the Tools menu and choose Address Book.

3. When the Address Book window appears, click the New Group button on the toolbar.

4. When the New Group dialog box appears, enter the name of the group in the Group Name box.

5. To add individual names to the group, click the Select Members button, select names from the Address Book list, and then click the Select button. Click OK to proceed.

6. Click OK when done.

Searching for an E-Mail Address on the Internet

If you don't know someone's e-mail address, you can use Outlook Express to search the Internet for that person's address.

1. From the Address Book window, click the Find button.

2. When the Find People dialog box appears (see Figure 24.10), select the directory to use from the Loo_k_ In pull-down list. You can choose from several major Internet-based directories, including 411, Bigfoot, InfoSpace, Switchboard, and WhoWhere.

3. Enter the person's name in the _N_ame box and click _F_ind Now. All e-mail addresses matching this name will be displayed.

FIG. 24.10

Use one of several Internet directories—such as Switchboard—to look up specific e-mail addresses.

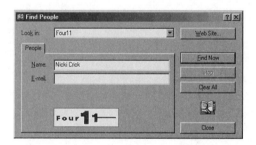

Part

VI

Ch

24

Participating in USENET Newsgroups

The New Newsgroup Features of Windows 98

USENET is a part of the Internet that manages close to 20,000 different *newsgroups*. A newsgroup is like a giant message board, where users exchange messages in a group devoted to a particular topic.

Windows 95 did not include a newsgroup reader. Windows 98 does. Outlook Express (described in Chapter 24, "Sending and Receiving E-Mail with Outlook Express") functions both as an e-mail program and a newsgroup reader for USENET newsgroups. The operation is similar between the two functions. If you know how to use Outlook Express for e-mail, you can probably figure out how to use it for newsgroups.

Configuring Outlook Express for USENET Newsgroups

In addition to being an e-mail program, Outlook Express also functions as a newsreader for USENET newsgroups. Newsgroups are like giant message boards, where users exchange messages in a group devoted to a particular topic.

Before you can use Outlook Express to read and send newsgroup messages, you first must configure it for your specific Internet connection. If you used the Internet Connection Wizard to create your Internet connection, Outlook Express was automatically configured at that time. If you didn't use the Internet Connection Wizard, you need to configure Outlook Express manually.

▶ **See** "Creating a New Connection with the Internet Connection Wizard," **p. 221**

1. Click the Launch Outlook Express icon on the Quick Launch toolbar to launch Outlook Express.

2. Pull down the Tools menu and select Accounts.

3. When the Internet Accounts dialog box appears, click the News tab, click the Add button, and then select News.

4. Outlook Express now launches a subset of the Internet Connection Wizard. When the Your Name dialog box appears, enter the name you want to use with this account and click Next.

5. When the Internet News E-Mail Address dialog box appears, enter the e-mail address given you by your ISP, and then click Next.

6. When the Internet News Server Name dialog box appears, enter the name of your ISP's news server (it should be provided by your ISP), and then click Next.

7. When the Friendly Name dialog box appears, enter the name you want to give this account, and then click Next.

8. When the Choose Connection Type dialog box appears, select Connect Using My Phone Line if you're using a dial-up connection; select Connect Using My Local Area Network if you're connecting via a company-wide network. Click Next to proceed.

9. When the Choose Modem dialog box appears, select your modem from the pull-down list and click Next.

10. When the Dial-Up Connection dialog box appears, select Use an Existing Dial-Up Connection, select your connection from the list, and then click Next.

11. When the Congratulations dialog box appears, click Finish.

12. Outlook Express now warns you that you're not currently subscribed to any newsgroups. When asked if you want to subscribe now, answer No. (See "Connecting to a Newsgroup Server" for information on connecting and subscribing to newsgroups.)

Connecting to a Newsgroup Server

After your newsgroup account is set up, you need to connect to the server and download a list of all available newsgroups.

1. Click the Launch Outlook Express icon on the Quick Launch toolbar to launch Outlook Express.

2. Click the icon in the Folder List for your particular news server.

3. The first time you connect to the news server, you are prompted to download a list of all the newsgroups available on your news server. Choose Yes, although this could take some time because most servers carry more than 25,000 newsgroups.

4. After Outlook Express downloads the complete list of newsgroups, you can select a newsgroup to read—go directly to Step 2 in the next section, "Selecting and Subscribing to Newsgroups."

Part

VI

Ch

25

Selecting and Subscribing to Newsgroups

After you're connected to your news server, you can choose from over 25,000 newsgroups to monitor. You can simply go to selected newsgroups, or you can subscribe to selected newsgroups. When you subscribe to a newsgroup, there is no formal registration process; this simply means you've added this newsgroup to a list of your favorites that you can access without searching all 25,000 groups.

To select and subscribe to newsgroups:

1. From within Outlook Express, click the icon in the Folder List for your particular news server. (If you already have the newsreader section of Outlook Express open, just click the Newsgroups button on the toolbar.)

2. If you are not currently subscribed to any newsgroups, you are prompted to view a list of all newsgroups. Click Yes to proceed.

3. When the Newsgroups dialog box appears (see Figure 25.1), click the All tab (at the bottom of the dialog box) and select a newsgroup from the main list. You can scroll through the list or search for a specific group by entering key words in the Display Newsgroups Which Contain box.

FIG. 25.1

Search through more
than 25,000 different
newsgroups for
the topic you're
interested in.

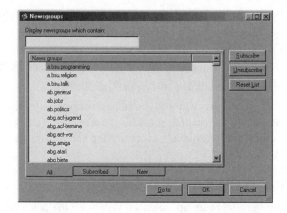

4. If you want to add this newsgroup to your subscribed list, click the Subscribe button.

5. To choose a newsgroup from your subscribed list, click the Subscribed tab and select the newsgroup you want to read.

6. To go directly to the selected newsgroup, click the Go To button.

Reading Newsgroup Articles

After you're in a newsgroup, you're presented with dozens (if not hundreds) of different messages. In USENET lingo, a message is called an *article*, and responses to an article form a *thread*. For your reading convenience, Outlook Express automatically combines all the articles in a thread under a single heading.

To read a newsgroup article:

1. After you've gone to a newsgroup, all current articles appear in the message pane. Click the article header you want to read to display the contents of the article in the preview pane (see Figure 25.2).

2. If an article is part of a thread, a + appears next to the article header. Click the + to display the other articles in this thread.

3. To display an article in a separate window, double-click the article header in the message pane.

Viewing and Saving Files Attached to Articles

Some newsgroups specialize in graphics. (These newsgroups generally include the word *binaries* somewhere in their name.) Articles can include both text and attached graphics files. Outlook Express lets you view graphics files right in the preview pane; you can also save attached files to your hard disk.

FIG. 25.2

To view an article in a newsgroup, click the article header in the message pane; the contents are displayed in the preview pane.

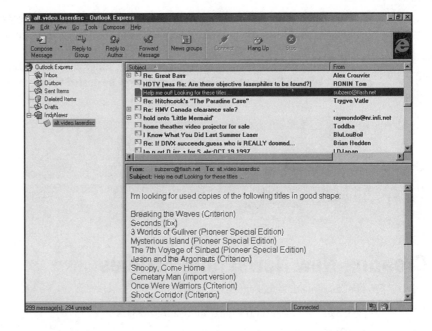

If an article contains an attachment, you see a paper clip icon in the article header. To view and/or save attached files to your hard disk:

1. To view a graphics attachment, click the article header that includes the attachment. The graphic should display in the preview pane.

2. To save an attachment to your hard disk, click the article header that includes the attachment. Pull down the File menu, select Save Attachments, and then select the file you want to save. When the Save Attachment As dialog box appears, select a location for the file and click Save.

Responding to Newsgroup Articles

When you read a newsgroup article, you can respond privately to the person who posted the article or publicly to the entire newsgroup.

1. After you've gone to a newsgroup, click the article header you want to respond to.

2. To respond privately to the person who posted this article, click the Reply to Author button on the toolbar. When the Re: window appears, note that the article's author is now listed in the To box, the original article's subject is referenced in the Subject box, and the original article is quoted in the text area of the window. Enter your reply above the quoted text and click the Send button. This e-mail message will be sent directly to your Outbox.

Part
VI

Ch
25

3. To respond publicly to all members of the newsgroup, click the Reply to Group button on the toolbar. When the Re: window appears, note that the article's author is now listed in the To box, the original article's subject is referenced in the Subject box, and the original article is quoted in the text area of the window. Enter your reply above the quoted text and click the Post button. This article will now be posted to the newsgroup you were reading.

> **CAUTION**
>
> Newsgroup users have a strict code of ethics that you don't want to violate. If you are unfamiliar with newsgroups, you may want to just read for a while before you start posting your own messages. When you do decide to participate, remember that advertising can be done only in the context of the topic (if in doubt, don't do it), and typing in uppercase is frowned upon.

Creating New Newsgroup Articles

To post a new article to a specific newsgroup:

1. Go to the newsgroup where you want to post.

2. Click the Compose Message button.

3. When the New Message window appears (see Figure 25.3), note that the current newsgroup is already entered in the Newsgroup field. If you want to post to a different newsgroup (or multiple newsgroups), click the icon in the Newsgroups field and choose other newsgroups from the Pick Newsgroups dialog box; then click OK.

FIG. 25.3

Click the Compose Message button to post a new newsgroup article.

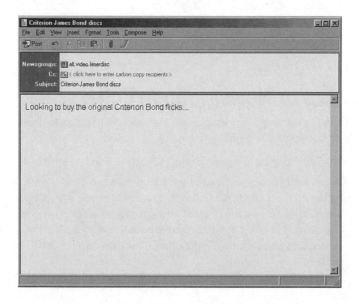

4. Enter the subject of the post in the Subject field.

5. Type the text of your article in the text area.

6. Click Post to post this article to the selected newsgroup(s).

Attaching Files to Newsgroup Articles

You can also attach files to newsgroup articles you post. (This is particularly useful if you frequent any of the "binaries" picture-oriented newsgroups.)

1. Create a new newsgroup article as described in the previous section.

2. Click the Attachment button (looks like a paper clip) on the toolbar.

3. When the Insert Attachment dialog box appears, locate the file you want to send and click Attach. The attached file appears as an icon in a new pane under the main text pane of your message.

4. Click the Post button to post the article with the attachment to the selected newsgroup(s).

Part
VI

Ch
25

Publishing Your Own Web Pages

The New Web Publishing Features of Windows 98

FrontPage Express is a new Web page authoring program included with Windows 98. It is a "lite" version of the more fully featured FrontPage program, available separately. With FrontPage Express you can create and edit Web pages without having to enter a single line of HTML code. (HTML is the code language behind all Web pages.) In fact, FrontPage Express includes special wizards to help you automatically create some common types of Web pages.

In addition, Windows 98 also includes the Web Publishing Wizard. This Wizard lets you take the Web pages you create with FrontPage Express and automatically publish them on a Web server.

Creating a Personal Web Page with FrontPage Express

It's easy to create a simple personal Web page with FrontPage Express; a special Wizard leads you through all the steps.

1. Click the Start button, select Programs, select Internet Explorer, and then select FrontPage Express.
2. When FrontPage Express launches, pull down the File menu and select New.
3. When the New Page dialog box appears, select Personal Home Page Wizard and click OK.
4. When the first screen of the Personal Home Page Wizard appears (see Figure 26.1), select the sections you want to appear on your home page, and then click Next.

FIG. 26.1
Use the Personal Home Page Wizard to create your own personal Web page.

5. When the next screen appears, type the Web address (URL) for your new page (this should be provided by your ISP) and the title you want to give it. Click Next to proceed.
6. If you elected to include Employee Information, you are now prompted as to what job-related information you want to include. Click Next to proceed.

7. If you elected to include Current Projects, you're prompted to include information about the projects you're currently working on. Click Next to proceed.

8. If you elected to include a Hot List of interesting Web sites, select how you want the Web links to appear, and then click Next.

9. If you elected to include Biographical Information, select the format for your biography, and then click Next.

10. If you elected to include Personal Interests, enter some interesting items and click Next.

11. If you elected to include Contact Information, enter all or some of the following: postal address, e-mail address, Web page address (URL), office phone, FAX number, and home phone. Click Next to proceed.

12. If you elected to include Comments and Suggestions, you are asked how you want to store the feedback provided by visitors to your Web page. You can choose to store the results in a data file, store the results in a new Web page, or have the results sent to you via e-mail. Click Next to proceed.

13. When the next screen appears, move the sections of your Web page up or down as appropriate, and then click Next.

14. When the final screen appears, click Finish. FrontPage Express now generates the HTML code for your page and displays the resulting page in its main window (see Figure 26.2).

FIG. 26.2

After you complete the Personal Home Page Wizard, FrontPage Express automatically generates your own personal Web page.

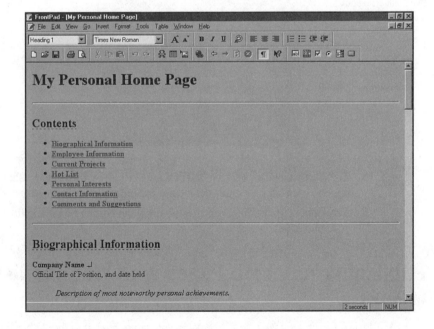

Part
VI

Ch
26

Customizing Your Web Page with FrontPage Express

You can also move beyond the confines of a wizard and use FrontPage Express's other tools to edit and customize Web pages.

1. Open a Web page by pulling down the File menu and selecting Open. When the Open File dialog box appears, select From File and enter the location of the file you want to edit.

2. To change text attributes, highlight the text to change and then click one of the following buttons on the toolbar: Increase Text Size, Decrease Text Size, Bold, Italic, Underline, or Text Color. (When you click the Text Color button, you must choose a color from the Color dialog box.)

3. To insert a horizontal line, pull down the Insert menu and select Horizontal Line.

4. To insert a new hypertext link, highlight the text that will contain the link, and then click the Create or Edit Hyperlink button on the toolbar. When the Create Hyperlink dialog box appears (see Figure 26.3), click the World Wide Web tab, enter the URL for the link in the URL box, and click OK. (If you want to link to another page on your personal site, click the Open Pages tab, select a page from the Open Pages list, and click OK.)

FIG. 26.3
Use the Create Hyperlink dialog box to link selected text to another Web page.

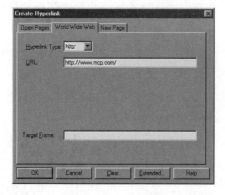

5. To insert a picture, click the Insert Image button on the toolbar. Click the Other Location tab, select From File, enter the location of the graphics file to insert, and click OK.

6. Remember to save the page when you're done editing by pulling down the File menu and selecting Save.

Publishing Your Web Pages with Web Publishing Wizard

After you've created your new Web page, you can publish it to the Web, where it will reside on a Web server and can be viewed by other Web users. You'll need to arrange with an Internet

Service Provider to provide online storage for your Web page (some ISPs charge for this service, some don't), and use Windows 98's Web Publishing Wizard to do the dirty work.

 TIP If you're posting a Web page to your company's Intranet, ask someone in your information services department for instructions.

To publish your page to the Web:

1. Click the Start button, select Programs, select Internet, and then select Web Publishing Wizard.

2. When the first screen of the Web Publishing Wizard appears, click Next.

3. When the Select a File or Folder screen appears, enter the Web page file or folder you want to publish. Use the Browse Folders and Browse Files buttons to find the folder or file, if necessary. Click Next to proceed.

4. When the Name the Web Server screen appears, enter the name you want to give your Web server, and then click Next.

5. When the Specify the URL and Directory screen appears, enter the Internet address (URL) that your ISP has assigned to your Web page; also enter the directory on your hard disk that corresponds to the Internet address. Click Next to proceed.

6. When the Enter Network Password dialog appears, enter the user name and password given you by your ISP, and then click OK.

7. When the Specify a Service Provider screen appears, click Next, and then select your ISP from the Service Provider list. If your ISP is not listed here, select Automatically Select Service Provider.

8. When the Publish Your Files dialog box appears, click Finish. The Wizard will now connect to the Internet and copy your file(s) to the server you specified. Watch the screen for any instructions specific to your situation.

Part
VI
Ch
26

CHAPTER 27

Talking to Other Internet Users with NetMeeting and Microsoft Chat

The New Chat Features of Windows 98

Windows 98 includes two new programs you can use for chatting over the Internet:

■ *NetMeeting*. This is a full-featured conferencing program that not only includes standard chat features, but also lets you exchange audio and video messages between users. NetMeeting also includes a *whiteboard* feature that lets multiple users draw on a shared virtual drawing surface—a great way to quickly exchange visual ideas.

■ *Microsoft Chat 2.0*. Formerly known as Comic Chat, Microsoft Chat 2.0 displays standard chat messages in a kind of comic strip format, with different comic characters representing each member of a chat room.

Setting Up NetMeeting for the First Time

NetMeeting is a "conferencing" application included with Windows 98. With NetMeeting you can chat with other Internet users using plain type from your keyboard, audio from a microphone and speakers, or video from a video camera. You can even exchange drawings in real-time with the special Whiteboard utility.

The first time you run NetMeeting, you need to configure the program for your system. This is done automatically via the Microsoft NetMeeting Wizard.

1. Click the Start button, select Programs, and then select Microsoft NetMeeting.

2. The Microsoft NetMeeting Wizard appears. Click Next to proceed.

3. When the next screen appears, check Log On to a Directory Server When NetMeeting Starts, and then select a directory server from the pull-down list. (The default server, ils.microsoft.com, is a good one to select.) Click Next.

4. When the next screen appears, enter your personal information (including e-mail address), and then click Next.

5. When the next screen appears, categorize your personal information as For Personal Use, For Business Use, or For Adults-Only Use. Click Next.

6. When the next screen appears, check the speed to which you're connecting to the Internet, and then click Next.

7. The Wizard now attempts to tune the audio settings of your system. Click Next to proceed.

8. The next screen highlights the audio devices in your system. Confirm or change these and click Next.

9. If you have a microphone attached to your system, click the Start Recording button and read aloud the message on the screen. Click Next to proceed.

10. When the final screen appears, click Finish.

Using NetMeeting to Chat with Other Users

Chatting with NetMeeting is as simple as connecting to a server, picking someone from a list of current users, and starting to type.

1. Click the Start button, select Programs, and then select Microsoft NetMeeting.

2. The main NetMeeting window appears while the program connects to your default directory server. (To change to another server, pull down the Server list and select another server.)

3. Click the Directory button to display the list of users on this server (see Figure 27.1).

FIG. 27.1

To chat with an individual user, highlight their name and click the Call button.

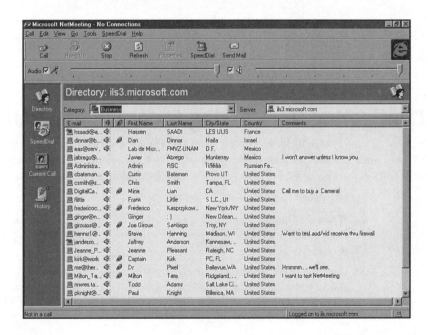

4. Highlight the user you want to talk to, and then click the Call button. The New Call dialog box appears; confirm the information and click Call.

5. The main window now displays a list of everyone participating in the current call. To open a chat session, click the Chat button. This displays the Chat window (see Figure 27.2).

6. To chat with everyone in the session, pull down the Send To list and select Everyone In Chat. To have a private chat (called a *whisper*) with an individual, pull down the Send To list and select that person's name.

7. Type your message in the Message box and press Enter.

Part

VI

Ch

27

FIG. 27.2

A typical chat session—you type your messages in the Message box and read all messages in the top pane.

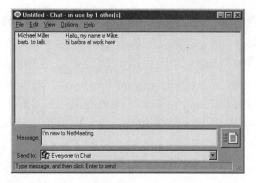

8. Your message—along with messages from other users—appears in the top pane of the Chat window.

9. To end a call, click the Hang Up button on the toolbar.

Configuring NetMeeting for Audio and Video Use

If your system includes a microphone and a sound card with speakers, you can chat using voice communications. If your system includes a video camera and appropriate video hardware, you can chat using live pictures. To set up NetMeeting for audio/video use:

1. Pull down the Tools menu and select Options.

2. When the Options dialog box appears, click the Audio tab and make sure Enable Full Duplex Audio is checked (if you have a full-duplex audio card). Adjust any other parameters as needed.

3. Click the Video tab and configure the options for your particular system. If you want to send a video image immediately at the start of each call, select Automatically Send Video at the Start of Each Call. To receive video images from other uses, click Automatically Receive Video at the Start of Each Call.

4. Click OK when done.

Using Audio, Video, and the Whiteboard

Calls using audio and video proceed along the lines described in "Using NetMeeting to Chat with Other Users," earlier in this chapter. The differences are:

■ Video is displayed in a small My Video window. You can change the size of the window by pulling down the View menu, selecting Window Size, and then selecting the size you want.

■ If you have a half-duplex sound card, only one person in a conversation can talk at a time. (You have to wait for the other person to quit talking before you start.) To both hear and talk at the same time, you need a full-duplex sound card.

- Even though you can have more than two people in a chat, you can exchange audio and video with only one other user at a time. To switch to another user, pull down the Tools menu, select Switch Audio and Video, and choose another user from the list.

- To stop sending audio and video to a user, click the audio or video icons next to the name of the user you want to stop sending to, and then click Stop Sending Audio and Video from the pop-up menu.

- You can also send drawings back and forth in a chat session by use of NetMeeting's *Whiteboard* utility (see Figure 27.3). Just click the Whiteboard button on the toolbar while you're in a chat session. Other users immediately see what you draw on the whiteboard—and vice versa.

FIG. 27.3
Drawing with Whiteboard is just like drawing on a piece of paper—and other users see what you're drawing as you draw it!

Configuring Microsoft Chat

Microsoft also includes a different type of chat program with Windows 98, called Microsoft Chat. Unlike the chat found in NetMeeting, which is text only, Microsoft Chat takes the messages floating around a Chat channel and uses them to create a continuous comic strip, with different cartoon characters representing the various Chat members.

To configure Microsoft Chat for first-time use:

1. Launch Microsoft Chat by clicking the Start button, selecting Internet Explorer, and then selecting Microsoft Chat.

2. When Microsoft Chat launches, you're presented with a Connect dialog box. Click Cancel to configure Microsoft Chat without going online.

3. Pull down the View menu and select Comic Strip. This lets you view Chat sessions as a "live" comic strip.

Part
VI

Ch
27

4. Pull down the View menu and select Options.

5. When the Microsoft Chat Options dialog box appears, select the Personal Info tab and enter your real name, a nickname for yourself, and a brief description.

6. Click the Comics View tab to select the font used in your comic strip and how many panels you want to display horizontally on-screen.

7. Select the Character tab and choose a character for yourself.

8. Click the Background tab and select a background for your comic strip.

9. Click OK when finished.

Using Microsoft Chat

Aside from its "live" cartoon aspect, Microsoft Chat operates pretty much the same way as NetMeeting Chat. Just follow these instructions:

1. Launch Microsoft Chat by clicking the Start button, selecting Internet Explorer, and then selecting Comic Chat.

2. When you first launch Microsoft Chat, you're presented with the Connect dialog box. Select a Chat Server from the pull-down list, select Show All Available Chat Rooms, and then click OK. (To connect to a new Chat server after Microsoft Chat is already running, pull down the File menu and select New Connection.)

3. When the Chat Room List dialog box appears, select the room you want to go to and click the Go To button. (To go to another Chat room, pull down the Room menu and select Room List.)

4. As shown in Figure 27.4, messages from other Chat members are automatically transformed into a multi-paneled comic strip. Enter your message in the bottom pane, and then click the Say button. Your character will appear in the comic strip, saying your message.

 For best results, use Microsoft Chat on a Chat server that supports Microsoft's Comic Chat format. While Microsoft Chat works with any Chat server, users on a non-Comic Chat server won't be able to see your character—and the comic strip action on your screen might not always make sense.

FIG. 27.4

Chatting in a Microsoft Chat comic strip—select an expression from the Emotion Wheel to express emotion.

Other Chat members and their characters

Chat messages

Your Chat character

Say button   Emotion Wheel

Network and Mobile Computing with Windows 98

Network Computing with Windows 98

The New Networking Features of Windows 98

From an end user's perspective, Windows 98 has few new networking-related features. Although Windows 98 has several new features of value to a network administrator, about the only new features end users will see are

■ The capability to change users (log off from one and log on to another) directly from the Start menu, without going through the Windows shutdown procedure.

■ Easier connection to Novell networks, thanks to an improved NetWare client.

■ The capability for your network administrator to remotely administer, monitor, and view the configuration of your PC.

Understanding Networks

A network is nothing more than a group of connected computers. When your computer is connected to a network, you can share data and devices with other network users. That means you can put a single resource—a specific data file, printer, or fax modem—in one location, and it can be shared by multiple users across the network. In addition, networks enable users to communicate with each other through services such as electronic mail.

You need several things for a network to work. The simplest networks require that each computer on the network have a network adapter card and a physical connection between the machines. You then have to make sure all computers on the network are configured with the proper network software and protocols.

Windows 98 provides support for all major network configurations, as well as handy utilities to make networking easy. This chapter provides basic information for configuring and connecting your computer for network use.

Connecting to an Existing Network

Windows 98 enables you to connect easily to an already existing network. Windows 98 is capable of working with a variety of network clients, adapters, and protocols.

The general steps for connecting your computer to an existing network are as follows; more specific instructions are detailed throughout the balance of this chapter.

1. Install your network adapter card according to its directions. Connect your computer to the network, as directed by your network administrator.

2. Make sure that you have the logon information you need, such as user name and password. If not, talk to your network administrator.

3. Install the network client(s) you need for your network.

4. Install the network protocols you need for your network. Install any Peer-to-Peer services you need for your network.

5. Restart your computer when prompted.

Installing a Network Client

A Network Client enables your computer to connect to other computers on a network, or over multiple networks. You can use one network across the company for electronic mail and applications, and another small workgroup network in your department for file and printer sharing. You need to have a Network Client installed on your system for each type of network you need to use.

To install a new network client on your system:

1. Click the Start button, select Settings, and then select Control Panel.
2. Click the Network icon.
3. When the Network dialog box appears, select the Configuration tab and click the Add button.
4. When the Select Network Component Type dialog box appears, choose Client from the list of network components and click the Add button again.
5. When the Select Network Client dialog box appears (see Figure 28.1), choose your client manufacturer from the Manufacturers list, and then choose your individual client from the list of Network Clients. If the client isn't listed or you have a newer version of the client, insert the vendor-supplied disk and click the Have Disk button.

FIG. 28.1
Use the Select Network Client dialog box to choose your network manufacturer and client.

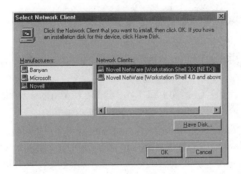

6. Click OK until you return to the Control Panel. Restart the computer if prompted.

Installing a Network Protocol

In networking, as in real life, successful communication requires that both parties use the same language. In the computer network world, the language that two computers use to communicate is called a *protocol*. You need to install a protocol for each type of "language" needed by your computer to "speak" with other computers on your network.

1. Click the Start button, select Settings, and then select Control Panel.
2. Click the Network icon.

Part
VII

Ch
28

3. When the Network dialog box appears, select the Configuration tab and click the Add button.

4. When the Select Network Component Type dialog box appears, choose Protocol from the list of network components, and click the Add button again.

5. When the Select Network Protocol dialog box appears, choose your network protocol manufacturer from the Manufacturers list, and then choose your individual protocol from the list of network protocols. If the protocol isn't listed or you have a newer version of the protocol, insert the vendor-supplied disk and click the Have Disk button.

6. Click OK until you are returned to the Control Panel. Restart the computer if you are prompted.

Installing a Peer-to-Peer Network

Peer-to-Peer networks don't have computers that are *dedicated servers*, which everyone uses for storing files, running applications, or routing print jobs. Instead, every computer is accessible to every other computer on the network as a peer; members within the group share their resources as they choose. If you want to share the files or printer on your machine with other network members, you need to install the appropriate service.

To install peer-to-peer network services on your computer

1. Click the Start button, select Settings, and then select Control Panel.

2. Click the Network icon.

3. When the Network dialog box appears, select the Configuration tab and click the Add button.

4. When the Select Network Component Type dialog box appears, choose Service from the list of network components, and click the Add button again.

5. Choose your network service manufacturer from the Manufacturers list, and then choose your individual service from the list of network services. If the service isn't listed or you have a newer version of the service, insert the vendor-supplied disk and click the Have Disk button.

6. Click the OK button until you return to the Control Panel. Restart the computer if prompted.

Logging On to a Network

After you have configured your network settings, you will be prompted to log on to the network each time you start your computer. Logging on enables you to access all your network resources.

1. Configure your computer to work with the network, as described in the previous sections.

2. Choose your primary network, as described in the next section, "Selecting the Primary Network Logon."

3. Enter your user name, password, and other requested information when prompted as your machine starts up.

4. If you want to log off and log back on under a different user name, click the Start button and select Log Off. When the Log Off Windows dialog box appears, click Yes. Windows will close, start back up, and display the New User Password dialog box. Enter the new user name and password, and click OK.

Selecting the Primary Network Logon

The Primary Network Logon determines the network that will validate your logon and enable you to use the network. When Windows 98 starts, it will prompt you for a name, password, and possibly a *domain name* or other information.

To select your Primary Network Logon:

1. Click the Start button, select Settings, and then select Control Panel.

2. Click the Network icon.

3. When the Network dialog box appears (see Figure 28.2), select the Configuration tab, and then select the network you want to have as your primary network from the Primary Network Logon list.

4. Click OK.

FIG. 28.2
Choose your primary network from the Primary Network Logon list.

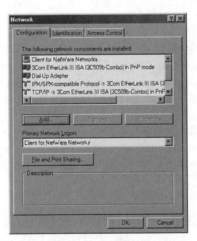

Accessing Other Computers on the Network

When you install Windows 98 on a computer connected to the network, you get an extra icon on your desktop—the Network Neighborhood icon. Network Neighborhood is kind of like a Windows Explorer for your network; opening Network Neighborhood displays all the contents of your computer network.

Part
VII

Ch
28

Using Network Neighborhood is a convenient way to explore the other computers on your network. You also can use Network Neighborhood to view files, folders, printers, and other network resources.

Use Network Neighborhood to access your network as follows:

1. Click the Network Neighborhood icon on your desktop to open the Network Neighborhood window (see Figure 28.3).

FIG. 28.3

Viewing the computers on your network with Network Neighborhood; click the Entire Network icon to view everything on the network.

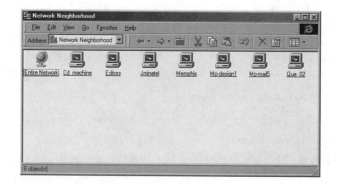

2. You can now see everything that is on your network—computers, printers, you name it—by clicking the Entire Network icon.

3. Click an object to open a workgroup, file server, computer, or folder. You may be prompted for a password; if you are, simply enter it and click OK. If you do not know the password, you need to contact the party responsible for maintaining that connection.

4. After you locate the files you want, you can copy, move, or open the files as you would in My Computer. If you have permission, you can also delete files, create new directories, copy files into the directory, plus edit the files that are in the directory.

 If you do not have permission to edit files—called *write access*—and you want to edit a file, you can always copy the file to your local machine and do the editing there. If you must be able to save the file into its network location, you need to speak to the owner of that directory to obtain write access.

Finding Other Computers on the Network

Computers on a network can be identified by their name, but even if you know the name, you may still have difficulty locating that computer on the network. The Windows 98 Find utility can help you locate different computers on a network.

1. Click the Start button, select Find, and then select Computer.

2. When the Find: Computer dialog box appears, type the name of the computer you're searching for into the Named box, and then click the Find Now button.

3. All computers with a matching name will appear in a list below the <u>N</u>amed box. Click the computer you want to access.

 TIP You can use *wildcard* characters in the computer name if you are not exactly sure of the computer's name. For example, to search for any combination of multiple characters, use an *; searching for **BOB*** will return BOBS, BOBBIE, or BOBBY.

Going Directly to a Folder on Another Computer

If you regularly grab files from your co-worker's computer or continually need files from a folder that's buried under several other folders on the file server, you may want to *map* a drive letter to the location. When a drive is mapped, you no longer have to navigate through all the layers of Network Neighborhood to access commonly visited folders. It's now a simple matter of clicking the appropriate drive in My Computer or Windows Explorer.

To map a frequently used drive:

1. Click the Network Neighborhood icon on the desktop and browse until you find the machine you want.

2. Click the icon for the selected computer and choose a default folder that will be opened when you open the drive. Right-click the folder and choose <u>M</u>ap Network Drive from the pop-up menu.

3. The Map Network Drive dialog box will appear with the first available drive letter already selected. If you want to use a drive letter other than the first available, click the drop-down arrow and select the appropriate letter. Any drive that has a description to the right of the letter has already been mapped.

4. Check the path to make sure it is correct. If you want the mapping to be permanent, make sure the Reconnec<u>t</u> at Logon box is checked. Click the OK button.

5. This folder/drive will now be visible in both My Computer and Windows Explorer. Click the drive icon to go directly to the selected computer and folder.

Limiting Access to Files on Your Computer

One nice feature of networks is the capability to let other users on the network access files on your computer (and vice versa). However, you probably don't want to give everyone on the network complete access to every file on your computer. To limit access to your computer resources, configure Windows 98 to share your computer only with those users to whom you grant permission.

You can grant permission to other network users in two ways—by *user* or by *password*. With user-level access, you choose specific users who can access your system. With password-level access, any user can access your system—as long as he knows the password.

To limit access to your computer:

1. Click the Start button, select Settings, and then select Control Panel.

2. Click the Network icon to display the Network dialog box. Click the Access Control tab (see Figure 28.4).

FIG. 28.4
You can limit access to particular users or to anyone who knows the password.

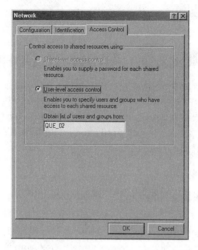

3. To enable access by *user*, check User-Level Access Control. Type the name of the server that contains the user list and click OK. Restart the system when prompted.

4. To enable access by *password*, check Share Level Access Control. Click OK and restart the system when prompted.

5. After your system has restarted, enable sharing for specific folders, as described in the next task.

 If you are concerned about your password being compromised, you may want to consider using user-level access for your resources. Although this method is more difficult to configure and maintain, you have complete control over who can access your resources and what individual privileges each user has.

Letting Others on the Network Share Your Files

If you have some files on your system that other users need to read or edit, you can put those files into shared folders and specify who has what access to those folders.

1. Open My Computer by clicking the My Computer icon.

2. If you haven't already, create a folder to hold the files you want to share, and then move the files you want to share into that folder.

3. Right-click the folder you want to share; when the pop-up menu appears, select S<u>h</u>aring.

4. When the Properties dialog box appears, select the Sharing tab, and then select the Shared As option. Click the A<u>d</u>d button to display the Add Users dialog box (see Figure 28.5).

FIG. 28.5

Determine the network users who can share your files.

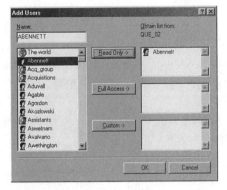

5. The names of users who can access this directory will be listed in the <u>N</u>ame list. Select a user or group of users from this list.

6. If you want the user or group to have read-only access, click the <u>R</u>ead Only button. If you want the user or group to have full access, click the <u>F</u>ull Access button. If you want to customize the type of access for a user or group, click the <u>C</u>ustom button. (If you click the <u>C</u>ustom button, when you click OK the Change Access Rights dialog box will be displayed. Check the rights you want the user or group to have, and click OK. See the bulleted list below for explanations of these different types of access.)

7. Continue adding users until everyone who needs access is listed and then click OK.

If you use long file names but users across your network do not have systems that support long file names (or your network doesn't support long file names), you may want to rename your files with the "8 + 3" file name convention. Otherwise, your file names will contain ~ symbols when others try to access them.

▶ **See** "Understanding Files and Folders," **p. 94**

The Add Users function lets you choose from three different types of access:

- ■ *Read Only.* Users can only look at your files, not edit them.
- ■ *Full Access.* Users can edit the files on your computer.
- ■ *Custom.* Turn on or off a variety of custom access options, including the capability to read, write, create, delete, or list files.

Part

VII

Ch

28

> **CAUTION**
>
> Think twice before allowing other users full access to your files; do you really want strangers changing or deleting files on your computer?

Installing a Network Printer

The simplest way to allow multiple users to use a single printer is to make it available through the network. Before you can print to a network printer, however, you have to install that printer on your machine.

1. Click the Start button, select Settings, and then select Printers to open the Printers folder. Click the Add Printer icon.

2. The Add Printer Wizard will guide you through installing the network printer. Make sure you choose Network Printer and not Local Printer when prompted.

3. When you have finished answering the Wizard's questions, click the Finish button.

Printing to a Network Printer

If you have a printer installed on your network, you can use it as if it is a local printer and print to it whenever you choose. To print to a network printer:

1. Make sure the network printer is installed on your system (see previous section).

2. If you are in an application and you want to print to a network printer, pull down the File menu and select Print. This opens the Print dialog box. Choose the network printer from the Name list.

3. When you've chosen the printer, click OK to initiate printing.

N O T E If you frequently print to a specific network printer, you can make that printer the default used by all applications. ■

Viewing Pending Print Jobs on the Network

If you have a selection of network printers, you may want to check their respective queues before printing so that you can choose the printer that is the least busy. Conversely, if you have only one network printer and it's on the other side of the building, you may want to check the queue after you send your print job so that you don't have to go over and waste time waiting.

To view all pending print jobs:

1. Click the Start button, select Settings, and then select Printers to open the Printers folder.

2. Click the icon for the printer you want to check.

3. You can then view the status of all the print jobs within the queue. If you want to delete your print job, simply select it and press the Delete key.

N O T E Remember that you can delete only your own print jobs—not the print jobs of others. ▪

Letting Other Network Users Share Your Printer

The previous sections involved printing from your computer to a common network printer. You can also configure your printer so that it can be used by other users on your network.

1. Click the Start button, select Settings, and then select Printers to open the Printers folder.

2. Click the printer that you want to share and choose Sharing from the pop-up menu.

3. When the Properties dialog box appears, select the Sharing tab, and then select the Shared As option. Enter a name for this printer in the Share Name field, and then click the Add button to display the Add Users dialog box.

4. Select a user or group of users from the Name list, and then click the Full Access button to enable access.

5. Continue adding users until everyone who needs access is listed, and then click OK.

CAUTION

Allowing others to use your printer can slow down your own print jobs.

Part
VII

Ch
28

Mobile Computing with Windows 98

The New Mobile Computing Features in Windows 98

Few new features in Windows 98 relate directly to mobile computing—although the improved capabilities of Outlook Express do make it easier to retrieve e-mail while you're on the road. About the only new mobile computing-related feature of note is the improved power management capabilities of Windows 98; it's much easier to configure your portable PC to power down when it's not in use.

Setting Power Management Properties on Your Portable PC

To extend battery life, most portable PCs have special energy-conserving features—such as deactivating the monitor or hard drive when the system is turned on but not in use (usually determined by mouse or keyboard activity).

To take advantage of Windows 98's power management features:

1. Click the Start button, select Settings, and then select Control Panel to open the Control Panel.

2. Click the Power Management icon to open the Power Management Properties dialog box.

3. Click the Power Schemes tab and select Portable/Laptop from the Power Schemes pull-down list.

4. Click the Advanced tab. Select the Show Battery Meter on Taskbar option, and then click OK.

It's also possible that the manufacturer of your portable PC has included its own power management utilities. You should use these utilities either in addition to or in place of Windows 98's power management features, as they are most often tailored to your specific hardware.

Installing a PC Card in Your Portable PC

Most newer portable PCs use standard *PC Cards* (also called PCMCIA cards) to add functionality. You can purchase a variety of PC Cards, including card-based modems and cards that add extra memory to your portable PC.

PC Cards can generally be added to your portable PC at any time, even if your PC is currently turned on and running. Because most PC Cards are Plug and Play-compatible, Windows 98 will recognize the card when it is inserted into your portable PC.

To install a new PC Card:

1. Insert the PC Card into the appropriate slot on your portable PC.

2. Windows 98 should recognize the new card automatically. If it doesn't, you need to restart your PC by clicking the Start button, selecting Shut Down, and then selecting Restart.

3. If Windows does not recognize the new card upon restart, you need to launch the Add New Hardware Wizard. To do so, click the Start button, select Settings, and then select Control Panel. Click the Add New Hardware icon, and follow the on-screen directions.

▶ **See** "Installing New Hardware," **p. 166**

Connecting Your Portable PC to Your Desktop PC with a Direct Cable Connection

One way to share files between your portable and your desktop PC is to connect the two computers directly, using a cable. Windows 98 provides a special Direct Cable Connection utility to facilitate communication between two computers connected in this fashion.

To use Windows 98's Direct Cable Connection

1. On each computer, click the Start button, select Programs, select Accessories, and then select Direct Cable Connection.

2. When the Direct Cable Connection Wizard appears (see Figure 29.1), select Host for your desktop PC and Guest for your portable PC. Click Next on both computers to proceed.

FIG. 29.1.
Use the Direct Cable
Connection Wizard to
connect your laptop PC
to your desktop PC.

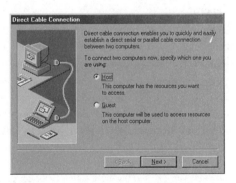

3. Select the port that is being used on each computer, and then connect the cable between your two computers, using either a serial or parallel cable as appropriate. Click Next on both computers to proceed.

4. If you want to password protect the data on your host computer, select Use Password Protection on your desktop PC, and then click the Set Password button and enter your password. Otherwise, click Finish to complete the connection.

5. Your two PCs are now connected. The host computer now appears in the guest computer's My Computer window, and vice versa. You can now drag and drop files from one computer to another by using My Computer or Windows Explorer.

6. To close the direct connection, click the Direct Cable Connection button on each PC's Taskbar, and then click the Close buttons.

Synchronizing Files Between Two Computers with Briefcase

If you take files back and forth between PCs, you probably get tired of figuring out where the most current files are located. With Windows 98's Briefcase, you simply pop the files from your primary machine into the Briefcase folder, work from your Briefcase floppy disk when you are at another machine, and then copy the Briefcase back to your primary machine when you return. You no longer have to track changes manually; Windows 98 and Briefcase will do the work for you.

N O T E   If you do not have a Briefcase icon on your desktop, create one by right-clicking any open desktop space. When the pop-up menu appears, select New, and then select Briefcase. ▪

To use Briefcase, follow these steps:

1. To add files to your Briefcase, start My Computer and navigate to the folder that contains the files you want to put in your Briefcase. Drag the files from My Computer and drop them on the Briefcase icon on your desktop.

2. To copy your Briefcase on a floppy disk, open My Computer, and then drag the Briefcase icon from your desktop and drop it onto the selected floppy drive in My Computer. (The desktop icon won't disappear.)

3. To use your Briefcase folder on another computer, simply insert the floppy that contains Briefcase into your secondary PC. Use the files directly from the Briefcase floppy disk, opening and saving them directly from the Briefcase.

4. To synchronize your Briefcase files with the originals on your primary PC, insert the Briefcase floppy disk into your main PC's floppy disk drive. Start My Computer and open the specified floppy disk drive. Drag the Briefcase icon from the floppy drive and drop it onto the Briefcase icon on your desktop. Windows 98 will automatically synchronize your files so that you are always using the most current version.

N O T E   To view the files in your Briefcase, click the Briefcase icon on your desktop. ▪

Setting Up Your Office Computer for Remote Operation

When you're on the road, you can still access your office's network, thanks to Windows 98's Dial-Up Networking utility. When you're connected in this fashion, you use your portable PC to run your office PC—and connect to your office network—just as if you were there in the office.

Before you can connect to your office PC, you need to establish a new dial-up networking connection.

1. Click the My Computer icon on your desktop, and then click the Dial-Up Networking icon.

2. When the Dial-Up Networking window appears, click the Make New Connection icon.

3. From the first screen of the Make New Connection Wizard, type a name for your new connection, select your modem from the list, and click Next.

4. When the next screen appears, enter the area code and telephone number of the computer you'll be dialing into, and then click Next. When the final screen appears, click Finish. (You should obtain the correct telephone number from your network administrator.)

Connecting to Your Network from a Remote Location

After you've created a new dial-up networking connection, you can dial into your network from any telephone line. To connect to your office network from your portable PC

1. Click the My Computer icon on your desktop, and then click the Dial-Up Networking icon.

2. When the Dial-Up Networking window appears, click the icon for the dial-up networking connection you previously created.

3. When the Connect To dialog box appears (see Figure 29.2), enter your user name and password, and then click the Connect button.

FIG. 29.2
Connecting to your office PC; make sure you enter the correct network user name and password!

4. When the connection is completed, enter any passwords required, and then proceed to work on your network as if you were using your office computer.

5. When you're finished working remotely, log off from your network as usual, and then click the Disconnect button.

Using a Windows CE Handheld PC

A handheld PC—or H/PC—is a mini version of a normal desktop or portable computer. H/PC devices, manufactured by Casio, Compaq, and others, are about the size of a small paperback book and are powered by two AA batteries.

H/PCs run a special version of the Windows operating system called Windows CE. Windows CE operates similarly to Windows 98 and enables you to use special "pocket" versions of your favorite desktop applications, such as Microsoft Excel and Microsoft Word.

Using an H/PC is a viable alternative to using a standard portable PC on the road. With a fully equipped H/PC, you can do basic application work as well as send and receive e-mail and browse the Web. Although not as fully functional as a standard portable PC, H/PCs are "good enough" for many users away from the office.

For more information on H/PCs and the Windows CE operating system, check out the following Web site: **http://www.microsoft.com/windowsce/**.

 T I P Add increased functionality to your H/PC with Microsoft's PowerToys for Windows CE. PowerToys includes such utilities as Windows CE Paint, Cascading Menus, AutoMute, and new sound schemes and background bitmaps. Use your desktop PC to download the Windows CE version of PowerToys from **http://www.microsoft.com/windowsce/hpc/software/wcel/powerr.htm**.

Synchronizing H/PC Files with Windows CE

One of the key features of Windows CE is the capability to synchronize files between your desktop PC and your H/PC device. You synchronize files—that is, update files that may have been changed on one or the other PC—by using a special Windows CE version of Windows Explorer called H/PC Explorer (see Figure 29.3). H/PC Explorer is installed on your hard disk from a CD-ROM supplied with your H/PC device.

FIG. 29.3

Use H/PC Explorer to synchronize files between your desktop PC and H/PC device.

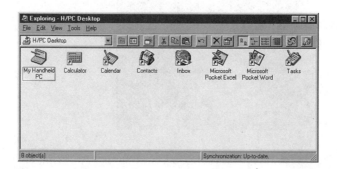

The Calendar, Contacts, and Tasks applications on your H/PC are compatible with Microsoft's Schedule+ and Outlook applications. When you connect your H/PC to your desktop PC, all data on your H/PC will be automatically updated with the latest data from your desktop application.

To synchronize data between your H/PC and your desktop PC:

1. On your desktop PC, click the Start button, select Programs, select HPC Explorer, and then select Handheld PC Explorer. This launches H/PC Explorer.

2. Turn on your H/PC and connect it (via the supplied cable) to a serial port on the back of your desktop PC. (If you're using a permanent H/PC docking cradle, insert your H/PC device into the docking cradle.)

3. Your desktop PC and your H/PC will automatically establish a connection; both units should acknowledge the connection.

4. Appointments, tasks, and contacts should be automatically synchronized between your two units after the connection is established. If you want to manually synchronize this data, go to H/PC Explorer on your desktop PC, pull down the Tools menu, and select Synchronize Now.

5. To update any Word or Excel files you've copied to your H/PC, you need to manually copy the latest versions of the files from your desktop PC. You do this by copying the selected files from My Computer on your desktop PC, and pasting them into H/PC Explorer. Standard desktop PC file types will be automatically converted to the "pocket" file types used by Windows CE.

6. When you're done synchronizing files, close H/PC Explorer and disconnect your H/PC from your desktop PC.

N O T E If you have one of the first H/PC devices, you may be running an earlier version of the Handheld PC Explorer program. The latest version of H/PC Explorer (version 1.1 as of this writing) is available for download from **http://www.microsoft.com/windowsce/hpc/support/wcel/ hpcexplorer.htm**. ■

P A R T

VIII

Troubleshooting Windows 98 Problems

Getting Help with Windows 98

The New Help Features of Windows 98

The Windows 98 Help system has changed much from the one in Windows 95. The big difference is that Windows 98 Help now includes a Web-based component called Web Help. If you can't locate the topic you want in the normal disk-based Help, you can click a button, connect to the Internet, and search for Help on a new Microsoft Windows 98 Help site.

Using the Windows 98 Help System

Help for Windows topics is available from the Start menu. Windows 98 incorporates both the standard hard disk-based Help you're used to from previous versions of Windows, and a new online Help system called Web Help.

1. Click the Start button and select Help.
2. When the Help window appears, you see two panes (as shown in Figure 30.1). The left pane guides you through various types of Help (through the use of tabs), and the right pane displays the specific Help contents.

FIG. 30.1

The local Windows Help system has many facets—click the Contents tab to get a good overview of Windows 98 features.

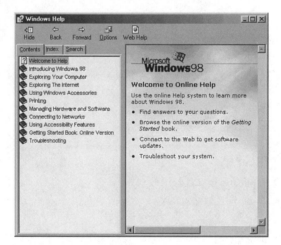

Click the following tabs to get different types of help:

- *Contents tab*. View a topical list that includes an introduction, how to, tips and tricks, and troubleshooting. This is a good place to start if you don't know quite what to look up.

- *Index tab*. Locate help by typing the first few letters of the word for which you are looking. The index locates topics related to what you type, searching only its list of topics.

- *Search tab*. Locate items by full text search of the Help files, not just the topic titles. (The first time you use Find in an application, the Setup Wizard needs to build a database of the Help text. This will take a few minutes.)

Print a topic from a Help window by clicking the <u>O</u>ptions button at the top of the Help window and selecting <u>P</u>rint.

Getting Help Online with Web Help

If the local Windows Help system doesn't contain enough information on a specific topic, you can use Windows 98's new Web Help to find information online. When you click the Web Help button in the main Help window, you're taken online to a special Microsoft Web page. This page contains links to various online Help resources, including the Knowledge Base. This is a large Web-based database of problems and solutions; chances are you can find the answer to your problem there.

1. Click the Start button and select <u>H</u>elp. When the main Help screen page appears, click Web Help.

2. The right pane of the Help window will now turn into a Web browser, connect to the Internet, and display a special Microsoft Technical Support Web page. You can click any link on this page to display specific types of Help information.

3. To search the Knowledge Base for a particular problem, click the Knowledge Base link and follow the on-screen instructions.

4. To troubleshoot particular problems, click the Troubleshooting Wizards link and follow the on-screen instructions.

 You can also find answers to Windows-related questions in the microsoft.public.* newsgroups. (See Chapter 25, "Participating in USENET Newsgroups," for more information.)

Getting Help from ToolTips

You don't have to pull down the <u>H</u>elp menu to find out about various parts of the Windows interface. Windows uses ToolTips—little pop-up boxes—to briefly describe the parts of the interface, such as buttons and toolbars.

N O T E In Office 97, ToolTips are called ScreenTips. ▨

1. Move your cursor over an object in the Windows or application interface, such as an icon or a Taskbar button.

2. After a moment, the ToolTip will pop up (as shown in Figure 30.2), displaying the name of the chosen object.

FIG. 30.2.

Move your cursor over the My Computer icon to display a rather comprehensive ToolTip.

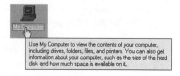

Getting Help in Dialog Boxes

In most Windows applications, a Help button appears in the top-right corner of the dialog boxes. The Help button looks like a question mark. You can use this Help button to learn about the various parts of a dialog box.

1. Open any dialog box and click its Help button (the button with the question mark on it). A question mark attaches to the pointer.

2. Click the object within the dialog box about which you want information. For example, click a list box or option button.

3. A pop-up description box appears. Click again to remove the message and the help feature from the pointer.

 You can also display information about parts of a dialog box by moving your cursor over the specific part and then right-clicking your mouse. This displays a pop-up menu; select <u>W</u>hat's This? to find more information.

Getting Help in Windows Applications

No matter which Windows application you're using, you should be able to get Help in pretty much the same fashion. Whether you need help in Word or Excel—or with Windows itself—when you access the Help system, all dialog boxes and operations should be similar.

To access Help in most Windows applications, follow these steps:

1. Pull down the <u>H</u>elp menu.

2. Select <u>C</u>ontents and Index.

3. When the Help Topics dialog box appears, select the appropriate tab.

N O T E If you're using Microsoft Office 97, you'll notice a new type of Help—the Office Assistant. This is an animated character that functions as a friendly "front end" to the standard Help system. You can use the Office Assistant to find specific Help topics or access Office's Help system in the standard fashion. ▪

Troubleshooting Hardware Installations

The New Troubleshooting Features of Windows 98

Finding and fixing hardware problems was difficult in Windows 95; things get easier in Windows 98. There are several new utilities in Windows 98 that help you troubleshoot problems with your system hardware:

- *Troubleshooter Wizards*. These Wizards lead you step-by-step through a diagnostics procedure for problems with common system components, such as your display, modem, and printer.

- *System Troubleshooter*. This system-level diagnostic tool uses the same steps used by Microsoft Technical Support staff when they're trying to diagnose difficult-to-find system configuration problems.

Running Windows Troubleshooters

Windows 98 includes several Troubleshooter Wizards to help you troubleshoot device conflicts on your system. Using one of these Troubleshooters is an easy way for non-technical users to find and fix hardware problems. You're led step by step through a series of questions designed to track down the solution to your specific problem. All you have to do is answer the interactive questions in the Troubleshooter, and you'll be led to the probable solution to your problem.

As of beta version 2.1, the following Troubleshooters were slated to be included with Windows 98:

- Dial-Up Networking
- Direct Cable Connection
- DirectX
- Display
- DriveSpace
- Hardware Conflict
- Memory
- Modem
- MS-DOS Programs
- Networking
- PC Card
- Print
- Sound
- Startup and Shutdown
- The Microsoft Network

To track down a particular problem with a Troubleshooter:

1. Click the Start button and select Help.

2. When the Help window appears, click the Contents tab click Troubleshooting, and then click Windows 98 Troubleshooters.

3. Select the Troubleshooter for your specific problem in the left pane. The Troubleshooter itself will be displayed in the right pane, as shown in Figure 31.1.

4. Follow the interactive directions to troubleshoot your particular hardware problems.

FIG. 31.1.

Use the Print Trouble-shooter to track down any printing problems with your system.

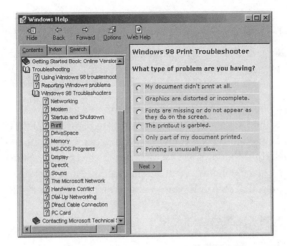

Fixing Big Problems with System Troubleshooter

If your problems are so big that the standard Windows Troubleshooters can't find solve them, you need to turn to a more powerful tool. Included with Windows 98 is just such a tool: System Troubleshooter.

System Troubleshooter is a tool that uses the same steps used by Microsoft Technical Support staff when they're trying to diagnose system configuration problems. You work through a series of steps that, one-by-one, disable various system components until you track down the one that's causing your specific problem. Use System Troubleshooter when you have major problems with your system, particularly problems that appear after you've installed a new piece of hardware.

> **CAUTION**
>
> Because System Troubleshooter modifies key system files, it should be used only by technically savvy users.

To use System Troubleshooter:

1. Launch System Troubleshooter by clicking the Start button and selecting Run. When the Run dialog box appears, type **tshoot** in the Open box, and then click OK.

2. Before you begin diagnosing problems, create a backup of all your system files by selecting the General tab and clicking the Create Backup button.

CAUTION

If something goes wrong while you're using System Troubleshooter, simply click the Restore Backup button to replace any changed system files with the originals you backed up earlier.

3. Begin by running a general diagnostic test of your system at startup. Select the General tab and check the Diagnostic Startup option (see Figure 31.2). Click OK, and then click Yes when prompted to restart your computer. When your computer restarts, you are presented with the Windows 98 Startup menu. Select Step-by-Step Confirmation from the menu; this will start Windows 98 one item at a time. If your system started with no problems, proceed to step 4. If your system didn't start properly, proceed to step 6.

FIG. 31.2.

Use System Trouble-shooter to diagnose series hardware and system problems.

4. Select the General tab and select the Selective Startup option. Start with the first startup option—Process Config.sys File—and, one at a time, enable each option. If your problem reappears after selecting a specific option, click the tab associated with that item and proceed to step 5.

5. Go to the tab associated with the problem option identified in step 4. Start with the first option and, one at a time, enable each option. When you identify the problem item, click the Edit button to edit the line or uncheck the line to keep it from loading.

6. If you continue to have problems, select the General tab and click the Advanced button. Experiment with the options in the Advanced Troubleshooting Settings dialog box to determine which, if any, option is causing your problem.

7. If you are unable to isolate the cause of your problem, consult with a support technician.

CAUTION

You may want to consult with a support technician before using the Advanced Troubleshooting options.

Finding and Fixing Hardware Conflicts

The System Properties dialog box is used to review hardware settings and to determine where devices may have conflicts. When you select the Device Manager tab, problems are displayed in the Class/Device list with an exclamation point.

To identify hardware conflicts:

1. Click the Start button, select Settings, and then select Control Panel to open the Control Panel. Click the System icon to open the System Properties dialog box and select the Device Manager tab, as shown in Figure 31.3.

FIG. 31.3
Click the System icon in Control panel to check for hardware conflicts on your system.

2. If there is a resource conflict, Windows will automatically open the problematic Class group. Scroll down the list until you see an exclamation point icon; this identifies the device with a conflict or other problem.

3. Highlight the device with the problem and click the Properties button to display the Properties dialog box.

4. Click the General tab and you'll see a message indicating the basic problem and the steps Windows recommends to solve the problem. The message may also display a problem code and number that can be useful when consulting with a technical support specialist.

5. When you have made the desired changes, click the OK button in each dialog box to close the box, apply the changes, and return to the desktop. Click the Cancel button in any dialog box to cancel the changes and close the box.

Changing Resource Settings Manually

If you have the appropriate technical expertise (and confidence!), you may want to change the resource settings for a hardware device manually.

1. Click the Start button, select <u>S</u>ettings, and then select <u>C</u>ontrol Panel to open the Control Panel. Click the System icon to open the System Properties dialog box, and then select the Device Manager tab.

2. Click the + sign next to the hardware device type to view all corresponding devices.

3. Highlight the device you want to reconfigure and click the P<u>r</u>operties button to display the Properties dialog box.

4. When the Properties dialog box appears, select the Resources tab, as shown in Figure 31.4. (If your device does not have a Resources tab, either you cannot change its resources or it isn't using any resource settings.)

FIG. 31.4

Use the Properties dialog box to change settings for video adapters and other devices.

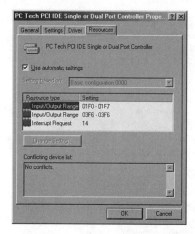

5. Select the resource you want to change, deselect <u>U</u>se automatic settings (if selected), and then click the <u>C</u>hange Setting button.

6. When the Resource Edit dialog box appears, edit the system resources appropriately. Click OK when done.

CAUTION

Windows may not allow you change settings on some resources. This is probably true if <u>U</u>se Automatic Settings is selected.

Editing and Repairing the Windows Registry

The New Registry Features in Windows 98

The Windows 98 Registry is essentially unchanged from Windows 95, as is the Registry Editor. However, Windows 98 has added a new utility called Registry Checker that automatically scans the Registry for errors on system startup. Registry Checker can also be used to replace a corrupted Registry with a backup copy. (Windows 98 now automatically keeps a backup copy of the Registry on hand.)

All this makes for a safer system; it's harder for a corrupt Registry to take down your system in Windows 98.

Understanding the Windows Registry

All important configuration information for your system is stored in a special file called the Windows Registry. This file includes the properties set in the Control Panel, settings installed by all of your Windows applications, and hardware detected by the Add New Hardware Wizard. When you configure these properties via normal means (dialog boxes and the like), the changes are automatically stored in the Registry.

You can also make changes directly in the Registry by using a utility called Registry Editor. Editing the Registry directly is recommended only if you are a very experienced Windows user and know how to recover from any mistakes.

> **CAUTION**
>
> Because the Registry is where all configuration information is stored, including many items that you can't configure anyplace else, editing the Registry is a dangerous thing. Editing the Registry should be attempted only by experienced computer users. If you mess up a Registry entry, you could seriously affect the way Windows operates!

Fixing a Corrupted Registry with Registry Checker

In Windows 98, a backup copy of the Registry is always made when you start your computer. This way you always have a "clean" copy of the Registry available, in case it gets corrupted while you're using Windows. Every time Windows starts, a hidden program called Registry Checker automatically scans your Registry for errors; if it notices a problem, it replaces the current version of the Registry with the "clean" backup copy.

You can also run Registry Checker manually to fix a corrupted Registry.

1. Click the Start button and select <u>R</u>un.
2. When the Run dialog box appears, type **scanreg** in the <u>O</u>pen box, and click OK.
3. Registry Checker will now scan your Registry for errors, fixing them automatically.
4. When it is done scanning your Registry, it will ask if you want to make another backup of the Registry. Click Yes to do so.

Restoring a Previous Copy of the Registry

If your Registry appears to be beyond fixing, you can use Registry Checker to manually restore the backup copy made the last time you started your computer.

1. Click the Start button and select Shut Down.

2. When the Shut Down Windows dialog box appears, select Restart in MS-DOS Mode and click OK.

3. Your computer will now restart in a special non-Windows MS-DOS mode. When you see the `c:\>` prompt, type **cd c:\windows** and press Enter.

4. You should now see a prompt that reads: `c:\windows>`. Type **c:\scanreg /restore** and press Enter.

5. Registry Checker will now restore the backup copy of the Registry. When it finishes doing so, press Ctrl+Alt+Del to restart your computer.

Using Registry Editor

The Registry Editor gives you power to configure Windows 98 features that are available only by editing the Registry. The settings in the Registry are called *keys*, and all keys have numerous *subkeys*. Each subkey has a specific set of values; the values store the configuration information for that item.

If you want to learn more about editing the Registry, you need to read beyond this book. I recommend *Windows 95 and Windows NT 4.0 Registry and Configuration Handbook,* published by Que. It covers the Registry in extreme detail and gives multiple examples of useful changes you can make using the Registry Editor.

Part
VIII

Ch
32

> **CAUTION**
>
> You will not find the Registry Editor on any menu because inexperienced tampering with it could render your computer unusable.

Here is how you use Registry Editor to edit the Registry:

1. Click the Start button and select Run.

2. When the Run dialog box appears, type **regedit** in the Open box and click OK. The Registry Editor window opens, as shown in Figure 32.1.

3. Open the levels of keys and subkeys the same way you open folders and subfolders in Windows Explorer. Highlight the subkeys in the left pane and edit the values in the right pane.

4. Close the Registry Editor by clicking its Close button. You may have to restart Windows to see the effect of some edits.

FIG. 32.1

Using the Registry
Editor; the left pane
shows the hierarchy of
keys and subkeys, and
the right pane shows the
values for the selected
subkey.

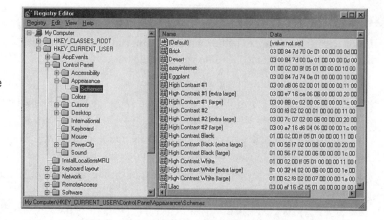

CAUTION

Use the Registry Editor carefully. There is no Undo command, nor any opportunity to close without saving.
Every change is the real thing!

CHAPTER 33

Solving Common Problems

In this chapter

Windows Won't Start

If Windows locks up when you start your computer, you need to restart your computer with Windows in Safe mode.

1. Press Ctrl+Alt+Del to restart your computer. (If your computer is completely frozen, you may need to press your computer's reset button, or turn your computer off and then back on manually.)

2. While your computer restarts, watch the on-screen messages. When you see the line Starting Windows..., press the F8 key.

3. You are presented with a Windows 98 Startup Menu. Select 3. Safe mode from the menu by pressing the 3 key and then pressing Enter.

4. Follow the instructions outlined in the next section, "Windows Starts in Safe Mode."

If Windows won't launch in Safe mode, you need to insert your Windows 98 Startup disk and restart your computer from your A drive. The Windows Startup disk lets you start Windows even if you have a problem with your hard disk or with your Windows system files on your hard disk.

▶ **See** "Creating a Startup Disk," **p. 107**

Windows Starts in Safe Mode

Safe mode is a special mode of Windows that uses a very simple configuration which should run on all computer systems—even those that are experiencing most operating problems. Safe mode is *not* your standard operating mode; it's a mode you use when Windows won't work otherwise.

If your computer starts in Windows Safe mode, follow these steps:

1. Exit Windows by clicking the Start button and selecting Shut down. When the Shut Down Windows dialog box appears, select the Restart option. Many problems are fixed by simply restarting your computer.

2. If Windows still starts in Safe mode, examine Windows 98's various configuration settings. In particular, check your system's display and device settings. (See Chapters 3 and 14 for more information on configuring your system.) Correct any misconfigured settings and repeat step 1.

Windows Freezes

When Windows freezes, your computer freezes. Follow these steps to get back up and running:

1. Wait a few minutes to make sure that Windows is really frozen. Some older applications are a little slow to respond and may simply be running a task in the background that makes it look like Windows is frozen.

2. Press Ctrl+Alt+Del.

3. If the Close Program dialog box appears, look for an application on the list with the words not responding next to it. If you find a frozen program, highlight it and then click the End Task button. After a few seconds a Wait/Shutdown window appears; confirm that you want to shut down the selected application.

4. If there is no frozen application, or if step 2 doesn't unfreeze your system, click the Shut Down button in the Close Program dialog box.

5. If this doesn't restart your computer, press Ctrl+Alt+Del twice.

6. If this doesn't restart your computer, press your computer's reset button.

7. If this doesn't restart your computer, manually turn your computer off, wait 30 seconds, and then turn the computer back on again.

N O T E When Windows restarts after an abnormal termination, it automatically runs ScanDisk to check for any potential disk problems. ■

▶ **See** "Perform a Hard Disk Checkup with ScanDisk," **p. 114**

What causes Windows to freeze? There could be any number of problems, although the most common culprit is too many programs using too much memory. If your system freezes on a regular basis, consider upgrading the amount of memory on your computer system.

Active Desktop Quits

Windows 98's Active Desktop is nothing more than an HTML Web page serving as background wallpaper; live links—such as the Channel Bar—reside on this page. If you experience any sort of problem with either Internet Explorer, Windows Explorer, or My Computer, it can affect any items residing on your Active Desktop. When this happens, Windows displays a new background page that lets you know you had a problem, and asks whether you want to restore your Active Desktop. When this happens, follow these steps:

1. Click the Restore My Active Desktop link.

2. After your desktop has been restored, shut down and restart your computer.

An Application Freezes

Windows 98 is a much safer environment than previous operating systems. When an application freezes, it seldom freezes your entire system. You can use a special command to close the frozen application without affecting other Windows programs.

When a Windows application freezes, follow these steps:

1. Press Ctrl+Alt+Del.

2. When the Close Program dialog box appears, select the application that is frozen from the list. (It probably has the words not responding next to it.)

Part
VIII

Ch
33

3. After a few seconds, a Wait/Shutdown window appears; confirm that you want to shut down the selected application.

4. Click the End Task button.

This will close the offending application and let you continue your work in Windows.

 TIP Even though you can continue working in Windows after an application freezes, it is safer to close all remaining applications, exit Windows, and then restart your computer. This will protect you just in case Windows has become unstable due to the application problem.

Frozen DOS programs can result from a number of different causes, most of them related to the configuration of the DOS program itself. Many DOS programs simply don't run well in Windows and require a special configuration—of memory, or display properties—to work at all. See Chapter 13, "Using DOS Software," for more details.

A Windows Application Won't Run

Several factors can cause a Windows application to refuse to run:

■ *The program may not be compatible with Windows 98.* Some Windows 3.x programs are incompatible with Windows 98. If a Windows 3.x application won't run and gives you a General Protection Fault error message, you probably have an incompatible program. You'll need to upgrade this software to a Windows 95 or Windows 98 version.

■ *Your system may not have enough memory available to run the program.* Try closing other Windows applications before you start this one, or try adding more memory to your system.

■ *Your computer may not have enough disk space to run the program.* Windows employs extra disk space as virtual memory. If there isn't enough free disk space available, you may not be able to run some programs. Try deleting unused files from your hard disk before you restart the program.

If you've tried everything the preceding list suggests but the application still doesn't run, exit Windows, restart your computer, and try launching the program again. You'd be surprised how often this works.

A DOS Application Won't Run

As is true of Windows applications, DOS applications may not load for any number of reasons. These include the following:

■ *The program may not be compatible with Windows 98.* There are some types of DOS programs that just won't run under Windows because they need full control of your system to do their job. These programs—which include Disk Doctor and anti-virus programs—simply shouldn't be used under Windows.

■ *Your computer may not have enough memory available to run the program.* Try closing any other open programs, and then restart the DOS program. Examine the program's configuration settings as described in Chapter 13, "Using DOS Software," with particular attention to memory-related settings. Note that most DOS programs require at least 512K to run efficiently.

■ *You may be running the program in a window when it needs to run full-screen.* Change the program's configuration settings (described in Chapter 13, "Using Dos Software") so that it always runs in full-screen mode.

You Can't Launch a Document File

The number one cause for this problem is that the program file is no longer where it was. For example, if you've deleted or moved a file, the file name can still appear in the <u>D</u>ocuments menu (off the Start menu); clicking the file name for this deleted file will simply result in an error message.

It's also possible that the document file type is not associated with a program type. To associate a program file with a file type, follow these steps:

1. Click the My Computer icon on your desktop to launch My Computer.

2. When My Computer launches, pull down the <u>V</u>iew menu and select Folder <u>O</u>ptions.

3. When the Folder Options dialog box appears, select the File Types tab.

4. Add a new file type by clicking the <u>N</u>ew Type button and filling in the blanks in the Add New File Type dialog box.

▶ **See** "Selecting Which Program Opens a Specific File Type," **p. 103**

You Accidentally Delete a File

Windows 98's Recycle Bin makes it easy to undelete an accidentally deleted file. Because files are not really deleted—they're sent to the Recycle Bin for a period of time and then eventually deleted—you can open the Recycle Bin and retrieve any files residing there:

1. Click the Recycle Bin icon on your desktop.

2. When the Recycle Bin window appears, right-click the icon for the file you want to undelete, and then select R<u>e</u>store from the pop-up menu.

This will restore the deleted file to its original location on your hard disk.

Windows Runs Slower Than Normal

The most likely culprit behind a system slowdown is memory—or rather, the lack of it. Check for the following:

■ *Are you running any new applications—or upgrades of older applications—that may consume more memory?* You may need to add extra memory to your system to accommodate the needs of some newer programs.

Part
VIII

Ch
33

- *Are you running more programs than usual at the same time?* Try closing some programs to free up extra memory.

- *Do you leave Windows running all the time?* If so, your computer may have a great deal of *unreleased memory.* Because not all Windows programs release all the memory they've used after they're closed, little chunks of unreleased memory are left floating around in your system's RAM. Other programs can't access this hoarded memory, which in turn slows down your system. The only way to release this leaked memory is to exit and restart Windows.

Any of these factors consumes more memory and forces Windows to slow down. If you're dissatisfied with the performance of Windows on your system, the answer is simple: Add more memory!

The Windows Display Doesn't Look Right

You can experience many different kinds of display problems. Some of the more common ones are listed as follows:

- *You're using the wrong video display driver.* (This is the most common source of display problems.) You may be using a SuperVGA driver, for example, even though you have only a normal VGA video card. For the best results, you must select the correct driver in Windows—the one that matches your system's card/monitor combination.

▶ **See** "Configuring Your Desktop Display," **p. 45**

- *Your selected video driver is the correct one, but you need an updated version to work with your current version of Windows.* If so, contact your video card manufacturer to obtain the latest version of the proper driver.

- *You're using a screen saver or wallpaper that Windows doesn't like.* Screen savers and Windows wallpaper sometimes can cause display problems. Some screen savers leave garbage on-screen when you close them. Try disabling your screen saver and see if that rectifies the problem. In addition, installing a wallpaper that requires a higher screen resolution can sometimes mess up your display. Choose a different wallpaper and see if the problem corrects itself.

- *You have a loose connection or a bad cable.* Check all your connections and cables between your system unit and your monitor.

You Have Trouble Printing

Printing can sometimes be a problem in Windows. Here's a list of some of the more common printing problems:

- *You may have the wrong printer driver installed.* Follow the instructions in Chapter 15, "Configuring and Using Printers," to make sure your printer is configured correctly.

- *You may not have enough disk space to print.* Windows sometimes uses temporary disk space to store data while a print job is in progress. Try deleting some old files to free up disk space.

- *Your programs may not be configured correctly.* Some Windows programs provide additional printer configuration options that go beyond those available through the standard Windows printer setup. Check your programs to make sure they're set up correctly.

- *You could be trying to print from both a DOS and a Windows program at the same time (or even from two DOS programs).* You can't do this because the output becomes garbled. Stop printing, and then restart with just one program at a time.

- *You may be out of paper.* If you receive an error message to this effect, reload your printer, and then select the Retry option to restart the print job.

- *Your printer connections may be faulty.* Remember to check all your cables, and make certain that the printer is plugged in and turned on.

Windows Won't Let You Exit

The most common cause for this is that you have a Windows program that has frozen, or an open DOS program. You need to close all your programs (and save all your documents) before Windows will let you exit. If you've closed all applications and you still can't exit Windows, follow these steps:

1. Press Ctrl+Alt+Del.

2. If the Close Program dialog box appears, look for an application on the list with the words not responding next to it. If you find a frozen program, click the End Task button. After a few seconds, a Wait/Shutdown window appears; confirm that you want to shut down the selected application.

3. If there is no frozen application, click the Shut Down button in the Close Program dialog box.

Part
VIII

Ch
33

> **CAUTION**
>
> Avoid shutting down your computer without exiting Windows properly; this can cause problems with your system configuration.

CHAPTER 34

Decoding Windows 98 Error Messages

In this chapter

Application is still active

You're trying to exit Windows while a DOS application is still running. Close the DOS program and then exit Windows.

▶ **See** "Closing a DOS Application," **p. 154**

Cannot communicate with modem

For some reason, Windows cannot access your modem. Check all connections and setup configurations to make sure that your modem is working and properly set up.

▶ **See** "Diagnosing Modem Problems," **p. 185**

Cannot find the file "*XXX*" or one of its components

The most common cause for this message is that the file in question is either missing or corrupted. Click the Start button and select Find to search for the file. Reinstall the program in question if necessary.

▶ **See** "Finding Files," **p. 95**

Cannot format disk

Windows generates this message when you try to format a disk that is write-protected. Change disks or uncover the write-protect notch (on 5 1/4-inch disks) or slide the write-protect tab into the down position (on 3 1/2-inch disks).

This message can also appear when you're trying to use a damaged disk, or if the disk contains a virus. If either of these are the case, you probably want to throw away this particular disk and start again with a new one.

Cannot run program—No application is associated with this file

If no program file is associated with a document you're trying to launch, you receive this message. To associate a program file with a file type, start My Computer, pull down the View menu, and select Folder Options. When the Folder Options dialog box appears, select the File Types tab. Add a new file type by clicking the New Type button and filling in the blanks in the Add New File Type dialog box.

▶ **See** "Selecting Which Program Opens a Specific File Type," **p. 103**

Cannot start application

Windows cannot start the desired application. Check to make sure the correct directory path and filename was specified. It's also possible that sufficient memory was not available to run this application.

▶ **See** "Finding Files," **p. 95**

Deleting this file will make it impossible to run this program

This message appears when you try to delete a program file. Make sure you *really* want to delete this program before you proceed.

Destination disk drive is full

You receive this message when you're trying to copy data to a floppy disk that has run out of free space. Either delete files from the floppy disk, or use another floppy disk that has more free space.

Disk error

If Windows generates a disk error message, it's normally because you're trying to use a bad or unformatted floppy disk. If you receive a disk error message, try another floppy disk.

Extremely low on memory, close applications and try again

This message results when your system doesn't have enough memory to run the application or perform the operation you specified. Just like the message suggests, close some applications and try the operation again. You may also need to exit Windows (to free up some unreleased memory), restart Windows, and then run the application or perform the operation.

This message can also be caused when you have too little free space left on your hard disk. (Windows uses your hard disk for virtual memory; too little hard disk space equals too little virtual memory.) Try deleting unnecessary files to free up hard disk space.

File already exists. Overwrite?

You're trying to create or save a file with a name that already exists. Windows is asking if you want to overwrite the existing file. If so, answer yes. If no, answer no and assign a new name to your file.

Part
VIII

Ch
34

Invalid system disk, replace the disk, and then press any key

This message appears when you've tried to start your system with a non-bootable floppy disk (anything other than a Windows 98 Startup disk) in your A:\ drive. Remove the floppy disk and press any key to continue.

Not enough memory

This error occurs when you try to launch an application but your system is low on available memory. Here are some solutions to try:

- Close any open applications and then restart the latest program. The more applications you have open, the less system memory you have available for additional applications.

- Close all applications, exit Windows, and restart your computer. Sometimes Windows applications don't free up all their memory when they close. This memory "leakage" can build up over time and drain your system resources. Exiting and relaunching Windows frees up this stolen memory.

- Free up extra disk space on your system. You can do this by emptying the Recycle Bin or deleting unused files or applications. Because Windows uses extra disk space as virtual memory, having too little disk space free can result in insufficient memory problems.

It's also possible that you are trying to launch a DOS program that needs more memory. See Chapter 13, "Using DOS Software," for instructions on how to configure Windows to better run DOS programs.

▶ **See** "Running a Troublesome Application in MS-DOS Mode," **p. 158**

Open With

Windows displays this message when you double-click a file type that isn't associated with a program. Choose a program to open the file from the list in the dialog box, or click the Other button to choose from other programs on your system.

▶ **See** "Selecting Which Program Opens a Specific File Type," **p. 103**

The file or folder that this shortcut refers to cannot be found

When you see this message, it means that the file associated with this shortcut has been moved or deleted. If the file's location has changed, right-click the shortcut icon, select Properties from the pop-up menu, select the Shortcut tab when the Properties dialog box appears, and enter a new location in the Target box. If the file has been deleted, delete the shortcut by dragging the shortcut icon into the Recycle Bin.

▶ **See** "Finding Files," **p. 95**

There is no viewer capable of viewing this file

You see this message when you use the Quick View option to view files in My Computer or Windows Explorer, but Quick View isn't capable of viewing this particular file type. Use the file's application to view the file instead.

▶ **See** "Previewing Files with QuickView," **p. 95**

There was an error writing to LPT1:

This message appears when something is wrong with your printer or your printer setup. Here are some possible solutions to the problem:

■ Make sure your printer is actually turned on and is online.

■ Make sure you have paper in your printer. If not, refill your paper tray.

■ Check your printer for paper jams.

■ Double-check all cable connections; make sure both ends of the printer cable are securely fastened.

If these simple solutions don't fix your problem, check your printer configuration as described in Chapter 15, "Configuring and Using Printers."

▶ **See** "Setting Printer Properties," **p. 174**

This filename is not valid

This message appears when you type an illegal name for a filename. An illegal name would include characters that you can't use for file names. Remove any illegal characters from the file name and save the file again.

▶ **See** "Renaming Files and Folders," **p. 97**

 The following characters (called "illegal" characters) cannot be used to name a file in Windows 98: / \ * | < > ? " :

This program has performed an illegal operation and will be shut down

This message appears when a program has ceased proper operation. Click the Close button to close the offending program.

Windows was not properly shut down

Windows displays this message when you restart your computer without properly exiting Windows. Remember to shut down Windows properly next time by clicking the Start button, selecting Shut Down, and—when the Shut Down Windows dialog box appears—selecting the Shut down the computer? option.

X:/ is not accessible. The device is not ready

This message appears when a disk drive is not yet ready; the *X* represents the drive with the problem. If the problem is with a floppy disk drive, insert the proper floppy disk in the drive. If the problem is with a hard disk drive, you may have some major problems with your system; consult a technician for more information. ●

Appendixes

Installing Windows 98

In this chapter

What You Need to Install Windows 98 on Your Computer

To run Windows 98, Microsoft specifies the following minimum system requirements:

- 80486DX-66 processor
- 16 MB RAM
- 150 MB free disk space
- Mouse or other pointing device
- VGA or higher resolution display

If your system does not conform to or exceeds these specifications, you should either upgrade your computer hardware or postpone the upgrade to Windows 98.

Upgrading to Windows 98 from Windows 95

To upgrade your Windows 95 system to Windows 98:

1. Start Windows 95. Put the Windows 98 Upgrade CD in the CD-ROM drive.
2. The CD-ROM should start automatically. You will be asked to accept the license agreement and provide various bits of information; follow the on-screen instructions to proceed.
3. Before the actual installation begins, you will be given an opportunity to create a Windows 98 Startup disk. Insert a blank disk in your A: drive and follow the on-screen instructions to proceed.
4. After the Startup disk is created, Windows 98 files are automatically copied to your system, and Windows is configured according to the existing components in your system. The total installation time will run anywhere from 30 to 90 minutes.

 When prompted to save your Windows 95 files, answer yes—that way you'll be able to easily uninstall Windows 98 and return to Windows 95, if you later decide to do so.

CAUTION

After you install the Windows 98 upgrade version, you should retain your old Windows 95 disks or CD-ROM, even if you do not intend to use them again. You will need the Windows 95 disks/CD if you install the Windows 98 upgrade version on a new or reformatted hard drive.

Removing Windows 98

If you had Windows 95 on your computer and you selected the option to save your old Windows 95 system files during Windows 98 setup, then you can remove all traces of Windows 98 to return to your Windows 95 installation.

One way to know if you can safely remove Windows 98 is to see if Windows 98 is on the list of files that can be removed in the Install/Uninstall page of the Add/Remove Programs dialog box (accessed within the Control Panel). If Windows 98 is on the list, then you can remove it.

1. Click the Start button, select Settings, and then select Control Panel.

2. Click the Add/Remove Programs icon. When the Add/Remove Programs dialog box appears, select the Install/Uninstall tab.

3. Select Windows 98 from the list and then click Add/Remove. A warning box informs you that you are about to remove Windows 98 and restore your previous version of Windows.

4. Click Yes to remove Windows 98. Click No if you changed your mind and don't want to remove Windows 98.

N O T E If you want to uninstall Windows 98 but can't start your computer in Windows 98 mode, start your system with the Windows Startup disk you created during setup. At the A: prompt, type **uninstall** to begin uninstalling Windows. ■

Adding and Removing Windows Components

You can use the Add/Remove Programs icon in the Control Panel to add or remove the accessories and other components of Windows.

N O T E In the Windows Setup Components list box, a check mark next to an item indicates that the component is already installed on your system. If the check box is gray with a check mark in it, then one or more subcomponents are installed. If there is no check mark, the item is not installed. You can install all or part of the unchecked items and their components. ■

To uninstall specific Windows components:

1. Click the Start button, select Settings, and then select Control Panel.

2. Click the Add/Remove Programs icon.

3. When the Add/Remove Programs dialog box appears, select the Windows Setup tab.

4. Select the component you want to add or remove from the Components list. (Click the name, not the check box.) The Description box near the bottom of the dialog box displays a description and the number of components that are selected.

5. If the component you selected has subcomponents, click the Details button to view the subcomponents. (Some subcomponents even have additional subcomponents, which you can view by clicking Details again.)

6. Choose OK to confirm changes on subcomponent selections. When you have finished selecting components and subcomponents, choose OK in the Add/Remove Programs dialog box.

7. If prompted, insert your original Windows 98 CD. You also may be prompted to restart your computer to complete the installation.

Installing Unlisted Components

You can add and remove listed Windows components from your system, but at some time you may want to install a Windows component that is not listed in the Components list in the Windows Setup page of the Add/Remove Programs dialog box. For example, there are several system management utilities contained on the Windows 98 CD-ROM that are not listed in the Components list.

To install an unlisted Windows 98 component:

1. Click the Start button, select Settings, and then select Control Panel.

2. Click the Add/Remove Programs icon.

3. When the Add/Remove Programs dialog box appears, select the Windows Setup tab, and then click the Have Disk button.

4. In the Copy Manufacturer's Files From box, type the path to the setup information file (.INF file) for the Windows component that you want to install. Choose Browse if you need to look for the file, and then choose OK to select it.

5. In the Have Disk dialog box, select the items you want to install from the Components list. Choose Install.

6. Click OK to install the component.

Windows 98 Glossary

1024×768 pixels   High-resolution screen display. Displays more windows in smaller icons and text than 800×600 mode.

16 color   Up to a maximum of 16 shades of color are displayed on-screen.

16-bit OS   Operating systems (OS) that address memory 16 bits of data at a time, such as Windows 3.x and earlier versions.

256 color   Up to a maximum of 256 shades of color are displayed on-screen.

32-bit OS   Operating systems (OS) that address memory 32 bits of data at a time, such as Windows 98.

640×480 pixels   Standard resolution screen display, also known as VGA.

800×600 pixels   High-resolution screen display. Displays more windows in smaller icons and text than 640×480 mode—but not as many as 1024×768 mode.

Active Channel   Content from a Web site that is "pushed" directly to the Windows 98 desktop.

Active Desktop   An HTML-enabled interface that turns the Windows 98 desktop into a Web document.

annotation   An informative note or comment added to a document, sometimes displayed as an icon that represents the note. Windows Help permits the addition of annotations, represented by paper clip icons.

ANSI characters   The regular character set that is found on the keyboard, plus more than 100 other characters, including symbols such as the registered trademark symbol and the copyright symbol.

application   A computer program.

.avi   File format for full-motion video files.

backup   The process of creating a compressed copy of the data on your hard disk, to be used in case of an emergency.

BBS   Bulletin Board System; a type of non-Internet online service.

beta   Pre-release version of a software program. Programs are often *beta tested* before their ultimate release by groups of experienced users. Beta testers are expected to find all the *bugs* in the program before it is released to the general public.

beta tester   Someone testing a pre-release version of a software program.

bit   The smallest measurement of disk space or memory. Eight bits comprise a *byte*.

boot   The process of turning on your computer system.

bps (bits per second)   Indicates the speed of a modem and the amount of data. One bit equals one character of text that can be transmitted.

bug   A software problem.

button   Raised objects in a dialog box that can be "pressed" (by clicking it with a mouse) to perform certain operations.

byte   A measurement of disk space or memory; one byte is just about equal to one character. One thousand bytes make up a kilobyte (Kb); one million bytes make up a megabyte (Mb).

cache   A place of storage. Web pages are often cached (stored) on your hard disk for rapid access at a later time.

card   A device that plugs into your system unit and performs auxiliary functions.

click   What you do with a mouse button.

CD-ROM   Compact Disc Read-Only Memory; a high-capacity storage device, read by a small laser in the CD-ROM drive.

channel   Content from a Web site that is "pushed" directly to the Windows 98 desktop.

client/server network   A type of network where servers store files and allocate resources. Servers typically control who can access the information and use the resources; clients connect to the servers and request information or resources.

client   An application in which you can create a linked object or embed an object through object linking and embedding (OLE). Also a subsidiary computer that connects to a computer server on a network.

Clipboard   Memory where cut or copied data is temporarily stored.

commercial online service   An online service, accessible via telephone line or through the Internet, with proprietary content. The three leading commercial online services are America Online (AOL), CompuServe Interactive (CSI), and the Microsoft Network (MSN).

compound document   In object linking and embedding (OLE), a document containing objects from one or more other applications.

Control Panel   The Windows component that contains additional components that enable you to configure various Windows options.

controls   In a dialog box, features such as check boxes, option buttons, and list boxes that allow the user to choose options.

cover page   The first page of a fax that provides basic information like the sender name, recipient name, fax numbers of the originator and intended receiver, purpose of the fax, and the total number of pages.

CPU   Central Processing Unit. Your system's microprocessor.

cursor   The on-screen pointer; the cursor indicates where you are either on-screen or in a document.

DBS   Direct Broadcast Satellite. The direct-to-home satellite system using small (18", typically) satellite dishes.

defragment   To restructure a disk so that files are stored in contiguous blocks of space, rather than dispersed into multiple fragments at different locations on the disk.

desktop   The entire screen area on which you display all of your computer work. The Windows 98 desktop can contain icons, a Taskbar, menus, and windows—and, if the Active Desktop is enabled, it can also include active channels and HTML objects.

device   A Windows file that represents some object—physical or nonphysical—installed on your system.

dial-up networking   The ability to connect one computer to another computer (or network of computers) using a modem and traditional phone lines.

dialog box   An on-screen window that either displays a message or asks for user input.

DirectShow   Formerly known as ActiveMovie, a streaming-video technology built into Windows 98 that delivers high-quality video playback of a variety of popular media file types, including MPEG, WAV, AVI, and QuickTime.

DirecTV   One of the broadcasting services for the DBS system; broadcasts the Program Guide used in TV Viewer.

disk   A device that stores data in magnetic format.

disk compression   To take the information that is stored, or will be stored, on a disk and compact it so that it takes less space to store. Disk compression in Windows 98 is handled by the Disk Defragmenter utility.

diskette   A 3.5-inch or 5.25-inch portable disk, also known as a floppy disk.

Domain Name Server (DNS)   A computer that translates physical addresses into logical addresses and vice versa; specifically, it can take the alphanumeric name for a location on the Internet, like **http://www.mcp.com**, and convert it into the location's actual IP Address.

DOS   Disk Operating System; an older, non-graphical 16-bit operating system, preceding Windows.

drag and drop   A method of copying or moving items by selecting and dragging with the mouse.

drivers   The program support files that tell a program how to interact with a specific hardware device, such as a high-performance hard disk controller or video display card.

DVD   A new optical storage medium, similar to CD-ROM but with much higher storage capacity. (The acronym DVD actually doesn't stand for anything anymore; at one time it stood for Digital Versatile Disk, and at another time Digital Video Disk.)

e-mail   Electronic mail; messages stored and sent digitally over a network or the Internet.

embed   Placement of an object created in one application into a document created with another application; the embedded object can be edited within the new document.

Enhanced IDE (EIDE)   An improved drive controller designed to handle hard drives with a capacity higher than 500 megabytes and to be used with IDE-interfaced CD drives, as well as standard floppy disk drives.

Enhanced Television   Future television signals that include an embedded data component used to transmit HTML Web pages to a Windows 98 computer.

EPROM   Erasable Programmable Read-Only Memory. Changeable memory that is stored on a computer chip.

FAT32   The 32-bit File Allocation Table used in Windows 98.

file   A collection of data, with its own unique name and location; files can be documents or executable programs.

File Allocation Table (FAT)   A table used to chart a file's name to the file's actual physical location on a disk.

File Manager   The file management component of Windows 3.x

file type   A specific type of file, associated with a specific application.

file name   The formal name assigned to a file; in Windows 98, a file name can be up to 256 characters long.

folder   A way to group files on a disk; each folder can contain multiple files or other folders (known as subfolders).

format   The process that prepares a disk for use.

FrontPage Express   HTML editor included in Windows 98; used to create and edit Web pages.

full-motion videos   The display of movie clips in as realistic a form as possible.

gigabyte   One thousand million bytes. Abbreviated Gb.

hard disk   The data storage device located inside your system unit.

hardware   The physical parts of your computer system—those you can actually touch.

high color (16 bit)   Up to a maximum of 64,000 shades of color are displayed on-screen.

home page   The default page you see when you first open your Web browser. Also the default, or top, page for a Web site.

hover   In Windows 98, the act of placing your cursor over an icon *without clicking* to select it.

H/PC   Handheld Personal Computer; a small computer, about the size of a paperback book, that runs the Windows CE operating system.

HTML   HyperText Markup Language; the scripting language used to create Web pages.

icon   A small picture that represents another object, typically a software application.

IDE   A drive controller designed to handle hard drives with a capacity not greater than 500M, as well as standard floppy disk drives.

insertion point   The vertical cursor line, probably blinking, that indicates where the next entry will be made in a document.

IntelliMouse   The new mouse from Microsoft that includes a special dial used to scroll through windows and Web pages.

Internet   The "network of networks" that connects millions of computers worldwide.

Internet Explorer   Microsoft's Internet browser; its chief competitor is *Netscape Navigator*.

Internet Service Provider (ISP)   A company that provides Internet access via modem or direct lines for a fee.

IP address   The unique number that identifies individual computers on the Internet; every computer on the Internet has its own IP address.

IPX   Internetwork Packet Exchange; IPX is the native protocol for Netware and is used on the majority of local area networks.

ISDN   Integrated Services Digital Network; an ultra-fast digital alternative to traditional telephone service.

ISP   Internet Service Provider; a company that provides Internet access via modem or direct lines for a fee.

Java   A programming language used to create applications that run over the World Wide Web.

Jaz drive   A portable storage medium from Iomega that can hold up to 1 gigabyte of data.

Knowledge Base   A database accessible from Microsoft's Web site that contains information on common software and operating systems problems. The Web address for the Knowledge Base is **www.microsoft.com/kb/default.asp**.

legacy   Older computer hardware that does not have model-specific information embedded in its ROM, requiring manual software setup. Also refers to older software.

link   A connection between two files or objects so that a change in one causes an update in the other. Also, links in Web pages that allow the user to quickly move to another page or area of the Web site.

Local Area Network (LAN)   A network and its components within one organization.

local printer   A printer attached directly to a computer.

Macintosh   A type of computer and operating system created and sold by Apple Computer; Macintosh programs are not compatible with Windows.

megabyte   One million bytes. Abbreviated Mb.

megahertz (MHz)   One million hertz—a measurement of frequency, which is how microprocessor speed is measured.

memory   Digital, chip-based storage for transient data.

Memphis   Microsoft's code name for Windows 98.

menu   The part of a windows screen that contains lists of commands in pull-down fashion.

Microsoft   The company that created Windows, MS-DOS, Office, and many other software programs.

MIDI (Musical Instrument Digital Interface)   A protocol for high-quality digital sound, used in various computer applications and by musicians.

modem   A device that lets your computer communicate with other computers via telephone lines.

monitor   Your computer system's video display unit.

MS-DOS   Microsoft-specific version of the DOS operating system; see *DOS*.

multimedia   The incorporation of audio, wave, and MIDI data with video data to create a program that is closer to reality.

My Computer   One of the file management utilities in Windows 98.

Netscape Communicator   A suite of Internet tools—including a Web browser—created and sold by Netscape Communications.

Netscape Navigator   Netscape's Web browser; competitor to Microsoft's *Internet Explorer*.

Netware   The most popular type of local area network in use today.

network   A group of computers connected to one another.

network printer   A printer shared by multiple users over a local area network.

newsgroup   Collection of topic-related messages on the Internet.

Object Linking and Embedding (OLE)   The Microsoft standard for creating dynamic, automatically updated links between documents; also the standard for embedding a document created by one application into a document created by another.

object   A document or portion of a document, such as a picture or graph, that can be pasted into another document.

online service   A commercial service providing access to the Internet and often to proprietary online content.

operating system   The core system software that communicates directly with your computer hardware.

Outlook Express   The e-mail and newsgroup software included with Windows 98. Outlook Express is a scaled-down version of the Outlook program included with Microsoft Office 97.

PC Cards (PCMCIA)   Small, credit card-sized devices that are installed in special slots in computers, usually laptops and other portable devices.

peer-to-peer   A type of network where all the connected computers can share files and resources; computers on a peer-to-peer network typically serve as a local workstation as well as a network computer.

peripheral   Add-on hardware device for a computer system, such as a printer or a modem.

pixel   The unit of measurement for screen displays.

Plug and Play   Hardware that includes its manufacturer and model information in its ROM, enabling the computer to recognize it immediately upon startup and install the necessary drivers if not already set up.

pop-up menu   The menu that appears when you right-click an object in Windows 98.

port   A connection between your computer and a peripheral device.

PostScript   A page description format used with many output devices, such as some laser printers.

print job   A document sent to a printer.

Print Manager   The Windows component that manages all print jobs.

print queue   In Print Manager, the list of print jobs that are ready for printing, paused, or currently printing.

Program Manager   The program organizer and launcher in Windows 3.x.

property   A characteristic of a file, program, or object, such as appearance and behavior.

protocol   A set of standards for exchanging data between two computer systems or communication devices.

push technology   Internet-based technology that "pushes" information from a content supplier directly to your desktop.

QuickTime   A video playback technology developed by Apple Corporation.

RAM   Random-Access Memory; a type of temporary memory used by your computer.

Registry   The Windows 98 registration file that stores all configuration information.

restore   Return a maximized or minimized window to its previous size. Also, return a backed-up file to its previous location, often from a disk or tape to a hard drive.

right-click   The act of hovering over an item in Windows 98 and then clicking your right mouse button. This often displays a pop-up menu of commands related to the object selected.

Safe mode   A special mode of Windows 98 that operates without many of the specialized configuration options. When Windows encounters a major configuration problem, it will often restart in Safe mode; you can then correct the problem and restart Windows in normal mode.

scroll bars   The moving bars at the side and bottom of a window that enable you to "scroll" through the complete window area.

SCSI (Small Computer System Interface)   An interface standard used to control hard drives, CD-ROM drives, and many other special devices; commonly used in high-performance machines because the attached drives may have higher performance than models used with IDE and EIDE controllers.

server   The "lead" computer on a computer network.

shortcuts   The icons on the desktop that are used to start applications; double-click a shortcut to start an application, or right-click to view and modify its properties.

Start menu   The menu used to start most Windows programs and utilities; visible when the Start button is clicked.

Startup disk   A special diskette used to start Windows if something is wrong with the information on your hard disk.

subkey   A component part of a key in the Windows 98 Registry.

submenu   A subsidiary menu accessed from a main menu.

system unit   That part of your computer system that looks like a big beige box and contains the main system internal components.

tab   A "page" in a dialog box; many dialog boxes display multiple sets of data on a series of tabs.

Taskbar   The bar at the bottom of the screen (normally) in Windows 98; the Start button and temporary buttons for active applications appear on the Taskbar.

TCP/IP   Transfer Control Protocol/Internet Protocol; the set of rules or standards that governs Internet communication.

toolbar   A menu bar, containing icons representing programs or commands, that can be "docked" to the Windows 98 Taskbar.

transfer protocol   A set of rules that determines or specifies how data is to be moved from one computer to another.

troubleshooter   A Wizard-based utility that helps users hunt down hardware problems.

true color (24 bit)   Up to a maximum of 16 million shades of color are displayed on-screen.

TweakUI   An unsupported utility from Microsoft that enhances and expands the standard Windows interface.

UNIX   A multiprocessing, multitasking operating system used by a significant number of servers on the Internet; UNIX programs are not compatible with Windows.

URL   Uniform Resource Locator; a URL is an address of a World Wide Web page, such as **http://www.mcp.com**.

USENET   The controlling body that manages newsgroups on the Internet.

virus   A rogue computer program that can cause damage to parts of your computer system.

virtual memory   Hard disk space used by Windows 98 as transient memory.

.wav   An audio file format.

Web Broadcast Architecture   Future technology that will allow Windows 98 to receive special Internet-related content embedded as part of special Enhanced Television signals.

Web browser   A program that displays the contents of Internet sites; popular browsers are *Internet Explorer* and *Netscape Navigator.*

Web Help   Part of the Windows Help system that uses information stored on a special Microsoft technical support Web site.

Web server   A computer that houses a Web site.

Web view   A display mode for My Computer or Windows Explorer that displays all icons and files as Web links.

Windows 3.x   A 16-bit operating system; the predecessor to Windows 95. (The *x* indicates any of the Windows versions that start with 3, such as 3.1, 3.11, and 3.12.)

Windows 95   A 32-bit operating system with a graphical user interface, released in August, 1995; the predecessor to Windows 98.

Windows 98   Microsoft's latest 32-bit operating system, due for release in mid-1998.

App

B

Windows CE   A version of Windows designed specifically for handheld personal computing devices.

Windows Explorer   One of the file management utilities in Windows 98. (Not to be confused with the *Internet Explorer* Web browser.)

Windows NT   A 32-bit operating system, specifically designed for networked environments.

wizard   An automated utility within Windows that leads users step-by-step through complicated or tedious configuration tasks.

workgroup   A group of computers typically connected on a peer-to-peer network.

workstation   A computer that is connected to a network, but does not act as a file server. Workstations can share information on a peer-to-peer network, but are primarily used for local processing.

World Wide Web   The graphical, multimedia, hypertext-linked part of the Internet; you access the Web with a *Web browser*.

Zip drive   A portable storage medium from Iomega that can hold up to 100Mb of data.

Index

Check out Que® Books
on the World Wide Web
http://www.quecorp.com

As the biggest software release in computer history, Windows 95 continues to redefine the computer industry. Click here for the latest info on our Windows 95 books

Make computing quick and easy with these products designed exclusively for new and casual users

Examine the latest releases in word processing, spreadsheets, operating systems, and suites

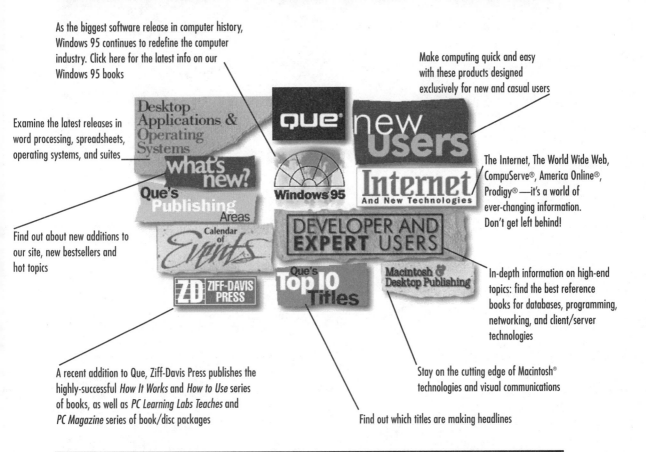

The Internet, The World Wide Web, CompuServe®, America Online®, Prodigy® —it's a world of ever-changing information. Don't get left behind!

Find out about new additions to our site, new bestsellers and hot topics

In-depth information on high-end topics: find the best reference books for databases, programming, networking, and client/server technologies

A recent addition to Que, Ziff-Davis Press publishes the highly-successful *How It Works* and *How to Use* series of books, as well as *PC Learning Labs Teaches* and *PC Magazine* series of book/disc packages

Stay on the cutting edge of Macintosh® technologies and visual communications

Find out which titles are making headlines

With 6 separate publishing groups, Que develops products for many specific market segments and areas of computer technology. Explore our Web Site and you'll find information on best-selling titles, newly published titles, upcoming products, authors, and much more.

- Stay informed on the latest industry trends and products available
- Visit our online bookstore for the latest information and editions
- Download software from Que's library of the best shareware and freeware

Complete and Return this Card
for a *FREE* Computer Book Catalog

Thank you for purchasing this book! You have purchased a superior computer book written expressly for your needs. To continue to provide the kind of up-to-date, pertinent coverage you've come to expect from us, we need to hear from you. Please take a minute to complete and return this self-addressed, postage-paid form. In return, we'll send you a free catalog of all our computer books on topics ranging from word processing to programming and the internet.

Mr. ☐   Mrs. ☐   Ms. ☐   Dr. ☐

Name (first) ☐☐☐☐☐☐☐☐☐☐☐☐   (M.I.) ☐   (last) ☐☐☐☐☐☐☐☐☐☐☐☐☐☐☐

Address ☐☐☐☐☐☐☐☐☐☐☐☐☐☐☐☐☐☐☐☐☐☐☐☐☐☐☐☐

☐☐☐☐☐☐☐☐☐☐☐☐☐☐☐☐☐☐☐☐☐☐☐☐☐☐☐☐

City ☐☐☐☐☐☐☐☐☐☐☐☐☐☐☐   State ☐☐   Zip ☐☐☐☐☐   ☐☐☐☐

Phone ☐☐☐   ☐☐☐   ☐☐☐☐   Fax ☐☐☐   ☐☐☐   ☐☐☐☐

Company Name ☐☐☐☐☐☐☐☐☐☐☐☐☐☐☐☐☐☐☐☐☐☐☐☐☐☐

E-mail address ☐☐☐☐☐☐☐☐☐☐☐☐☐☐☐☐☐☐☐☐☐☐☐☐☐☐

1. Please check at least (3) influencing factors for purchasing this book.

Front or back cover information on book .... ☐
Special approach to the content .... ☐
Completeness of content .... ☐
Author's reputation .... ☐
Publisher's reputation .... ☐
Book cover design or layout .... ☐
Index or table of contents of book .... ☐
Price of book .... ☐
Special effects, graphics, illustrations .... ☐
Other (Please specify): _____ ☐

2. How did you first learn about this book?

Saw in Macmillan Computer Publishing catalog .... ☐
Recommended by store personnel .... ☐
Saw the book on bookshelf at store .... ☐
Recommended by a friend .... ☐
Received advertisement in the mail .... ☐
Saw an advertisement in: _____ ☐
Read book review in: _____ ☐
Other (Please specify): _____ ☐

3. How many computer books have you purchased in the last six months?

This book only .... ☐   3 to 5 books .... ☐
books .... ☐   More than 5 .... ☐

4. Where did you purchase this book?

Bookstore .... ☐
Computer Store .... ☐
Consumer Electronics Store .... ☐
Department Store .... ☐
Office Club .... ☐
Warehouse Club .... ☐
Mail Order .... ☐
Direct from Publisher .... ☐
Internet site .... ☐
Other (Please specify): _____ ☐

5. How long have you been using a computer?

☐ Less than 6 months   ☐ 6 months to a year
☐ 1 to 3 years   ☐ More than 3 years

6. What is your level of experience with personal computers and with the subject of this book?

	With PCs	With subject of book
New	☐	☐
Casual	☐	☐
Accomplished	☐	☐
Expert	☐	☐

Source Code ISBN: 0-7897-1543-0

7. Which of the following best describes your job title?

Administrative Assistant .... ☐
Coordinator .... ☐
Manager/Supervisor .... ☐
Director .... ☐
Vice President .... ☐
President/CEO/COO .... ☐
Lawyer/Doctor/Medical Professional .... ☐
Teacher/Educator/Trainer .... ☐
Engineer/Technician .... ☐
Consultant .... ☐
Not employed/Student/Retired .... ☐
Other (Please specify): _____ ☐

8. Which of the following best describes the area of the company your job title falls under?

Accounting .... ☐
Engineering .... ☐
Manufacturing .... ☐
Operations .... ☐
Marketing .... ☐
Sales .... ☐
Other (Please specify): _____ ☐

9. What is your age?

Under 20 .... ☐
21-29 .... ☐
30-39 .... ☐
40-49 .... ☐
50-59 .... ☐
60-over .... ☐

10. Are you:

Male .... ☐
Female .... ☐

11. Which computer publications do you read regularly? (Please list)

_____
_____
_____
_____
_____
_____
_____
_____
_____
_____

Comments: _____
_____
_____

Fold here and scotch-tape to mail.

MACMILLAN COMPUTER PUBLISHING USA

A VIACOM COMPANY

Technical

Support:

If you need assistance with the information in this book or with a CD/Disk accompanying the book, please access the Knowledge Base on our Web site at **http://www.superlibrary.com/general/support**. Our most Frequently Asked Questions are answered there. If you do not find the answer to your questions on our Web site, you may contact Macmillan Technical Support **(317) 581-3833** or e-mail us at **support@mcp.com**.